Punishing Places

Punishing Places

THE GEOGRAPHY OF
MASS IMPRISONMENT

Jessica T. Simes

UNIVERSITY OF CALIFORNIA PRESS

University of California Press
Oakland, California

© 2021 by Jessica T. Simes

Library of Congress Cataloging-in-Publication Data

Names: Simes, Jessica T, 1987- author.
Title: Punishing places : the geography of mass imprisonment /
   Jessica T. Simes.
Description: Oakland, California : University of California Press, [2021] |
   Includes bibliographical references and index.
Identifiers: LCCN 2021014013 (print) | LCCN 2021014014 (ebook) |
   ISBN 9780520380325 (cloth) | ISBN 9780520380332 (paperback) |
   ISBN 9780520380349 (epub)
Subjects: LCSH: Imprisonment—Social aspects—United States. | Prisons—
   Social aspects—United States. | Segregation—United States.
Classification: LCC HV9471 .S574 2021 (print) | LCC HV9471 (ebook) |
   DDC 365/.973—dc23
LC record available at https://lccn.loc.gov/2021014013
LC ebook record available at https://lccn.loc.gov/2021014014

30 29 28 27 26 25 24 23 22 21
10 9 8 7 6 5 4 3 2 1

CONTENTS

ILLUSTRATIONS

FIGURES

MAPS

TABLES

PREFACE

This book reports findings from an eight-year project investigating the consequences of mass incarceration for neighborhoods and communities in the United States. A vast research literature has revealed the large demographic trends in imprisonment, usually at the state or national level, and reported on the long-term, even generational consequences of mass incarceration for individuals and their families. Drawing on insights from community and urban sociology, my research builds on this foundation to understand how mass incarceration became part of the deep and durable forms of disadvantage concentrated in America's poorest and most vulnerable neighborhoods. Several experiences, both within and beyond the academy, led me to write this book about the spatial context of mass incarceration.

The 2014 National Academy of Sciences report on the causes and consequences of mass incarceration called for more research—like that in the following pages—on the community-level effects of mass incarceration: "Much of the research on the effects of incarceration has focused on individual-level outcomes for formerly incarcerated individuals and sometimes their families. Yet because of the extreme social concentration of incarceration, the most important effects may be systemic, for groups and communities."[1] In its review of the extant literature, the NAS committee recommends deeper research on community-level conditions and effects of incarceration, and specifically, a rigorous study of neighborhood-level conditions of criminalized behavior, disadvantage, and criminal justice processing.[2] I have responded to the call both by drawing attention to community-level conditions of incarceration at the neighborhood and county levels and by presenting new measures that capture the social and political costs of mass incarceration.

The spatial distribution of incarceration has attracted increased attention from social science researchers in recent years.[3] Criminal justice mapping by Eric Cadora and Lauren Kurgan shows that prison admissions in several major cities are drawn from a small number of what they call Million Dollar Blocks. Their maps create a visualization of a neighborhood's share of a state's prison budget.[4] Cadora and colleagues also find that incidences of reported crime are more evenly distributed across neighborhoods than are imprisonment rates. That is, crime is more spread out compared to the concentrated pattern of imprisonment. In Brooklyn, for example, the crime rate in the precinct with the highest crime is three times higher than in the precinct with the lowest crime, but for the rate of incarceration, the difference is a factor of nine.[5] Kelly Lytle Hernandez and colleagues performed similar mapping with the Million Dollar Hoods project, documenting the fiscal and human costs of mass incarceration in Los Angeles County in terms of each zip code's total jail expenditures and the total number of days people from those zip codes spent in jail. Todd Clear's research in this area refers to high-incarceration neighborhoods in Tallahassee as "prison places," while Robert J. Sampson and Charles Loeffler call the segregated, impoverished neighborhoods with very high incarceration rates in Chicago "punishment's place."[6] All these case studies (and more) have demonstrated the extreme spatial inequities in incarceration *within* urban cities and metro areas. I hope to build on these insights to explore the community-level effects and conditions of mass incarceration *beyond* large cities.

I knew that in order to understand the effects of mass incarceration on communities, I needed to be able to identify the neighborhoods of incarcerated people and map those data along with other important community-level conditions. When I was a first-year graduate student, I applied for an unpaid internship at the Massachusetts Department of Correction. My initial work in the department would inspire this project with a surprise (to me, at least): the majority of people coming to prison were not from the urban core, but from small cities outside of Boston. Later in graduate school, while working on my dissertation, I helped to start a prisoner reentry nonprofit in Lowell, Massachusetts, a small city north of Boston. In this organization, I worked with service providers, social workers, and residents of the city of Lowell and surrounding areas; many of our conversations inform the arguments and analyses in these pages. From them, I learned the importance of remaining close to the populations and places sociology studies, especially if we hope to identify emerging and understudied patterns.

In the pages of this book, I bring attention to the devastation caused by racism, poverty, violence, and mass incarceration in places throughout the United States and specifically in Massachusetts. In drawing attention to these conditions, I also run the risk of deepening stigmatization. What initially motivated this research—to shine a light on understudied places affected by mass incarceration—led to a concern I had in the process of writing about stigmatizing conditions. In chapter 4, I report on interviews I had with many social service providers about the conditions of their cities and what must be done to end poverty and the cycle of incarceration, but these places are much more than the poverty rates, policy neglect, policing, and incarceration that I write about. They are communities like any other, full of complexities and humanity, and each cannot be fully captured by my characterization, particularly as I choose to share what challenges they face.

As I was finishing up my first draft of this manuscript in late May 2020, police officers brutally murdered George Floyd and Breonna Taylor, bringing out millions to protest police violence. As communities raised signs affirming Black Lives and chants of "I Can't Breathe" echoed throughout the country, a space opened up for robust debates over what justice means under current conditions of mass incarceration. In this watershed moment for social movements and racial justice, proposals for abolition and reparations became commonly proposed solutions to police violence and mass incarceration. In my initial draft, I wrote that while abolition and reparative justice remain marginalized from mainstream policy reform discussions, my findings suggested them as necessary next steps to resolve the injustices of mass incarceration. I cautioned that even progressive-minded scholars and policy makers view reparative justice and abolition as radical and untenable approaches to justice and equity. However, in one summer of protest and reckoning, that fundamentally changed.

What began as a project uncovering new and understudied trends in imprisonment patterns led me back to one of the oldest facts of American society. Underlying incarceration rates—the highest and most concentrated being among Black and Latino people—is the legacy of racial residential segregation. In the context of ever-widening spatial patterns in recent years, incarceration rates still concentrate in Black communities in ways unseen in any White community. This finding leads me to ask: What must the state do to repair the injustices of policy choices affecting the most marginalized people in society? It is my hope that this book honors the lives and lifetimes lost to mass imprisonment and supports a continued struggle toward community-based justice.

ACKNOWLEDGMENTS

I wish to offer my sincere gratitude to Rhiana Kohl, Eva Yutkins-Kennedy, Nicholas Cannata, and Lisa Sampson from the Massachusetts Department of Correction, as well as the Massachusetts state prison system's research division, which supplied the majority of the data used for this book's analysis. Because of their work and assistance, today I am able to tell a mostly untold story of American punishment: the importance of small cities in the persistence of mass incarceration and social inequality.

I have had the good fortune to have superb advisers and mentors who have greatly improved this project. The work presented in this book is the result of many conversations and discussions with my dissertation committee: Bruce Western, Rob Sampson, Matt Desmond, and the late Devah Pager. Their combined expertise, generosity, and support brought energy and rigor to this project. I am especially grateful to Bruce Western for his unparalleled support, his many critical reads, and the resulting evolution of my scholarship.

In fall 2018, I participated in a symposium hosted by the Vera Institute of Justice (the data reported in chapters 3 and 5 come from the Institute's Incarceration Trends project). The participants in that symposium challenged and extended my thinking about place and punishment, and the discussions informed what became chapter 6 in this book.

In May 2019, a group of scholars carefully critiqued the first draft of this manuscript. I deeply admire each of these researchers: Monica Bell, Issa Kohler-Hausmann, Sarah Lageson, Heather Schoenfeld, and Bruce Western. Their participation in this book conference, guidance, and collective wisdom helped to reshape and focus this book, clarifying its contribution to the carceral literature.

Throughout 2020, I participated in a virtual writing collective that fueled my book writing. Thanks to Paula Austin, Cati Connell, Sultan Doughan, Saida Grundy, Jackie Jahn, Sarah Miller, Dana Moss, Merav Shohet, and Ana Villarreal for their support, generous laughter, and advice. I wish to express my deepest appreciation to Jackie for providing critical feedback on the entire draft, to Cati for offering her wisdom as a veteran book author, and to Dana for writing alongside me for a year and then some.

Braxton Jones, Heather Mooney, Erin Tichenor, Teresa Tran, and Jade Williams provided excellent research assistance for this book project. Erin, in particular, provided significant assistance with interviews used for the study of social service providers in chapter 4.

Maura Roessner, my editor at UC Press, believed in the project in its very early stages and offered support throughout the publication process. Letta Page expertly improved my prose and contributed greatly to the clarity of my ideas and arguments. Heartfelt thanks to Sharon Langworthy for excellent copyediting. I also wish to thank the anonymous reviewers of the manuscript who greatly improved the final draft.

The Rappaport Institute for Greater Boston, Boston University's Initiative on Cities, and Harvard's Institute for Quantitative Social Science, Taubman Center for State and Local Government, and Multidisciplinary Program in Inequality and Social Policy provided grant and fellowship support.

Portions of several chapters were published as "Place and Punishment: The Spatial Context of Mass Incarceration," *Journal of Quantitative Criminology* 34:513–33, and "The Ecology of Race and Punishment Across Cities," *City & Community* 19:169–90.

I would be nothing without the enduring support of my family and friends, who buoyed me throughout the book writing process. To my dear friends, parents, sister, and brother: thank you for all the ways you have profoundly shaped my life and work. Finally, my deepest gratitude to my husband Nate, whose love, support, and effortless kindness kept me going through this whole project, from dissertation to book.

My involvement in two field studies has had a deep and durable effect on my thinking on incarceration and neighborhood inequality. While in graduate school, I was a research assistant for the Boston Reentry Study, which interviewed 122 men and women who left prison and returned to the Greater Boston area. Formally a study of prisoner reentry, this project brought new evidence to bear on deep and extreme poverty in America, challenging my assumptions about patterns of neighborhood attachment and attainment at the extremes of urban marginality. And in 2017, I embarked on a field study of solitary confinement with Bruce Western. In our interviews with over 120 incarcerated people and prison staff, this exploration of solitary confinement expanded to a much broader discussion of the pains of imprisonment and the social isolation attending *all* prison life—whether in solitary or in the general prison population. So informed, the present project is anchored in an analysis of the fundamentally segregative quality of American public policy revealed by the extrication of individuals from particular geographies of vulnerability and social disadvantage. This process of removing people from neighborhoods to cages is largely hidden from public view. I dedicate this book to the incarcerated and formerly incarcerated men and women who have entrusted me with their stories of removal, isolation, and resilience in an era of mass incarceration.

Introduction

IN THE LATE TWENTIETH CENTURY, the United States embarked on an experiment in crime control that was both globally and historically unique. In response to rising rates of violence and unresolved matters of race and class, policy makers built and expanded a prison system to control social problems and impose group-level punishment. Today, nearly one in three Americans has a criminal record—about 110 million people in the United States.[1] From 1948 to 2010, criminal courts convicted more than 19 million people of felony charges.[2] By the close of the twentieth century, the US incarceration rate had grown by 500 percent over just a few decades. More than 7 million people had gone to prison or jail.[3]

During this unprecedented rise in incarceration rates, going to prison became a normal life event for many young Black men living in poor communities.[4] Researchers uncovered a shocking reality: nearly a third of all Black men would go to prison during their lifetimes, compared to 17 percent of Latino men and 6 percent of White men.[5] At a time in American history when so many people of one race will go to prison, scholars began to describe the US system as one of *mass incarceration*, in which the criminal justice system punishes entire communities rather than individual criminals.[6] Today's criminal justice system follows from the historical legacy of racism that underlies American public policy.

This astounding growth in the prison system represents a significant shift in how American society governs social and economic marginality, affecting poor communities in every region and state across the country. The extreme demographic concentration of punishment suggests *where* the most important effects may be felt by American communities and neighborhoods.[7] The enormous footprint of the criminal justice system and its ramifications now extends beyond prison walls. Punishment saturates households, neighborhoods, and communities. As millions disappeared from communities and entered prisons and jails, mass incarceration fundamentally impacted American community life, including those people left behind. Millions of children lost parents. Partners and family members lost loved ones. And neighborhoods experienced the hollowing out of entire groups as the cycle of incarceration destabilized their populations.

The immeasurable costs of these policy choices for disadvantaged communities, both in a fiscal sense and the human toll, outweigh any of the possible benefits. Uncovering, questioning, and addressing the profound historic injustices of mass imprisonment is both a scholarly and a moral imperative. As the consequences of this failed experiment will be felt within disadvantaged communities for decades to come, this book aims to chart and map the conditions of mass incarceration in those neighborhoods and communities across the country.

. . .

When I began exploring those neighborhoods most affected by mass incarceration, I noticed a tendency to discuss urban neighborhoods in large metropolitan areas such as New York City or Chicago. As scholars in the last thirty years aimed to explain the causes and consequences of mass incarceration, their sociological research agenda seemed crowded with concurrent social problems. The decline of labor in US cities, the rise (and fall) of violent crime, the concentration of poverty and housing insecurity, untreated mental illness and the closing of asylums, and the crack and heroin epidemics all begged for attention to the nature—and mitigation—of postwar social inequality. In hindsight, it became clear that incarceration was a primary policy response to this host of social problems.

In the public mindset and the scholarly research agenda, the social problems of violence, substance use, untreated mental illness, and poverty were intimately linked to the social structure of America's major cities. The policies and politics of crime control that emerged in the early 1970s linked crime and violence to specifically *urban* social problems, leaving little room for a more complex reality. The urban focus gained and sustained traction, and little attention was paid to the growing imprisonment rates found within small cities, suburbs, and rural areas. As a result, hyperincarcerated communities are often imagined almost exclusively as racially segregated neighborhoods with very high levels of poverty, violence, and other markers of socioeconomic disadvantage—in other words, part of a deep core of disadvantage in major urban cities. Such a place is envisioned as being marred by gang violence, substance use and sales, and public social disorder. And while this neighborhood signifies only a very narrow set of places, it has come to symbolize the relationship between neighborhood poverty, violence, and the criminal justice system, including policing and incarceration. These places' social problems—real or imagined—became public justifications for harsh and punitive policy responses, including a concentration of surveillance, frequent police contacts, and removals from the community to the criminal justice system.

Recent examples show the durability of the city as a metaphor for disorder. During Donald Trump's presidency, for example, Trump often used "Chicago" and "Baltimore" as shorthand for disorder, violence, and depravity, and to justify his reprise of law and order politics. For example, in 2019 he called Baltimore a "disgusting, rat and rodent infested mess" and said that its residents were "living in hell."[8] During a law enforcement roundtable in 2020, Trump called violence in Chicago "worse than Afghanistan."[9] These references to big cities ultimately served the purpose of justifying unbridled support for the police and later, their military-style deployment during Black Lives Matter (BLM) protests.

At the same time, cities like Chicago, Baltimore, and New York received the most attention from researchers and reformers. As scholars pointed to these places on maps, few questioned the urban character of mass incarceration. In 1992, the *New York Times* cited an extraordinary finding from a study by Eddie Ellis to convey the spatial character of mass imprisonment: "75 percent of the state's entire prison population comes from just seven neighborhoods in New York City."[10] About ten years later, a study replicated Ellis's earlier work, investigating the same seven neighborhoods: the Lower East Side, the South Bronx, Harlem, Brownsville, Bedford-Stuyvesant, East New York, and South Jamaica.[11] Ellis's discovery—and studies like it—proved durable; policy makers, prison reform advocates, and scholars have all seemed to embrace as gospel the idea that the spatial dimension of mass incarceration across the United States clearly highlighted a cause-and-effect cycle of urban problems and urban punishment.

The emphasis on urban neighborhoods and large cities pervades research and policy decades after Ellis's observations. It is etched into the entire theoretical discussion on the community-level causes and effects of mass imprisonment. Certainly some scholars have deliberately chosen urban imagery to draw attention to and critique the deleterious conditions of intense formal social control (by social control, I mean policing, court processing, and incarceration in prison or jail), particularly for Black populations living in segregated urban places. Across a number of disciplines, urban scholars have made explicit claims about the relationship between place and punishment, between Black urban spaces and policing and incarceration.[12]

At the same time, researchers studying mass incarceration tended to favor analysis of national and state-level trends; very few with a reform-minded research agenda have actually examined the local conditions of punishment, and fewer still the local conditions anywhere outside cities.[13] While urban scholars helped me to see the importance of *place* for understanding mass incarceration, I became increasingly curious about places beyond big cities and how place might be shaping population-level inequality in incarceration.

The realities of the place-and-punishment connection suggest that the narrow focus on urban centers overlooked emergent trends in nonurban areas. As of 2020, the majority of jail and prison admissions in the United States come from *non*metropolitan areas. In some places, these patterns have existed since the height of mass incarceration in the late 1990s. My investigation of the geographic contours of mass incarceration led to a surprising truth: the prison pipeline extends far beyond the bounds of inner-city neighborhoods and deep urban poverty.

A spatial perspective on punishment has several unexpected outcomes that I explore throughout the chapters of this book. First, it takes a full and unconstrained spatial view of punishment to see where mass incarceration flourishes today; the highest current rates of incarceration are in America's small cities and nonmetropolitan counties. Small cities, suburbs, and rural areas outside of American metro areas have the highest rates of incarceration (in either prison or jails) today, and in my case, Massachusetts, this has been true for at least the first twenty years of the twenty-first century. I find astronomical and unyielding incarceration rates in places like Lawrence and Holyoke, Massachusetts—small cities largely unknown to those who live outside the state. A deeper look at these places draws our attention to the effects of isolation and remoteness that locate the working population far from job centers. Stigmas associated with poverty and drug use stymie community supports to help people with housing and sobriety. Persistent economic decline leads to abandonment and population loss. The intuition of prior research that place matters holds true—but *where* place matters for punishment in America has evolved in recent years beyond large urban cities.

A second crucial implication, however, is that acknowledging mass incarceration unfolded in a broad set of places does not undermine the central role of race in American incarceration rates. Indeed, the central argument of this book is that *mass incarceration should be conceptualized as one of the legacies of racial residential segregation.* The criminal justice system arrests, convicts, and surveils people in *places*. The spatial organization of social control is embedded in the long-standing hypersegregation of American communities. Like neighborhood rates of poverty and violence, incarceration is a uniquely racialized experience in the United States. I find Black-White and Latino-White neighborhood disparities are significantly higher for rates of incarceration than for poverty or violence. I call this profound concentration of punishment in Black and Latino neighborhoods *communities of pervasive incarceration.* Thus, while mass incarceration evolved during a period of geographically broader social disadvantages, it also took hold during a period of deepening racial segregation. A broad spatial view, in fact, only enhances our sense of the disparate and racialized experiences of community-level punishment; when we look beyond big cities, not only do we observe the highest rates of incarceration, we also observe the lowest.

Third, this community-level study of imprisonment provides deeper insight into the largely unmeasured political and social effects of mass incarceration for communities. For example, I demonstrate mass incarceration's toll on communities by combining the total years in which the criminal justice system sent people to prison in a community. I find Massachusetts sentenced people to nearly 170,000 years of state prison in just a small portion of years under mass incarceration (and keep in mind that Massachusetts has one of the lowest incarceration rates in the country). This measure of *community loss* at the neighborhood level shows profound disparities by race and class. This time lost to imprisonment affects the economic stability of neighborhoods, family structure and connection, and the health and well-being of those communities. This level of loss expands upon previous conceptualizations of excessive incarceration that focus solely on counts of people and raises further moral objections to the current system of incarceration.

All of these findings expand our thinking away from individual understandings of crime and criminalization to the larger social forces of segregation and inequality that give rise to criminalizing and *punishing places*. This reframing asks not how to stop individuals from engaging in behaviors that will lead to their incarceration, but rather how policies could meaningfully improve community life under conditions of mass incarceration. Taking a broader view of the spatial context of imprisonment and its historical evolution adds much-needed precision and context as we try to understand the causes and consequences of mass incarceration.

Thus, the book's title, *Punishing Places*, has a double meaning. The main goal of this book is to describe the conditions of mass incarceration in communities, because rather than just punishing individuals, the American system of incarceration has been punishing neighborhoods on a globally and historically unprecedented scale. Moving beyond the individualized framework of the consequences of mass incarceration for incarcerated and formerly incarcerated people to think instead about the community-level effects points us toward a very different set of questions regarding the sources of inequality and injustice. Even more, it suggests radical changes in our ideas about how to ameliorate injustices. The second meaning embedded in the title, *Punishing Places*, is that living in a community where incarceration has become a normal experience produces durable disadvantages for *all* community members.[14] Punishing places deepen and compound the deprivations within and damage the well-being of America's most marginalized and disadvantaged communities.

STUDYING COMMUNITY RATES OF PRISON ADMISSIONS

Bringing a long-neglected spatial lens to the problem of mass incarceration helps me identify a key tension between urban inequality and social control perspectives, which I explore in detail in chapter 2. A largely urban focus in the research literature on the spatial pattern of incarceration simply does not fit with the overwhelming evidence presented by the sociology of punishment, which shows mass incarceration has taken hold in places far beyond those described in the urban disorder narrative. Thus, on the one hand, mass incarceration has affected areas significantly removed and distant from the places at which criminal justice policies have been aimed. On the other hand, a major theme from my research is the long-standing and deeply unequal exposure to punishing environments associated with one's home address. The pervasive incarceration that marks *punishing places* indicates the tension between punitive practices' concentration in neighborhoods and broad geographic distribution across states, bringing empirical and theoretical clarity to the unequal imprisonment rates across the country. This persistent neighborhood inequality in a context of changing geographic patterns speaks to the remarkable consistency of deprivation and state violence associated with segregated and disadvantaged communities in the United States. But we have to look beyond big cities to capture, understand, and end punishing places today.

In these pages, I aim to answer this question: How do inequalities of *place* produce disparities and high rates of *punishment?* To answer it, I embarked on an unprecedented data collection of geographic information about where individuals were living prior to their incarceration for an entire state and spanning the first two decades of the twenty-first century. Using a combination of qualitative, quantitative, and spatial methods, in this book I bring two distinct literatures—place disadvantage and punishment—to a single analysis, revealing how mass incarceration is a distinctive, place-based harm to a diverse set of communities across the United States. This effort has yielded several key findings that should change how scholars and policy makers think about mass incarceration's stubborn persistence and help identify pathways to its demise.

Throughout the book, I use spatial tools and concepts to analyze patterns of imprisonment. Mapping spatial patterns of incarceration by race and ethnicity sheds light on the differences in clustering by groups. This spatial clustering offers a way to analyze mass incarceration as it is experienced in communities, rather than just in terms of broad racial categories. Spatial regression analysis further elucidates the degree to which incarceration in one area affects the patterns found in surrounding areas. Spatial methods and concepts provide the necessary tools to resolve two seemingly paradoxical trends: incarceration is both more spatially diffuse in recent years and, in some neighborhoods, durably spatially concentrated. Prior to this study, incarceration had been primarily studied demographically—at the level of groups, states, or nations. Thinking *spatially* about punishment provides greater granularity and specificity that unlocks answers to important questions about where and why punishment occurs so commonly in one place and hardly at all in another.

What does it mean to study neighborhood prison admission rates? Figure I.1 is a simplified model of the links between community and prison. In this book, I observe neighborhoods immediately prior to a prison admission as recorded in the intake process. The corrections officer who conducts the prison intake registers background information, including the incoming resident's place of birth, race and ethnicity, educational background and religious affiliation, and last address prior to entering prison. The last item allows me to dig into geographic data to study the prior neighborhood environments of incarcerated people and community rates of imprisonment. The addresses

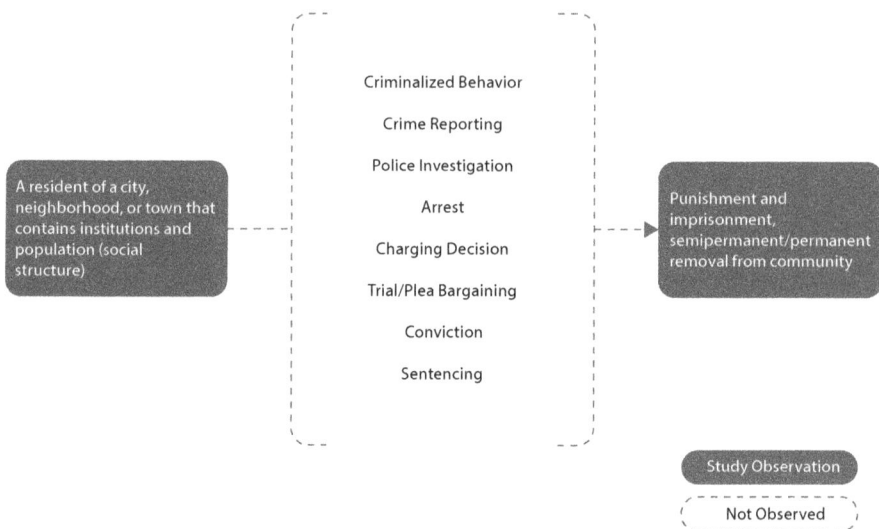

Criminalized Behavior

Crime Reporting

Police Investigation

Arrest

Charging Decision

Trial/Plea Bargaining

Conviction

Sentencing

A resident of a city, neighborhood, or town that contains institutions and population (social structure)

Punishment and imprisonment, semipermanent/permanent removal from community

Study Observation

Not Observed

FIGURE I.1. From prison to community.

reported at prison intake are also, in this analysis, linked to neighborhood, city, and county boundaries, which allow for mapping imprisonment in communities. For my purposes here, imprisonment—and removal from community—is a distinctive part of the criminal legal process directly affecting the stability and composition of neighborhoods.

Figure I.1 depicts the stages of the criminal process, each of which has been separately studied and linked to disparate outcomes in incarceration.[15] The stages have also been linked to a neighborhood context of concentrated disadvantage, which could in part explain and serve as mechanisms for the association between neighborhood context and imprisonment. The current study does not observe these intermediate steps—a limitation, given that the patterns of arrest and court processing play a role (possibly a significant one) in the neighborhood patterns of imprisonment and attending policy implications.

But like mortality in health research, imprisonment is the summation of the entire criminal legal process. Imprisonment is a social death, a disappearance, a final stage that follows from each prior stage. In order to be sent to prison and removed from society, one must have been criminalized, prosecuted, and sentenced. Further, unlike a conviction without a period of removal, imprisonment involves the *loss* of people, of members of families and communities, not just the mark of a criminal record. These two conditions of imprisonment—that it is cumulative and involves removal—suggest that it is an important and understudied condition of neighborhoods, potentially impacting community institutions and populations.

Describing incarceration for a diverse set of communities is a central concern throughout this book. Though state and federal policies formed around a narrative of "inner-city" violence and substance use in the late 1960s through the 1990s, punitive crime policy was applied to areas beyond the inner city. Patterns of policing, court processing, and punishment beyond the urban core of large metropolitan cities demand significant attention from researchers and policy makers because these are significant interventions. Using neighborhood, city, and county data from Massachusetts and across the United States, my analysis uncovers an almost universal shift in the spatial pattern of jail and prison admissions.[16] The near-total focus on large metropolitan cities in earlier studies has shaped perceptions among policy makers and the public about the nature of mass incarceration and its presumably urban impacts. Yet two decades into the twenty-first century, people who hailed from small counties constituted nearly half of the correctional population. These places are understudied, but they help explain the persistence of mass imprisonment and the rise and fall of imprisonment rates in various localities. A complete social and spatial mapping of mass imprisonment accounts for both the concentrated advantage in areas beyond city centers, largely untouched by mass incarceration, as well as the growing *regional* inequalities—such as the suburbanization of poverty—that demographers have observed for several decades.

THE PARADOX OF LIBERAL POLITICS AND PUNITIVENESS: THE CASE OF MASSACHUSETTS

I analyze data from across the United States, but to study neighborhoods, I use data from the Massachusetts Department of Correction (MADOC). My unique access to this resource stems from my response to a 2011 posting on the MADOC website for an unpaid intern. I was in my second year of graduate school when I attended training run by prison staff; most of my peers in the internship program hoped to one day work in corrections. I hoped to gain access to and learn about the prison system from the vantage of the research division. Since I engaged in that training, I have worked with the Research

Division to study patterns of imprisonment throughout the Commonwealth, but it took several months working on research briefs and projects before I earned permission to explore a key variable collected at intake: last known zip code. I tabulated the 2009 admissions data, expecting to find that the vast majority were zip codes in Boston's most disadvantaged neighborhoods. Instead, I was surprised to learn that a number of small cities reported the state's highest prison admission rates. I realized that because state prison systems do not concern themselves with individual cities or counties (their populations come from and their power presides over the entire state), I needed to adopt a fresh lens regarding what kinds of places matter for the study of imprisonment. Had I not worked in MADOC's Research Division, I may have followed other sociologists and studied only Boston neighborhoods.

Historically, the state has been known as a bellwether for progressive penal policy and reform. John Augustus, a Massachusetts bootmaker and Father of Probation, is credited with founding the early practices that would later become modern-day probationary community supervision. The Massachusetts Probation Service, the nation's first probation agency, was developed in 1878 as an alternative to prison. Another innovation was the establishment of the Norfolk Prison Colony in 1927, to address overcrowding in a Boston prison. Reformers at Norfolk sought to apply novel social, medical, psychological, and educational techniques and allowed incarcerated people to participate democratically in policy decisions at the prison.[17]

The progressive nature of early Massachusetts prisons is reflected in its contemporary institutions. Today, the state's imprisonment rate (146 per 100,000) is one-third the national rate (432 per 100,000).[18] In many respects, Massachusetts's penal history typifies Northeast and Midwest states: its criminal justice policy trajectory is both progressive and harshly punitive.[19] For instance, while the Norfolk prison has progressive roots, it has received widespread criticism for unsafe conditions as incarcerated people have voiced significant concerns about brown water coming out of the faucets (a *Boston Globe* investigation in 2017 found 43% of water samples taken from the prison contained dangerously elevated levels of manganese).[20] And while Massachusetts lawmakers conceived of probation as an alternative to penal confinement, expansions created a sort of parallel system to mass imprisonment—what Michelle Phelps calls "mass probation"—that nevertheless drew millions of people into the criminal justice system and generated an outsized presence of surveillance and control in poor communities.[21] These contradictions have come to define much of Massachusetts's and America's history of criminal

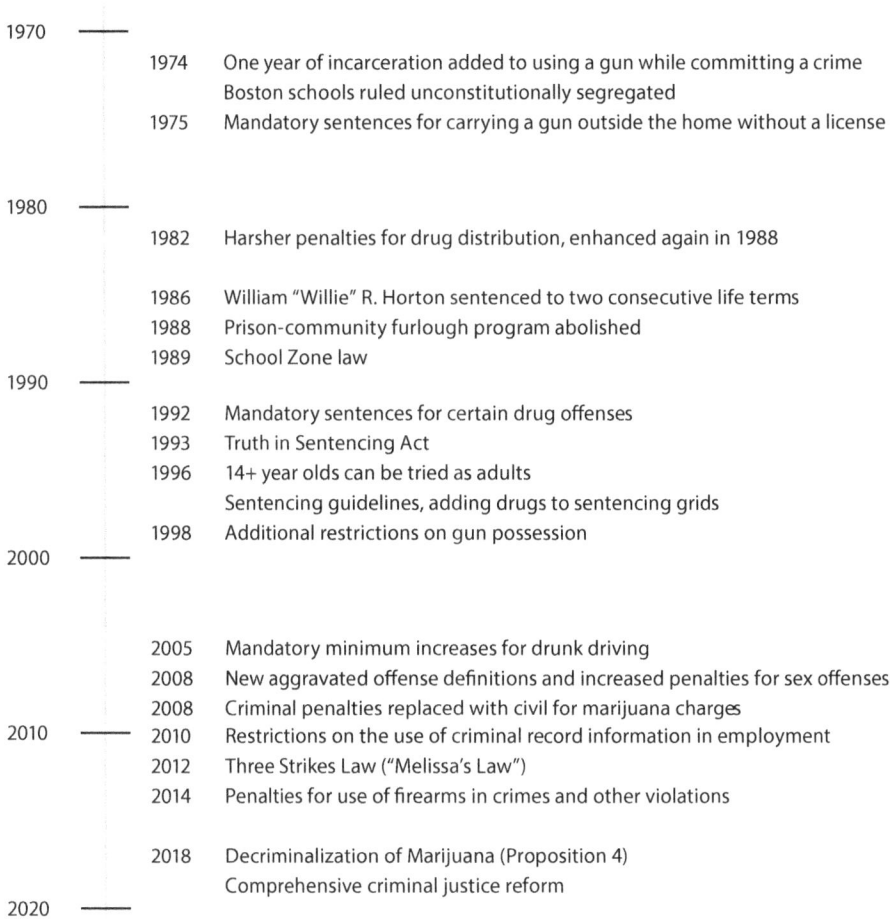

```
1970  ——

      1974   One year of incarceration added to using a gun while committing a crime
             Boston schools ruled unconstitutionally segregated
      1975   Mandatory sentences for carrying a gun outside the home without a license


1980  ——

      1982   Harsher penalties for drug distribution, enhanced again in 1988

      1986   William "Willie" R. Horton sentenced to two consecutive life terms
      1988   Prison-community furlough program abolished
      1989   School Zone law
1990  ——
      1992   Mandatory sentences for certain drug offenses
      1993   Truth in Sentencing Act
      1996   14+ year olds can be tried as adults
             Sentencing guidelines, adding drugs to sentencing grids
      1998   Additional restrictions on gun possession
2000  ——


      2005   Mandatory minimum increases for drunk driving
      2008   New aggravated offense definitions and increased penalties for sex offenses
      2008   Criminal penalties replaced with civil for marijuana charges
2010  ——  2010   Restrictions on the use of criminal record information in employment
      2012   Three Strikes Law ("Melissa's Law")
      2014   Penalties for use of firearms in crimes and other violations

      2018   Decriminalization of Marijuana (Proposition 4)
             Comprehensive criminal justice reform
2020  ——
```

FIGURE I.2. Timeline of Massachusetts tough on crime and justice reinvestment policies. *Sources:* Brownsberger (2015); Formisano (1991); Lerman and Weaver (2014a).

justice policy, in which liberal reforms have paradoxically led to increased carceral capacity.[22]

Figure I.2 displays a timeline of key policies that have made Massachusetts an important fixture in the political atmosphere of criminal justice policy and policy reform. One of the earliest nondiscretionary sentencing enhancement policies was implemented here in 1974; it increased the length of a sentence by one year for those convicted of a crime with a gun. Like much of the rest of the country, Massachusetts enacted a series of tough on crime policies in the 1990s. These included a series of sentencing enhancements, such as a "truth in sentencing" policy in 1993 and harsher guidelines for drug offenses in 1996, both of which forced imposition of longer prison sentences. The 2000s offered some reprieve; legislation lessened the harsh prosecution of cannabis-related offenses (which would be decriminalized by voters in 2018) but created new penalties and mandatory minimums for violent crimes and crimes involving a firearm. Lawmakers passed a three strikes law in 2012—a late entry among US states.

The context of persistent racial segregation in Massachusetts is another key to an understanding of neighborhood conditions and mass incarceration. By 1974, the overtly racist backlash against 1960s-era school integration (itself a response to intense racial segregation) had become plain, belying Massachusetts's ostensible integrationist superiority to southern segregation throughout the late nineteenth and early twentieth centuries. That summer, District Court judge Arthur Garrity ruled that the Boston School Committee had deliberately engaged in school segregation in defiance of federal policy. The finding exposed a roiling undercurrent of racial tension and discrimination in a city heralded for its educational and scientific excellence.[23] To achieve racial balance in the schools, Judge Garrity ordered that students be bused to schools in surrounding neighborhoods. The ruling focused primarily on schools in the predominantly White neighborhood of South Boston and the predominantly Black neighborhood of Roxbury. White residents of Boston erupted in violent opposition to the ruling, with mobs throwing bricks and rocks at school buses carrying Black children to school. After months of demonstrations, eventually the National Guard arrived in Boston to enforce court-ordered busing. Throughout openly racist protests and even under court order, conditions of segregation persisted in Boston and small cities in the state, as they do to this day.[24] Inequities in wealth by race and ethnicity remain profound and unabated; though Massachusetts still views itself as a leader in educational standards, it also leads in the achievement gap.[25] Again, the paradox of progressive policy ideals and lived realities of inequality characterizes much of Massachusetts's history.[26]

In the late 1980s, a series of events surrounding the furloughed release of William Horton from a Massachusetts state prison placed a spotlight on the state's criminal justice practices and led to a retrenchment of rehabilitative prison policies (the kind normally contrasted as progressive against what are known as punitive policies). A furlough program allows individuals who are incarcerated to leave secure facilities for short periods. During his furlough, Horton committed a series of violent crimes. Caught by police, he was sentenced to two consecutive life terms in prison, and the state ended the furlough program for good two years later. The political impacts of the Horton incident in Massachusetts, however, were far-reaching. George H. W. Bush famously used the case in racially charged television ads to undermine his presidential campaign opponent, Massachusetts governor Michael Dukakis, charging that he was dangerously "soft on crime." Scholars have attributed Bush's eventual election victory to the "Willie Horton" ad.[27]

Massachusetts's racist history maps onto racial disparities in who goes to prison. Racial disparities in incarceration are higher than national levels. In 2014, the state's Black-White incarceration ratio was 7.5 (meaning the Black incarceration rate is more than seven times the White incarceration rate), compared to a national ratio of 5.1, and its Latino-White ratio was the highest in the nation at 4.3, compared to a national ratio of 1.4.[28] Racial disparities are often higher in states where the Black population is predominantly urban and makes up a small percentage of the total state population (such as Massachusetts).[29] Accordingly, in the Bay State, the population is about 6 percent non-Hispanic Black and 10 percent Latino, yet its incarcerated population is about a quarter non-Hispanic Black and a quarter Latino.[30] Side-by-side intense racial disproportionality and liberal policy making mean that Massachusetts provides a unique and important context for understanding the community conditions of mass imprisonment.

The Massachusetts state legislature passed a comprehensive criminal justice reform bill in 2018, which reduced or eliminated some mandatory minimums, while again creating sentencing enhancements for crimes involving the distribution of fentanyl (implicated in a hefty increase in opioid-related deaths in Massachusetts since 2012). The Massachusetts District Attorneys Association staunchly opposed the 2018 reform bill. At a state judiciary committee hearing on criminal justice reform legislation, three DAs from counties representing central Massachusetts, Cape Cod, and part of Greater Boston testified in opposition to the elimination of mandatory minimum sentences for drug crimes. Specifically, they opposed the idea that treatment services could meaningfully reduce recidivism (i.e., that someone who has been convicted of a crime will commit one in the future). District Attorney Michael W. Morrissey testified that if reform passed, "You're going to remove the one safeguard that often protects the public on a sentence, on a truth-in-sentencing piece, a mandatory minimum sentence." To drive home their discontent, the DA association sent state senators a six-page letter firmly opposing many aspects of the bill, writing that Massachusetts's

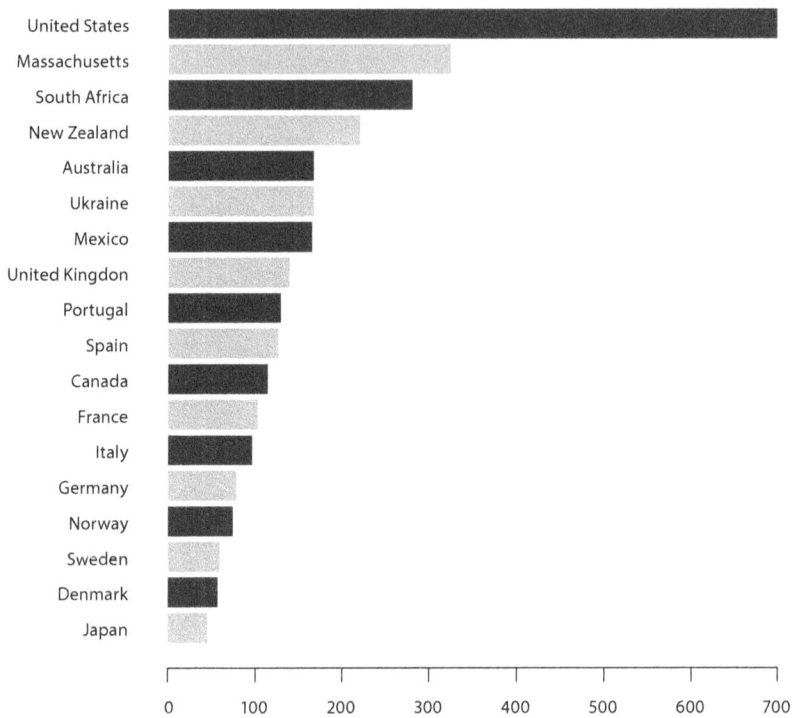

FIGURE I.3. Comparison of incarceration rates in Massachusetts, the United States, and a selection of countries, 2018. *Source:* Wagner and Sawyer (2018).

existing approach to public safety should be retained and arguing that it was an "unparalleled success" in the nation: "Massachusetts' success was achieved without resorting to the costly, draconian and self-defeating measures that other states embraced. As other states undertake criminal justice reform, they are most often trying to emulate what we have already had in place in Massachusetts. Our Commonwealth is one of the few places in the country that has achieved an incredibly low (and still declining) incarceration rate, one of the lowest rates of violent crime in the country, and even sharply declining arrest rates."[31] Massachusetts prosecutors often cite the state's low overall rate of imprisonment without acknowledging two important facts. First, Massachusetts's incarceration rate is still extremely high by any global standard (figure I.3). Its rate of imprisonment has grown considerably since the 1980s, tripling its prison and jail population. Half of this increase is attributable to growth in the incarceration of people convicted of drug-related felonies.[32] Second, as the rest of this book demonstrates, while the *state* has a low overall rate, cities, particularly those under the jurisdiction of the prosecutors who most vocally opposed the 2018 reform legislation, have incarceration rates more like the national average.

In some ways, and from a progressive social and criminal justice policy perspective, Massachusetts is a best-case scenario: it is, for instance, a wealthy state that spearheaded Medicaid expansion under Republican governor Mitt Romney in 2006, long before Obamacare became national policy. It does not ban formerly incarcerated people from voting. Executions ceased in 1947, and capital punishment was officially abolished in 1984. It has eliminated prison gerrymandering, a practice whereby governments count incarcerated people as residents of the areas where they are imprisoned and not their home communities, thus inflating the population count of the voting districts where prisons and jails are located and distorting the political influence of these areas while undermining it for incarcerated people's home communities.[33]

Nevertheless, my focal case of Massachusetts exhibits many of the important hallmarks of the American system of harsh punishment. Racialized policing in segregated neighborhoods, the passage of mandatory minimums for drugs and weapons crimes, harsh prison conditions, and the historic rise in imprisonment since the 1980s all resemble the national trend to govern social marginality and human vulnerability using the tools of punitiveness.[34] This case of very low incarceration overall, but very high disparities, offers an important window into the failure to address inequality in the context of a progressive state with a comparably robust welfare, health-care, and education system.

OVERVIEW

In what follows, I argue that mass incarceration is a broad mode of governance taking hold across a variety of community areas, including small cities, suburbs, and rural towns. The spatial distribution of US incarceration follows the contours of racial segregation, poverty, and rates of policed and criminalized behavior. The community-level conditions of pervasive incarceration reframe harsh punishment as harmful not just to the individuals who go to prison, but also to their family, friends, and neighbors.

In chapter 1 I lay out the distinctive way that a spatial view of punishment allows us to explore and deepen our understanding of the causes and consequences of mass incarceration. I discuss the two theoretical perspectives that have explained the spatial concentration of incarceration and synthesize them to build a more comprehensive theory of place and punishment.

Chapter 2 considers whether the theory produced through the urban sociology literature to explain the spatial pattern of incarceration holds up in a statewide analysis of Massachusetts data. Spatial regression yields three primary findings. First, incarceration is highly spatially concentrated; census tracts covering only 15 percent of the state's population account for half of all prison admissions. Second, across urban and nonurban areas, even after controlling for arrest and criminalized violence, incarceration is strongly related to concentrated disadvantage and the share of the Black population within census tracts. Third, admission rates in small cities and suburbs are the highest rates in the sample and far exceed what would be expected given assumptions about the neighborhood patterns of poverty, race, and criminalized violence.

Following from this third empirical finding in chapter 2, chapter 3 charts the historical trends in imprisonment, using city and county data to compare urban, suburban, small/midsized, and rural places. I focus on the places that have been understudied in the literature on imprisonment: small cities. The findings show that imprisonment has disaggregated spatially since the mid-1990s and that large metro areas no longer account for the majority of imprisonment in Massachusetts (or US) counties. In Massachusetts, prison admissions have declined since the early 2000s in a spatially concentrated way (the decline has been concentrated in Boston, its largest city). A final analysis in this chapter explores these patterns in US counties for both prison and jail, comparing the four main regions of the country.

I complement the quantitative analysis of small cities presented in chapter 3 with qualitative data derived from sixty-four in-depth, semistructured interviews with social service providers working in small cities across Massachusetts. In chapter 4 I present several mechanisms derived from these interviews. The data provide important links between the social context of high prison admission rates and spatial conditions of isolation and remoteness, social service needs and policy neglect, stigma, and the unique socioeconomic conditions of small cities.

Chapter 5 examines racial disparity in community rates of imprisonment. I present the concept of communities of pervasive incarceration to conceptually distinguish places of intense and widespread criminal justice contact. Considering racial disparity at different scales of geography, I estimate racial disproportionality—the ratio of the percentage of people who were sent to prison and the percentage of people in a geographic area—for

White, Black, and Latino people admitted to state prison in Massachusetts. Then I analyze and map the spatial clustering of prison admissions by race and ethnicity.

Measuring imprisonment rates is one thing; measuring the impact of imprisonment is another. Chapter 6 explores three new methods of measuring the latter. I first explore what it could mean to explicitly test and measure *excess incarceration*, or the idea that levels of punishment exceed norms of either a "crime-warranted" or "abolitionist" view of the current prison system. I draw from a concept in health research, "excess mortality," to develop the concept of excess incarceration as a way to imbue a measure of incarceration with moral commitments to either low or no incarceration and test how well the state meets those standards. Second, as I described earlier, I introduce the concept of community loss to measure the total years a community or neighborhood lost to the prison system during mass incarceration and reflect on what that loss means for community vitality and social bonds. Third, I offer a framework of *punishment vulnerability* as a way to conceptualize imprisonment as a community-level hazard. This measure zeros in not solely on the disadvantages observed in communities but also on the coping and resistance strategies within those communities. In doing so, I call for merging and opening cross-disciplinary data toward crafting solutions to problems surrounding the community-level effects of mass incarceration.

Chapter 7 summarizes this study's contributions to sociology and its policy implications for criminal justice reform. How might place-conscious reforms and initiatives put an end to mass incarceration?[35] What community-based models of justice respond to the state-sponsored injustice of mass incarceration? And how might abolition and reparative justice redress the harms associated with America's failed crime control experiment?

ONE

A Spatial View of Punishment

> But whatever the complex relationship between imagination, reality, and after-image, the city could never again be used as a symbol of order.
>
> —COHEN (1985)

POLICING, COURT PROCESSING, COMMUNITY SUPERVISION, AND INCARCERATION are methods of crime control that are fundamentally organized by place. Police officers are assigned to precincts; beats are broken up by blocks and other local markers.[1] Courts, probation, and parole offices preside over districts and counties, and halfway houses are carefully sited in areas of cities in accordance with presumptions about who lives where.[2] Sentencing can be enhanced when a person is convicted of a crime within school zones and other public institutions. The concentrations of arrests and prison admissions are deeply intertwined with the spatial logic of social control and the order of the city.

Throughout this book, I examine mass incarceration along multiple dimensions of place. This allows me to study how punishment is expressed in neighborhood and civic life, as well as what consequences mass incarceration may have for communities and our scholarly understanding of social disadvantage in neighborhoods. Adopting a spatial view of punishment acknowledges that, like the laws themselves, patterns of criminal justice contact are not limited by a single city or county boundary. They exist across a continuous set of places. This perspective offers new avenues for understanding patterns of social control, in a framework in which places are studied in connection as a network of neighborhoods and cities that influence and are influenced by one another.[3] Using methods in which all places are worthy of study reflects the true reach of the American criminal justice system; police, courts, prisons, and political institutions are each examined as parts of a whole, comprising the lived experience of all people within their reach, under their surveillance, and subject to their control.

To begin, I briefly describe the theoretical perspectives that have guided sociological thinking about the relationships between place and punishment. I consider the dimensions of space and place that directly or indirectly relate to patterns of social control. It is worth asking questions such as these: *Where are the most vulnerable populations located? What practices lead to concentrated incarceration? Are the conditions of exclusion and banishment a characteristic of the social ecology of urban life or the result of lawmakers' planful political calculus?*

SOCIAL CONTROL AND URBAN INEQUALITY

Two perspectives have dominated explanations of the concentrated spatial pattern of incarceration described in the criminological and urban sociology literature. The first is what I term the *social control perspective*. The second I call the *urban inequality perspective*. Both have long focused on the nature of social control and how it is enacted in places and communities, yet these two theoretical perspectives evolved largely in parallel, with little exchange or synthesis. Moreover, both perspectives make assumptions about the urban character of social control that developed into mass incarceration. Theorists from each perspective argue that the highest US incarceration rates are found in unstable, impoverished, and segregated urban neighborhoods.

Social Control Perspectives on Place and Punishment

From the social control perspective, the clustering of incarceration can first be attributed to the spatial organization of urban policing strategies, widely documented as disproportionately targeting poor and minority neighborhoods. In the 1960s, urban police forces began to inhabit an expanded role in crime prevention as well as response. Today we find a hybrid style of urban policing, which combines classic policing strategies from the latter half of the twentieth century, like misdemeanor arrests and sweeps, consent searches, and order maintenance, with the modern techniques of surveillance and spatial control in urban social contexts.[4] All these policing techniques are facilitated by the conditions and the built environment of urban places. The routine activities of urban drug dealing, for example, tend to occur in public, outdoor locations, making arrests and drug enforcement easier than in middle-class neighborhoods, suburbs, and rural areas, where drug and other criminalized activities tend to happen indoors and away from public view.[5]

Another possible explanation for the urban concentration of incarceration is the accumulation of city ordinances and criminal codes aimed at curbing urban disorder. Again, the public character of urban disorder (versus the more private character of crime and disorder in less-populated, less-built environments) has allowed for an explosion of codes and ordinances that specifically criminalize the activities of city dwellers. In response to visible crime, city and state lawmakers created urban policies imbued with spatial restrictions. This approach soon focused policing on (and expanded police power to regulate) homelessness, vagrancy, loitering, and public disorder within parks, downtown business districts, and other public areas—that is, on the behaviors most strongly associated with the experience of urban poverty and social isolation.[6] For example, the development and expansion of criminal codes for possession offenses established a precedent for threat elimination that looks strikingly similar to vagrancy laws. When policy turns to the pursuit of threat management, however, a criminalized person's culpability transforms into "nothing more than general, though cryptic, references to dangerousness."[7] The public quality of poverty and poverty-related criminalization in urban places, such as street homelessness, loitering and idleness, possession, and drug use, came to be framed in terms of security and criminality, expanding the purpose of crime control to govern social marginality.[8]

Enhancements in sentencing for criminal activity within school zones have further influenced the spatial pattern of policing to include not just schools but all public facilities, including public housing, parks, buses and bus stops, hospitals, and places of worship.[9] For example, Massachusetts General Law Section 32J stipulates mandatory minimum sentences of up to fifteen years if drug-related crimes are committed within three hundred feet of any school, or within one hundred feet of a public park or playground.[10] These areas are forbidden to people who have been convicted of certain crimes, both becoming zones of criminalization and exclusion and extending punishment beyond a criminal sentence and into free access to community space. Trespass law, once the purview of private property, has been increasingly used to monitor public places, including libraries, commercial properties and their adjacent sidewalks, welfare agencies, bus stops and train stations, and public housing.[11] The impulse of public officials to regulate the public activities of urban residents delineates who is a welcome resident of the city and who is banished.[12] Thus, scholars in the "social control" camp argue that what makes the prison distinctively urban is that public officials have designed criminal codes that strictly regulate the behavior of urban city dwellers, where the density of schools and public institutions makes nearly all space qualified for sentencing enhancements. By design, urban public places are the main targets of these codes, and the beneficiaries of these codes are mainly the businesses of the urban core, to make cities more comfortable and presentable places for the affluent.

As urban street crime and disorder came under the intensive focus of police and municipalities in the 1960s and 1970s, and ordinances that policed and criminalized people simply existing in urban public space exploded, segregative architectural forms such as the armored, fortress-like, gated community emerged in urban cities in the early 1980s.[13] Between 3 and 5 percent of residents in Chicago, Boston, and New York live in gated or walled communities.[14] Sometimes armed with private security, their walls and gates demarcate the private and public, those who belong and those who trespass, and thus who can ensure protection from violence, small disturbances and nuisances, and even police interactions. Thus, urban space and the built environment reinforce the sense of areas to which police should direct their attention and other areas where residents are given an assumed degree of privacy. Virtually all gated communities have homeowners' associations, with strict rules guiding their neighborhood environment; many have private security officers and neighborhood watch programs.[15]

The death in 2012 of Trayvon Martin took place at The Retreat at Twin Lakes, a gated community in Sanford, Florida. Martin visited the subdivision often and stayed with his father's fiancée. Martin's killer, who was eventually acquitted of all charges, led the community's neighborhood watch program. Zach Youngerman wrote in the *Boston Globe* about how the gated community may have been a factor: "Most of the Retreat at Twin Lakes lacks a conventional sidewalk—a public pedestrian thoroughfare parallel to vehicle traffic but protected by a curb. Together with a landscaped tree belt, parking lanes, and occasionally bike lanes, sidewalks and roads make up what is called the public right of way. Without public rights of way, we would all be constantly having to trespass on private land or pay tolls to get anywhere. This was the situation Martin faced inside and outside the gated subdivision."[16] As gated communities became more common in urban places after the 1980s, during the same period that mass incarceration unfolded in the United States, the social control perspective points us to the built environment's role in the policing of public space. With gated communities and gentrification, in combination with laws and ordinances banning trespass and loitering in the public realm of urban metropolises, the physical environment became an important expression of the state's orientation to violence and public safety.[17]

Beyond the built environment and community enforcement practices, a person's community context plays a role in court decisions and sentencing outcomes. Studies show that independent of individual or case characteristics, bias and discrimination on the basis of a stigmatized neighborhood residence may influence court decisions and provide a partial explanation for variation in incarceration rates across space. Research on sentencing finds that neighborhood disadvantage is a strong predictor of charging, prosecution, criminal sentencing, and incarceration, even when controlling for a defendant's economic status.[18] More recent research finds that defendants from Black and Latino neighborhoods are sentenced to prison at a significantly higher rate, even after adjusting for the potential prosecutorial focus on areas with high reported crime.[19] Neighborhood stigma, from this perspective, drives decisions of prosecutors and judges in sentencing practices.

Theorists in this tradition, as I mentioned previously, have implicitly argued that the prison itself is an urban institution. Loïc Wacquant makes an *explicit* case for an urban city-prison link. Unlike Michelle Alexander, who draws a historical parallel between Jim Crow and mass incarceration, Wacquant draws a historical link between the urban ghetto that emerged after Jim Crow in the industrializing North and the historic increase in imprisonment that followed. These institutions—ghetto and prison—are theorized by Wacquant to be symbiotic and functionally equivalent, following from two prior racist institutions of chattel slavery and Jim Crow: "As the walls of the ghetto shook and threatened to crumble, the walls of the prison were correspondingly extended, enlarged, and fortified. . . . Soon the black ghetto . . . became bound to the jail and prison system by a triple relationship of functional equivalency, structural homology, and cultural syncretism, such that they now constitute a single *carceral continuum* which entraps a redundant population of younger black men (and increasingly women) who circulate in closed circuit between its two poles in a self-perpetuating cycle of social and legal marginality with devastating personal and social consequences."[20] In turn, their reciprocity perpetuates the socioeconomic marginality and stigma of a dispossessed Black population and feeds the runaway growth of the carceral system.[21]

The Northeast and Rust Belt did not contain the only urban places afflicted by mass incarceration. Ruth Wilson Gilmore, in *Golden Gulag:*

Prisons, Surplus, and Opposition in Globalizing California, draws a connection between urban populations and the growth of the penal state in rural areas and explores "how urban social expense fits into the rural landscape."[22] In her account of the geographic demography of California's incarcerated people, she writes, "Most prisoners come from the state's urban cores—particularly Los Angeles and the surrounding southern counties. . . . In short, as a class, convicts are deindustrialized cities' working or workless poor."[23] An economic crisis of unemployment emerged as manufacturing hollowed out urban labor in postwar America. A surplus population in the West's urban core combined with surplus land in rural portions of California to produce a prison boom and mass incarceration. For Gilmore, like Wacquant, the urban city as the locus of racialized poverty and estrangement from the labor market merged with other political and economic forces to produce "the biggest prison construction program in the history of the world."[24]

Beyond the very real conditions of poverty, unemployment, and social control in cities, the city became an important political symbol, used to drive public support for punitive policies. In *Visions of Social Control*, Stanley Cohen investigates the city's role as a powerful metaphor used to justify punitive criminal justice policies: "With the industrial revolution, these metaphors gave way to reality and a darker, more complicated image emerged of the city as a problem, a form of evil in itself."[25] This image persisted well into the 1960s and 1970s, with the jail and the prison becoming the answer to the problem of social control in cities.[26] "As both metaphor and social fact, the city became identified with crime, racialism, poverty, unemployment, discrimination, violence, and insecurity," Cohen continues.[27] Thus the state assembled policies to compensate for the loss of *community* amid the violence and unrest that came to represent American cities. This metaphor was no accident. It played on concepts of order and community that had political salience, conveying the conversion of cities and the "streets" of urban life into an arena of social and racial crisis. The very communities most impacted by violence became those that were most impacted by crime control policy, burdened by the emerging penological consensus around managing social problems in disadvantaged urban neighborhoods.

Cohen specifically describes the early Chicago school's emphasis on crime as contagion and its particular focus on the urban areas that separate central business districts and outer working- and middle-class residential areas as concentrated areas of vice, poverty, violence, residential instability, and other social ills. "Within their complex moral geography of the city—those unforgettable concentric circles—the solution for the areas of disorganization was to restore community control."[28] In this way, Cohen critically assesses the urban literature's apolitical view of the social ecology of crime and punishment. The very analysis of the social disorganization of the city produced by the early Chicago school provided a map for intensified social control practices.

Many crime prevention policies reflected this metaphor of the city in crisis, evoked in the naming of programs aimed at crime prevention in neighborhoods. As historian Elizabeth Hinton recounts in her capacious accounting of anti-poverty policy and its relationship to mass incarceration, President Lyndon B. Johnson established the National Commission on Law Enforcement and Administration of Justice in 1967, and in the following year he passed a capstone of his Great Society: the Safe Streets Act. The act invested an initial $400 million in programs and agencies aimed at crime control projects throughout the county.[29] The commission's report underscored two facts that remain central to the design of crime policy today: "Two striking facts that the [Uniform Crime Reports] and every other examination of American crime disclose are that most crimes, wherever they are committed, are committed by boys and young men, and that most crimes, by whomever they are committed, are committed in cities."[30] Significantly, the entirety of the political spectrum perpetuated the urban crisis narrative. In this period of great social upheaval during the late 1960s and early 1970s, a broad coalition of conservatives, liberals, progressives, researchers, policy makers, and prisoner advocates used these metaphors to evoke national public concern over social problems in the so-called inner city. *Urban* became synonymous with *crime*, and both terms became synonymous with *Blackness*.[31] American social policy was transformed, yet still rooted in anti-Black sentiments.

The political salience of urban street crime rose as the candidates and elected officials of the late 1960s elevated urban street crime to the national platform. Many believed Johnson's Great Society and subsequent welfare policy in the United States had failed due to their inability to fully address urban unrest and violence.[32] As Michael Flamm writes, "By the fall of 1968, explosion after explosion had rocked the nation, leaving liberals on the defensive and conservatives on the march. By crafting a popular message and exploiting favorable circumstances, they had seized control of the most important domestic issue in American politics. The triumph of law and order was on the horizon."[33] States and local communities have followed suit, and recent examples invoking this vision of social control demonstrate the relationship between the city, criminalization, and punishment. For example, the 1968 Safe Streets Act was followed, in the mid-1970s, by the New Jersey Safe and Clean Neighborhoods Program. In 2001 the US Department of Justice announced its Project Safe Neighborhoods to address gun and gang violence at the local, state, and tribal levels (it has been implemented in cities and communities across the country). Four years later, Los Angeles launched The Safer Cities Initiative, a hallmark of LAPD chief William Bratton's broken windows approach, which deploys police officers to surveil homeless populations in Skid Row.[34] StreetSafe Boston was established in 2008 by the Boston Foundation and aimed to help reduce violence by focusing interventions on approximately twenty of the city's most active gangs in neighborhoods disproportionately affected by violence. Safe streets acts and initiatives have proliferated since President Johnson's administration, implicitly contrasting notions of "clean" or "safe" against the chaotic, violent, and dirty "streets" in need of cleaning and the restoration of order via formal state intervention. Highly marginalized and hypersegregated urban neighborhoods are persistent targets for social control.

At the 2016 Republican National Convention, it was clear that then-nominee Donald J. Trump would gleefully resuscitate law-and-order politics in the same vein as Johnson's Great Society programs. Accepting the party's nomination for the American presidency, Trump declared, "We will be a country of generosity and warmth. But we will also be a country of law and order."[35] Later in the speech, he remarked: "Americans watching this address tonight have seen the recent images of violence in our streets and the chaos in our communities. Many have witnessed this violence personally, some have even been its victims."[36] Not coincidentally, during the run-up to Trump's 2016 election, cities around the country were experiencing widespread protests against police killings and brutality. Two opposing political movements—one supporting the victims of police killings and the other supporting police officers under scrutiny—are tidily encapsulated by a pair of battle cries: "Black Lives Matter" and "Blue Lives Matter." Invoking the language of cities as a font of violence and fear and speaking directly to Blue Lives Matter supporters, Trump threatened: "I have a message to every last person threatening the peace on our streets and the safety of our police: when I take the oath of office next year, I will restore law and order our country."[37] During the early summer of 2020, when the entire world was grappling with the coronavirus pandemic, the police killings of George Floyd and Breonna Taylor spurred communities to action. The "streets" filled with an unprecedented number of public protests; between 15 and 26 million people protested during June 2020, with chants of "Black Lives Matter" in hundreds of protests.[38] In response, city and federal police, clad in riot gear and armed with tanks and other weapons of war, fortified whole neighborhoods to protect private property.[39] US senator Ron Wyden (D-Oregon) stated in response to the deploying of federal officers in Portland in July 2020: "What America does not need is Donald Trump parachuting federal law enforcement into U.S. cities as if they're enemy strongholds requiring an occupying army to suppress."[40] If Trump aimed to defeat activists and restore peace on "our streets" amid the BLM protests of 2015, he clearly missed.

The social control perspective provides a causal argument for the effects of state-sponsored disadvantage and incarceration, attributing the spatial concentration of incarceration to urban policing and order maintenance strategies aimed at controlling threats to social order—beyond violent crime—under historical conditions of concentrated urban disadvantage. In this view, mass imprisonment represents a regime of racialized urban poverty created through a series of shifts in criminal justice policy and practices directed at social problems associated with the urban poor. The public character of urban disorder opened the way for a proliferation of codes and ordinances that criminalize the activities of poor city residents, framing urban homelessness, possession, drug use, and vagrancy as matters of security and criminality. Hot spots policing and civil gang injunctions provide further examples of strategies aimed at particular locations to curb behaviors associated with urban marginality, such as gang activities deemed *dangerous*, though not explicitly criminal. The pattern of concentrated incarceration emerged from the activities of the state to govern urban social marginality beyond crime. Cities became important symbols for the state's legitimate use of violence, enacted upon its most marginalized populations.

In the vast and diverse body of work comprising the social control perspective, theories of punishment's spatial pattern tend to be wary or even critical of the implication that there is a relationship between incarceration and crime.[41] These scholars tend to argue that the concentration of social control efforts in disadvantaged places produced the pattern of punishment—significantly, independent of the spatial distribution of criminalized behavior and violence.[42] The combination of policing strategies, criminal codes, public ordinances, and sentencing practices that fueled mass imprisonment expanded the scope of criminal processing to the governance and management of urban social problems associated with economically and socially marginalized people and places.[43] In short, any measure of crime is endogenous to crime control practices: where police and other agents of social control direct their efforts and whom they criminalize. Further, social control scholars argue, the concentration of incarceration among the most marginal members of society is an expected result of suppressing an entire population from full membership in American community life.[44]

Taken together, these theories about the spatial distribution of punishment suggest imprisonment is a central part of racialized urban poverty, largely independent of crime patterns. Given the racist origins of crime statistics, the inaccuracy of those records, and the inconsistencies in reporting practices, crime is rarely considered an important factor shaping the ecology of imprisonment in this perspective.[45]

Urban Inequality Perspectives on Place and Punishment

The urban inequality perspective describes a multifaceted urban ecology in which rates of incarceration and violence are highest in neighborhoods of concentrated disadvantage. When studying variation in incarceration rates, urban inequality researchers typically first attempt to account for crime rates.[46]

Historically, urban violence rates have far exceeded rates recorded in rural and suburban areas.[47] In the urban inequality perspective, the spatial distribution of incarceration maps onto the spatial pattern of criminalized behavior, which concentrates in urban areas. This pattern of concentration is also found *within* urban cities themselves. In an examination of the association between incarceration and reported crime rates in Chicago community areas, the correlation is near unity (0.96), indicating there are virtually no high crime–low incarceration neighborhoods in the city of Chicago.[48] Within urban space, crime is highly spatially concentrated. As Sampson and Wilson (1995) discuss, however, that fact urges a deep consideration of the role of community context and the ecological concentration of poverty, racial segregation, population turnover, family disruption, and weak civic participation within urban space. Thus, urban social scientists and geographers who study the concentration of incarceration in place focus mainly on the imprisonment rate as a correlate of concentrated disadvantage and include incarceration among the measures of disadvantage typically used to define neighborhood deprivation.[49] The resulting scholarship has emphasized the ecological pattern of crime, neighborhood disadvantage (poverty, unemployment, reliance on public assistance), and incarceration.[50]

Race is a fundamental organizing principle that stratifies advantages and disadvantages in US neighborhoods and communities.[51] Extreme racial segregation and social isolation in urban locales profoundly impacts the spatial pattern of arrests and offending.[52] For instance, Black and Latino populations are most likely to live in places of extreme residential segregation and concentrated deprivation; they are disproportionately represented in arrest, conviction, and incarceration populations.[53] Those researchers adopting the urban inequality perspective note that racial segregation is correlated with a set of adversities pertaining to socioeconomic deprivation. These include the prevention of wealth accumulation, underresourced schools, limited access to social service infrastructure like hospitals and public transportation, and persistent poverty and joblessness. Racial segregation has also been discussed as the direct result of state policies, restrictive housing covenants and redlining, and White flight.[54] In short, in the United States, it is far more likely for a Black child's parent to have grown up in a poor, segregated neighborhood than for a White child's to have done so, and accumulated, generational disadvantage means that persistent segregation must be regarded as a key factor explaining racially differentiated life outcomes—including exposure to violence.[55]

High imprisonment rates are taken, in the urban inequality perspective, as one of the social disadvantages spatially clustering within urban areas. In this description of urban inequality, concentrated disadvantage and violent crime are the strongest predictors of neighborhood incarceration rates; indeed, scholars of urban inequality consistently find patterns of offending and arrest are highly concentrated in poor and racially segregated urban neighborhoods.[56] Moreover, the ecological structure of crime and formal social control has been theorized to "spill over" into contiguous surrounding neighborhoods, influencing patterns of criminal justice contact independent of the internal neighborhood context.[57] This spatial diffusion across neighborhoods suggests that prison admissions will be highly spatially correlated or clustered across neighboring areas.

The broken-windows policing described earlier in connection with one of its champions, LAPD chief Bratton, has at its core the broken windows theory advanced by criminologists James Q. Wilson and George L. Kelling. Drawing a direct link between crime and urban places, establishing another ecological basis for the relationship between urban disorder, crime, and later the concentration of incarceration, Wilson writes in *Thinking About*

Crime, "The citizen who fears the ill-smelling drunk, the rowdy teenager, or the importuning beggar is not merely expressing his distaste for unseemly behavior, he is also giving voice to a bit of folk wisdom that happens to be a correct generalization—namely, that serious street crime flourishes in areas in which disorderly behavior goes unchecked."[58] Prominent theories about the relationship between disorder and crime have spawned a long-standing debate over the effectiveness and indeed the constitutionality of the order-maintenance policing taken up by police departments in cities like Los Angeles and New York.[59] The theory itself is distinctly urban because it focuses on the public character of disorder—the view from the street—and suggests that disorder breeds crime because seemingly insignificant breaks in social norms (like unmended windows) are thought to accumulate in a breakdown of further social norms. Soon crime is high, trust is low, and someone needs to step in to nip things in the bud. Social scientists and policy makers drew direct links between urbanicity and crime and used broken windows theory to urge intensive, even deeply intrusive urban policing.

Social scientists from both the social control and urban inequality perspectives have criticized the broken windows ecological perspective. A great many believe the rise and prominence of stop-and-frisk, hot spots policing, and targeting of disadvantaged neighborhoods (all of which have a spatial character) were undue and disproportionate costs for paltry returns.[60] Throughout the 1980s and 1990s, police focused on disorder, enforcing codes through strategies designed for uneven implementation. Cops targeted specific neighborhoods based on concentrations of vacant lots and other symptoms of urban disorder, and they aggressively pursued misdemeanor crime. Scholars looking at this style of policing in retrospect (and some at the time) have argued that it relies on the shared meanings of and bias toward certain urban places and behaviors stigmatized through their association with race and class.[61] In addition, specific strategies, such as hot spots policing, intentionally create highly concentrated spatial patterns of police contact, arrest, and incarceration, ostensibly to focus on the few involved in criminalized activity.[62] Examining how not only the socioeconomic conditions and crime, but also the social control strategy responses, may be related spatially, compels an adaptation of the spatial approach to consider the web of geographically contingent conditions that drive high levels of incarceration. In short, *who* goes to prison from *where* should consider multiple community-level factors as well as state interventions.

The social control and urban inequality perspectives are not fundamentally opposed when it comes to explaining the spatial patterns of imprisonment. They do, however, differ in three key ways. First, each theory differently situates the explanatory role of the state in producing concentrated prison admissions. The social control perspective emphasizes the role of the state in generating patterns of social inequality, an imprint evidenced by the social structure of neighborhoods. The state's exertion of violent force and control over marginalized groups and places organizes the pattern of policing, court processing, and incarceration. Conversely, the urban inequality perspective deemphasizes the role of the state in favor of understanding the ecological relationships among structural social and demographic conditions.[63] While the state may be compelled to respond to the "natural" outcomes of certain combinations of social and demographic conditions, acknowledging the state's role in these unjust and discriminatory practices is notably absent from place-based reform efforts.

A second key difference concerns the broader implications of their views of place and punishment. Social control theorists focus on how incarceration is a fundamentally segregative social institution that reflects and reinforces the spatial and social exclusion of the most marginalized groups. The urban inequality perspective emphasizes the ecological pattern of social disadvantages and how patterns of incarceration are enmeshed with multiple neighborhood conditions within and across neighborhoods. The difference is subtle, but each suggests a different kind of policy response. The former emphasizes decarceration, less punishment, and shrinking the role of police in everyday life. The second might focus more on strengthening community bonds, or by increasing services and economic resources available in disadvantaged communities.

The third key differentiator between these theoretical perspectives is in their treatment of crime as an explanatory factor in patterned incarceration. Many social control theorists do not account for crime in their descriptions of the distribution of incarceration, while urban inequality researchers consider crime a fundamental and obvious driver of those patterns.

What unites these theoretical perspectives is their mutual focus on the city and distinctly urban social problems, urban social control institutions and practices, and the historical emergence of concentrated deprivation brought about by policy and the ecology of populations in American cities. Research has demonstrated the role of major urban cities in mass imprisonment as a matter of crime and conditions of concentrated disadvantage, yet little scholarly work has examined whether contemporary spatial patterns of imprisonment outside major urban cities are explained by crime alone or in conjunction with other factors.[64] To truly account for spatial patterns of incarceration, we need a unified theory of punishing places that draws from both perspectives *and* holds explanatory power when it comes to the emergent patterns of incarceration beyond large cities. The unstated assumption of those studying urban incarceration rates is that studying prison admissions, crime, and neighborhood concentrated disadvantage within large cities will capture most of the variation in the spatial distribution of penal confinement. My data suggest otherwise.

To establish a unified understanding of place and punishment, I draw on both perspectives. I follow the instinct of social control scholars to identify broad demographic trends and regional differences in punishment across a diverse set of states. I also follow urban inequality scholars who emphasize the importance of relationships among conditions within and across smaller geographic areas. Combining these two perspectives is significant for grasping the conditions and disparities of mass incarceration and crafting effective policy reforms. From this vantage point, we can see how a unified theory of place and punishment would argue that mass incarceration resulted from a panoply of harsh and punitive policy decisions made by an array of actors in the criminal legal system to manage broad social and economic problems most associated with non-White groups, particularly Black men. These similarly spirited practices and policies diffused across a diverse set of places and, since the start of the prison boom, have been implemented unevenly across space. As a result, poor communities across the rural-urban continuum, especially poor communities of color, exhibit extreme levels of neighborhood incarceration. Incarceration has become a strong force in the lives of people outside of the large cities that once symbolized the chaos and violence of American life and drew much-needed attention as the epicenters of reform efforts. Now, as punitive and criminalizing practices remain and intensify in small cities and rural areas, we can see that the spatial pattern of prison admissions follows the historical trajectories of *both* policy and population.

Where does crime, and in particular violent crime, come into a unified theory of punishing places? I am skeptical of any analysis of incarceration that ignores the reality of violent crime and its relationship to social control, but I am also deeply skeptical of an uncritical view of crime statistics in analyses of the criminal justice system. On the one hand, I believe criminological and urban inequality theories tend to *overestimate* the role of crime in predicting rates of imprisonment, largely because reported crime and arrest statistics are endogenous to the patterns and practices of policing. Put another way, what may be reflective of violence in part will also be reflective of policing; concentrations of violence in the official record are likely due, at least in part, to where police choose to look for them. Moreover, an analysis that accounts for violent crime could amount to a community-level "blaming the victim," in which policing and incarceration are the presumed responses to violence, when in fact a number of responses could be deployed by the state. Arrest and incarceration remain policy *choices*.

On the other hand, a study of the community-level conditions of mass incarceration that denies the experience of violence in impoverished neighborhoods and communities of color would be an incomplete analysis.[65] Moralizing individuals caught up in the criminal justice system via the inordinate focus on nonviolent drug offenders in reform efforts, say, place much focus on those criminalized activities with fewer obvious human costs, neatly sidestepping the far more morally complicated realities of harm and violence. Moreover, justice practices can acknowledge harm without inflicting more of it.[66] Denying that violence is spatially and socially patterned drives much-needed attention away from the generations and lifetimes of violence described in life histories of formerly incarcerated people and the intergenerational and contextual effects of exposure to violence on children.[67]

The social control and urban inequality perspectives each paint an incomplete portrait of concentrated disadvantage, and resolving this debate over the role of crime is further complicated by the possibility that high rates of imprisonment may also cause crime to increase, if broken community bonds and residential instability emanating from the churn of prison's revolving door leads to further criminalization.[68]

Throughout the book, I use the terms *criminalized behavior* and *criminalized violence* to account for both perspectives. In some instances I refer to *reported crime*. Criminalized behavior accounts for experiences of violence (behavior), but also shows that measures accounting for this behavior are in part driven by state actors and the stigma of people and places (criminalized), not a natural state of being violent or criminal. Criminalization of particular behaviors such as drug use or selling can be clearly attributed to social control theories of deviance and social marginality. I use drug *arrest* statistics (note that not all reported crime leads to an arrest, so arrest statistics more directly capture the social control environment) to account for drug enforcement by police at the community or neighborhood level, not as an objective measure of "drug crime." For behaviors that are more harmful and potentially correlated with imprisonment rates in communities, I use the Uniform Crime Reports (UCRs) on more serious violent crimes (murder, rape, aggravated assault, and robbery) in several chapters of this book to capture rates of criminalized violence in a neighborhood or city.

The Empirical Implications of a Unified Theory of Punishing Places

With a few exceptions, existing studies of urban neighborhood imprisonment rates have provided the main empirical evidence for understanding the relationship between neighborhood conditions and rates of imprisonment.[69] Driven in large part by the contributions of urban inequality and social control scholars I have described, incarceration is now largely defined as a facet of spatially concentrated disadvantage in urban places marked by poverty, joblessness, population turnover, racial segregation, heightened surveillance, and criminalized violence. These criminal and civil disorder codes, police practices, and economic blight fell upon the US urban population, so research on the social problem of spatially concentrated incarceration has been almost entirely conducted within the bounds of large urban areas and has resulted almost entirely in freestanding case studies of specific cities.

For those who hope to understand rates of criminal justice involvement, there are significant costs to studying just one type of geography. For example, studying areas with low levels of incarceration deepens and broadens our understanding of social inequality. We can learn much from comparisons of places with, say, similar socioeconomic conditions but different levels of incarceration, which might be instructive when it comes to policy reforms aimed at reducing the footprint of the criminal justice system. By limiting samples to large urban cities, scholars have essentially cut out whole swaths of the population in places at the extremes of the distribution—places with very low and very high rates of incarceration. Empirically, this practice has generated biased estimates of the social disadvantage–incarceration association, and it has certainly underestimated social inequality.[70]

Theory has yet to offer satisfying explanations of high rates of incarceration beyond major metro areas, though researchers—especially those reckoning with the surge of social movements aimed at police violence, reform, and even abolition—have begun to explore suburban contexts.[71] John Eason's research, for example, identifies what he calls the "rural ghetto" as a critical mechanism driving prison proliferation.[72] His work suggests that a web strung between the conditions of deep and systemic poverty, race, stigma, and prison largely explain the consequences of expansive carceral proliferation in impoverished rural areas. More simply, Eason writes that the rural ghetto and the urban ghetto are alike in their high levels of segregation and stigmatization. The Vera Institute of Justice reported in a 2015 report that the growth in the US jail population between 1970 and 2014 was mostly driven by the growth of jail populations in *small* counties (population less than 200,000).[73] And an article published in the *New York Times* in 2016 drew on work by John Pfaff to demonstrate the profound levels of jail incarceration affecting nonurban or less populous counties.[74] This small literature—especially Eason's crucial contributions to the study of the spatial distribution of criminal justice institutions into rural areas—is exciting and productive, begging us to consider whether prison admissions spatially concentrate in rural areas and which conditions explain the high levels of incarceration in other localities, like small cities and suburbs.

Poverty and social marginality take unique forms in rural areas, suburbs, and small cities. Some can be traced to the urban focus of prior policy interventions. Suburbs and rural areas today have a dearth of service provision organizations, particularly poverty-oriented social programs.[75] Substance use and criminalized violence, and the policing of such activities, is a relatively new phenomenon in these regions, propelled by trends including the spread of methamphetamine use and production in rural areas and small cities with high numbers of young, low-income Whites.[76] In Massachusetts, a recent increase in opioid related-deaths has brought significant attention to drug trafficking, and local news now heavily covers opioid drug enforcement in smaller cities and suburbs.[77] As a police spokesperson from Chicopee, a suburb of Springfield, Massachusetts, with a population of about 50,000, stated after a major heroin bust in October 2016: "The more we can confiscate, the more dealers we can arrest, we understand that it will help save lives. That's our goal to save lives and to get this stuff off the street."[78] Echoes of the city or the "streets" as a metaphor for disorder appear in these small towns and suburbs all across the country.

And though urban violence rates have historically far exceeded rural and suburban rates, this disparity has recently decreased dramatically across the United States.[79] By 2019, urban areas had a reported violent crime rate of 21 per 1,000 persons over age twelve, while suburban and rural places were at about 22 and 16 per 1,000 respectively, closing a gap that for decades was at least twice as large.[80] The increases in reported violent crime and drug use in suburbs, rural towns, and small cities can be explained by late-twentieth-century shifts in their populations and economies. Some larger cities like Boston have partially recovered from the economic decline driven by deindustrialization, yet the smaller, more isolated working-class cities, especially in New England, the Northeast, and the Midwest, struggle to find sustenance, let alone sustained economic growth. In addition, the suburbanization of poverty and rapid central-city gentrification have altered the geography of social inequality.[81] Between 2000 and 2011, micropolitan areas (those centered on a smaller city of 10,000 to 50,000 residents) experienced a near-doubling of their population in high-poverty neighborhoods (from about 520,000 to nearly 1 million people).[82] Independent of poverty and the supply of health-care options, one study found that rural status confers additional disadvantages that depress health-care access.[83] Another recent study shows that prosecutors from less-populous counties increasingly pursue harsher sentences than their urban counterparts.[84] These realities point to new sites for investigating racial bias and formal social control beyond the conditions of so-called inner-city neighborhoods.

What differentiates these smaller cities and towns from large urban cities like Boston or Chicago is not their demography or levels of concentrated disadvantage; in fact, the conditions are often much the same. No, their uniqueness is their *growing* role in the persistence of mass incarceration and socioeconomic decline. In 1973, Boston accounted for nearly 50 percent of Massachusetts's admissions to prison, despite only accounting for about 18 percent of the state's population. By 2014, with its population stable since the 1970s, Boston's share of new prison admissions had dropped to only about 18 percent. Small cities account for the vast majority of today's prison admissions, which historically speaking is new. To date, studies of the spatial pattern of incarceration beyond large-city case studies have yet to supplement descriptive accounts with statistical models capable of considering a variety of community-level conditions that may aid us in explaining these shifts.

AN ABRIDGED GLOSSARY OF PLACE AND PUNISHMENT

To provide shared terminology and conceptual clarity, the following discussion outlines a set of concepts in sociological research on place and how they are important for studying punishment. I describe a number of urban and community concepts, as well as spatial and geographic measures.

Neighborhoods and Community Areas

A considerable research literature has been devoted to the study of neighborhoods and their effects on life chances (individual level, e.g., poverty status) and rates of behavior or events in the neighborhood (neighborhood level, e.g., incarceration rate). As a construct and unit of analysis, neighborhoods come with opportunities and challenges. Scholars still widely debate the precise definition of the "neighborhood" as a theoretical construct, empirical unit of analysis, and lived community experience.

Early Chicago school luminaries Robert Park and Ernest Burgess characterize neighborhoods as having "close proximity, co-operation, intimate social contact, and strong feeling of social consciousness."[85] To them, a neighborhood was "a social unit which, by its clear definition of outline, its inner organic completeness, its hair trigger reactions, may be fairly considered as functioning like a social mind."[86] The capacity for the transmission of social norms or levels of social control in neighborhoods, they continued, was drastically undermined by economic isolation and residential instability. These scholars were proposing the salience of culture and structure within communities as they considered how these urban social processes influenced levels of reported delinquency and crime. The unit of analysis was not the individual, but rates of social behavior that varied by neighborhood-level culture and social structure. In Park and Burgess's 1925 book *The City*, neighborhoods operated within the larger city structure as "natural areas": communities defined in terms of the "common experience of the group." Neighborhoods in this perspective are interdependent, highly localized community areas engaged in processes of symbiosis, cooperation, competition, and conflict.

Half a century later, in his 1974 book *Symbolic Communities*, Albert Hunter defined the "city" as a functionally integrated whole, made up of interdependent local community areas (i.e., neighborhoods). To Hunter, the "community" concept carries distinctive ecological and normative roles. It is ecological in the sense that there exists a selective spatial distribution of populations and functions, and interaction is mediated through this physical environment. It is normative on the basis of the shared collective representations and moral sentiments, born out of the cultural and symbolic elements of "community."

Hunter defines the "neighborhood" via residents' perceptions of both physical and social boundaries. Within this unit, he writes, the individual "appears to have the most primary interaction but the least spatial distinctiveness. There are not likely to be any institutions so finely differentiated as to serve the collective needs of such a small unit. Furthermore, such a fine differentiation results in so many social blocks that they would cause a cognitive overland if they were used for symbolic identifications throughout the city."[87] In line with Hunter's logic, this book more precisely defines the neighborhood as *a social and spatial unit of social organization*, larger than a household and smaller than a city.

However complex and stylized the descriptions of place and space, quantitative social scientists, including myself, treat census tracts and other units such as block groups as proxies for neighborhoods. Census tracts, due to my desire to analyze census data in conjunction with data from large administrative datasets that often include imperfect geographic data for individuals contacted by the criminal justice system, are among the best available units for identifying neighborhoods. Still, much of what we know to be the neighborhood is based in shared meanings and associations that are poorly captured by designations like blocks and census tracts; these just aren't the intuitive ways people describe where they live. Nonetheless, the analyses throughout this book employ census tracts to analyze rates of incarceration in neighborhoods and use the terms *tract* and *neighborhood* interchangeably.

Urban, Suburban, Exurban, Rural

Urban, suburban, and rural designations often refer to perceptions and meanings as much as may they may correspond to geospatial measures. The word *rural* might conjure farmland, villages, and open space, while *urban* may conjure skyscrapers, business districts, and density of people. Urban places in the social sciences are often connected to cities and incorporated places; rural places are often associated with towns and unincorporated, noncity areas. Just in this short list of descriptors, the difference between urban and rural relates to administrative, land-use, and economic conditions.[88] How these terms are operationalized has been widely explored by the fields of geography, epidemiology, and sociology.[89] The most common method of identifying urban/rural is through population density.[90]

Census definitions are largely based on coarse population thresholds. By one definition, there are two types of urban areas in the United States: urbanized areas (UAs) of 50,000 or more people, and urban clusters (UCs) of at least 2,500 and fewer than 50,000 people. Rural is defined as all population, housing, and territory *not* included in a UA or UC. The most populous urban county in the country, according to 2010 Census data, is Los Angeles County, with 9.8 million residents. The least populous rural county is Loving County, Texas, with 82 residents. The Census also uses the terms *metropolitan*, *micropolitan*, and *nonmetropolitan*; qualification as a metropolitan statistical area (MSA), for instance, requires the presence of a city of 50,000 or more inhabitants *or* a Census Bureau–defined UA (of at least 50,000 inhabitants) and a total population of at least 100,000 (75,000 in New England, since cities are smaller there on average).

Suburban communities emerged during several decades of White, middle-class migration out of central cities.[91] However, today the American suburb is much more diverse than the traditional imaginary of suburbs.[92] Defining a suburb, particularly for quantitative studies, involves a combination of administrative designations, adjacency to central cities (e.g., inner ring, outer ring), and the density and age of the built environment.[93] A common strategy for defining suburbs is to designate all areas within an MSA or metropolitan area beyond the primary central city as suburbs.[94] This method is useful for comparing urban and suburban areas but does not allow for a comparison of different types of suburbs.[95] Jill K. Clark and colleagues offer the following definitions of exurbs: "Exurbia is conceptualized as a place of transition between urban and rural, located somewhere between the suburbs and truly rural areas and within the commuting zone of a large, urbanized area."[96]

Other work explores the concept of *neighborhood* in rural communities, a unit of analysis typically reserved for urban areas. Eason defines the rural ghetto as "the concentration of racial and economic disadvantage in a stigmatized neighborhood in a micropolitan town."[97] A systematic review of the measurement and conceptualization of rural neighborhoods identified only nineteen studies that examine neighborhoods in rural regions and found that typical measures of concentrated disadvantage, such as poverty or unemployment rates, may be less salient for rural neighborhood residents' life chances than other contextual measures, such as isolation, remoteness, and access to services.[98]

Indeed, cultural and social meanings associated with places and populations regularly determine how people define urban, suburban, and rural designations. Some regions of the country are understood as particularly urbanized (e.g., the Northeast), while other regions are associated with large rural areas (e.g., the South). The urban/rural dichotomy has a strong presence in the criminal justice literature on prison and jail sitings. Prisons tend to be located in rural areas, while jails can be found in city centers.[99] Geographers have drawn attention to the spatial mismatch of prison location (rural) and the populations entering prison gates (urban).[100]

Cities, Counties, States

Geography matters for criminal justice jurisdiction and control because it often determines the division of the state's coercive power across institutions and people. An encounter with the police in a *city* tends to mean an encounter with a *city jurisdiction*, whereas an encounter with the police in a *rural* area can mean an encounter with a *county or state jurisdiction*. Counties tend to run jail systems (though cities do have jails) and have an elected county sheriff. Only three states do not elect prosecutors; the rest hold local elections based on county or judicial district to determine who will lead their court systems. Similarly to neighborhoods, as I discussed earlier, cities and counties can be important sites for social cohesion and attachment, though this can vary regionally. For example, cities can be important sites for community belonging and a sense of attachment to place for people in the Northeast and Midwest states, whereas counties serve as a strong place-based identity for southerners and those in other parts of the country.

States manage the vast majority of people sentenced to prison in the United States (a small minority are sentenced to federal prison). So, while there is a strong focus on the national project of mass incarceration, there are unique state-level incarceration histories, regimes, and needs for reform.[101] States in the South and West have historically the highest rates of incarceration and relatively large correctional populations. The variation across states has provided social scientists ways to tease out the role of political and institutional processes in mass incarceration, such as comparing legislative moves to enhance punitive sentencing and build carceral capacity in different states.[102] Each of these jurisdictions—city, county, and state—is important for the study of place and social control, not only as a freestanding case study, but also in conjunction with other jurisdictions' data and results.

Sociology's Cities

The field of sociology, particularly sociologists who study criminalized violence, punishment, and the social conditions of neighborhood disadvantage, has a fascination with Chicago, Los Angeles, and New York City. This bias of generalizing social processes from a single place or region is reflected in the title of Zandria F. Robinson's 2014 book: *This Ain't Chicago: Race, Class, and Regional Identity in the Post-Soul South*. Mario Luis Small criticized the tilt toward these metropolitan areas as intrinsically generalizable in his essay "No Two Ghettos are Alike."[103] Numerous ethnographic and quantitative studies have used data from this triumvirate to draw conclusions about criminal violence and social control; a limited geography has created false notions.[104] With regard to Chicago specifically, these are the assumptions that (1) other large cities are fundamentally *like* Chicago; (2) poverty, violence, and racial inequality pattern in space in the same ways across geographic space, allowing Chicago data to be broadly generalizable; and (3) Chicago's neighborhood ecology is representative of most places.

In the present study, I endeavor to promote an agnosticism toward cities: the sense that when it comes to areas not yet prominent in the field of sociology, we cannot actually *know* what we do not actually *study*. This work in part pushes back on sociology's myopia in order to peer into the incarceration patterns of smaller cities, suburbs, and rural areas largely untouched by sociologists but inarguably impacted by the removal and confinement of their community members.

Forgotten, Declining, Gateway Cities

Urban planners and geographers have examined spatial patterns of abandonment, desertification, and forgotten places.[105] Gilmore offers a definition of "forgotten places" as fractured, spatially discontinuous, neither urban or rural, "between" or marginal collectivities that have been abandoned *and* intensely occupied by the state.[106] "In the United States, these people and locations are among the most vulnerable to the 'organized abandonment' that accompanies globalization's large-scale movements of capital and labor, and as such they are subject to many other processes that accumulate in and as forgotten places."[107]

State and regional governance has begun to attend to what are considered declining and left-behind cities, bringing to the fore issues such as affordable housing, transportation to job centers, and public funding for health care and education. In Massachusetts, the main research site for this book, the legislature (as of 2020) has defined twenty-six of what it calls, rather than declining or forgotten, "Gateway Cities": Attleboro, Barnstable, Brockton, Chelsea, Chicopee, Everett, Fall River, Fitchburg, Haverhill, Holyoke, Lawrence,

Leominster, Lowell, Lynn, Malden, Methuen, New Bedford, Peabody, Pittsfield, Quincy, Revere, Salem, Springfield, Taunton, Westfield, and Worcester. Some figure prominently in this book, because each boasts unusually high incarceration rates. Just these twenty-six cities account for a significant proportion of the state's prison admissions.

Size and Density

Throughout, I refer to some places as "small cities." In my studies of Massachusetts, this means places with a population under 250,000 (usually less than 100,000) that have commuting patterns, population densities, and proximity to MSAs but are comparatively small. The size of a city is important for understanding density and rates of incarceration within that city. For example, an incarceration rate may be very high because the population (the denominator) is quite low. While Boston is comprised of nearly two hundred census tracts (how neighborhoods are operationalized in this book), several small cities have fewer than twenty-five tracts. The size and density of population in cities is important for understanding the size of the criminal justice presence in that community and the role of its criminal justice institutions in serving a wide range of problems beyond reported crime and violence. I focus on small cities for three main reasons. First, though there are thousands of them, and 52 percent of city residents live in them, small cities are grossly understudied.[108] Second, small cities, like all other municipalities, have local governments, jails in some instances, and police forces, each of which may help explain their incarceration trends (if policing and court processing tend to be harsher, incarceration is likely on an upward trajectory). And third, the social transformation of deindustrialization took place in these small cities just as it did in large ones, and it has persisted in many of them since the early 1970s.

Remoteness and Isolation

Isolated communities form when there is a lack of transportation and infrastructure linking metropolitan centers and historically remote, rural areas. Sociospatial isolation involves physical and social dimensions. We can therefore consider remoteness or isolation when we assess health and workforce needs and the resources allocated to meet them. Don Parkes and colleagues, in their studies of rural and remote health in Australia, make the following distinction: "Isolation is essentially a construction of the senses: a pathological or undesirable component of human ecosystems. Remoteness, on the other hand, is a fundamentally geographical state that is derived from a measure of distance."[109]

The effects of geography alone pose serious problems for rural justice. Consider, for instance, that geographic isolation could plausibly increase the lethality of violence by slowing the response of emergency medical services, or that the problems of geographic remoteness and isolation are compounded by the dearth of resources in rural areas where the concomitant access to guns increases the chance of exposure to violence.[110] I explore these contexts and experiences of isolation and remoteness with data derived from interviews with social service providers in small cities and remote communities in chapter 4.

· · ·

This chapter lays the groundwork for analyzing the spatial pattern and distribution of imprisonment and incarceration in the United States. In order to turn, in the next chapter, to testing the urban hypotheses presented by the social control and urban inequality perspectives on this pattern, I have laid out these theoretical traditions and the main concepts I use in examining place as it relates to punishment. Chapter 3 examines these theories using a spatial view of punishment to see how well the urban theory predicts incarceration rates in a statewide analysis of neighborhoods.

Taken together, the perspectives discussed here describe a new regime of racialized urban poverty that comes with a host of carceral implications. First, urban neighborhoods account for a disproportionate share of incarceration. Second, much of the incarceration in urban areas can be explained by spatially concentrated patterns of criminalized violence, poverty, low educational attainment, and racial segregation. David Garland summarizes this perspective as analyzing "punishment not in the narrow terms of the 'crime problem' but instead as one of the mechanisms for managing the urban underclass."[111] This perspective moves beyond mass imprisonment as one among an array of structural disadvantages experienced by the urban poor or as a policy response to spatial patterns of criminalized behavior. The prison emerged to regulate specifically urban social problems through a complex array of activities on the ground—police, officials, judges, and prosecutors—that produced a new way of managing social marginality. Its regulatory powers hold beyond the cities it is meant to manage, and so, in the next chapter, I test this hypothesis with data for an entire state.

TWO

The Urban Model

We know that 75 percent of the people who will go to prison
in the State of New York will come from seven communities in
New York City. . . . Not only do we know where they are, but
we know geographically every single block in those communities. . . . We know what conditions are in those communities.

—ELLIS (1998)

IN 1979 A GROUP OF MEN INCARCERATED at Green Haven prison in
New York formed a group called the Think Tank. Together, they published a
study called "The Non-Traditional Approach to Criminal and Social Justice."
Informally called the "Seven Neighborhoods Study," this research, conducted
by a group of citizen-social scientists confined to a maximum-security prison,
examined the neighborhood concentration of state prison admissions in the
districts of New York City.

Edwin (Eddie) Ellis, a justice activist and spokesperson for the Black Panther
Party in the 1960s, had been sentenced to prison for twenty-five years in 1969.
He was transferred to Green Haven following the rebellion at Attica prison in
1971. Soon afterward, Ellis and his colleagues realized a preponderance of their
fellow prisoners in Green Haven hailed from only a handful of very poor and
segregated neighborhoods in New York City. Ellis, in an interview published in
Humanity & Society, reflects: "In order for the prison experience to make some
sense, we had to understand all the reasons people have for going to prison,
and we had to construct some activity in the prisons, which would serve to
resocialize people. . . . We tried to quantify who was in prison in terms of numbers, where they came from in terms of community or geographic location,
and some of the characteristics, demographic characteristics, of the people in
prison—age, gender, employment, and health statistics—to give us some better
sense of who we were dealing with and what the problems were."[1]

The Think Tank's sociological insights and methodological advance-
ments, and specifically their attention to *geographic* data collection, deeply

inform the work and research presented throughout this book. They used State Assembly districts for their geographic units of analysis, and they merged multiple sources of data, including census records, administrative records, and crime reports.[2] The publication in 1979 of their remarkable and unprecedented research study eventually received national attention when the *New York Times* featured the Seven Neighborhoods on its front page in 1992. The Think Tank report had identified an alarming trend: approximately three-quarters of all incarcerated people in the late 1970s and 1980s in New York State arrived from Harlem, Manhattan's Lower East Side, the South Bronx, South Jamaica, Bedford-Stuyvesant, Brownsville, and East New York in Brooklyn. Long before any such publications in academic journals of the social sciences, the Think Tank's report drew a direct connection between community and prison. It pointed to the disproportionate rates of prison admissions from these neighborhoods as an indication of the failures of the criminal justice system—and to these seven neighborhoods as important sites at which to direct policy reform.

. . .

Amid historically high incarceration rates, researchers investigating mass incarceration have worked to replicate the Think Tank's findings. Overwhelmingly, their observations confirm that people who are sent to prison and jail in the United States are being removed from poor and minority urban neighborhoods. In this context, the US penal system has gained a reputation as a distinctively urban institution, closely connected to the lives of poor young men in the American "inner city." Thus, the Think Tank inspired further groundbreaking work, focused on how major cities and metropolitan areas contribute to the prison system. Key among these is a data visualization project called Million Dollar Blocks; later, Chicago's Million Dollar Blocks, as well as the Million Dollar Hoods project, focused on Los Angeles County.[3] All of these projects aim to visualize the Think Tank's original insights—that a very small number of places contribute the greatest share of jail or prison populations—in ways that will capture attention from researchers, reformers, and everyday Americans.

In the previous chapter, I described two main theoretical perspectives that have emerged from social science to explain the spatial character of incarceration. One, the urban inequality perspective, observes that a small number of poor, contiguous neighborhoods in large urban cities experience very high incarceration rates, a pattern highly correlated with the spatial distribution of reported crime. Relatedly, the social control perspective observes high rates of incarceration in poor neighborhoods in large American cities, but attributes this pattern to a process of social control and confinement of racial minorities, who are residentially segregated and dislocated from mainstream social and economic opportunities.

Two empirical assumptions follow from these theoretical perspectives. First, incarceration will be significantly associated with socioeconomic disadvantage in urban neighborhoods, even after taking into account the spatial distribution of criminalized behavior. A second implication is that prison admissions will largely originate from poor and segregated urban neighborhoods within metropolitan areas.

In this chapter, informed by the Think Tank's model as well as scholars from the social control and urban inequality research literatures, I take this body of work a step forward by analyzing prison admissions according to the model presented by these views. Using a sample of neighborhoods comprising all census tracts within a state, I estimate rates of prison admissions and the degree to which these measures account for the levels of incarceration found in neighborhoods and communities across the urban-rural interface.

One benefit of exploring rates of prison admissions in a large sample of census tracts is the ability to test many of the hypotheses and assumptions built into the two theoretical perspectives presented in chapter 1. In addition, this chapter draws attention to an all but overlooked measure: the rates of prison admissions from small cities and suburbs. Earlier quantitative work relies on single, large-city case studies, reinforcing scholarly tendencies to build the substantively assumed *urban* character of mass imprisonment into the study of criminal justice encounters and contact. The resulting picture can mislead scholars and policy makers by leaving them with the impression that mass incarceration is best understood through close examination of the conditions within disadvantaged neighborhoods of large cities. My analysis of prison admissions for the state of Massachusetts, however, suggests just how necessary it is that we widen the scope of our inquiries by shifting the focus on mass incarceration in America beyond deep "inner-city" poverty. A main goal of this chapter is to study the full distribution of places with an expanded sampling frame of neighborhoods that reflect the *complete* spatial context of mass incarceration in a state jurisdiction. Note that this means not only not studying just cities, but also not studying only suburbs or only rural areas. Taking the Think Tank's insights seriously means going wherever the data take us, including asking whether the concentrations they observed in the 1980s and 1990s persist today. Taking all these factors together, the reader should finish this chapter with a better grasp of mass imprisonment in its full geographic extent: an institution unconstrained by city boundaries.

This effort relies on two innovations. In what follows, I analyze a statistical model that considers spatial variation in prison admissions as a function of reported crime, concentrated disadvantage, the share of the neighborhood population that is non-White, and spatial considerations. Second, I estimate this model with spatial data disaggregated to census tracts, with the explicit inclusion of all municipalities across urban and nonurban areas. The urban inequality and social control perspectives would hypothesize that, even in a statewide analysis, the overwhelming majority of places marked by extreme levels of prison admissions will be found in major cities, specifically in their poor, segregated neighborhoods. I test these hypotheses by analyzing statewide prison admission data from Massachusetts. This analysis unifies a fractured literature that identifies a strong relationship between the conditions of big-city urban life and imprisonment in one literature, the harshness of suburban policing in another, and the proliferation of jails and prisons amid rural poverty in a third. Across the spatial spectrum, I explore how local conditions shape prison admission rates in a context of a broad spatial distribution of social and economic disadvantage. I demonstrate that a statistical model using disaggregated data across the spatial distribution (as opposed to a single city or community area) can more accurately assess the model put forth by urban inequality and social control scholars, while attending to potential outliers or places largely unexamined by the mass incarceration literature.

This is one of the first broad demographic approaches to studying the links between place and punishment. Regression models estimate prison admissions in census tracts, accounting for reported crime and socioeconomic disadvantage across an entire state. I am able to conduct this analysis only through my access to a rare dataset of prison admissions for the state of Massachusetts (2009–2017), providing a complete map of the spatial distribution of incarceration in large cities, suburbs, satellite cities, and rural towns. (For a detailed description of the data, see the appendix.) My results provide support for the Think Tank's initial findings: prison admissions are related to conditions of extreme socioeconomic disadvantage in urban places. At the same time, my analysis also calls into question the idea that concentrated imprisonment is *solely* experienced in the disadvantaged cores of large cities like Boston in the present day.

TESTING THE URBAN MODEL WITH DATA ON PUNISHING PLACES

This kind of analysis has been elusive, because scholars have not had access to the data needed to study the problem. My dataset for the study of the spatial distribution of incarceration beyond urban cores leverages nine years of comprehensive admissions data for Massachusetts state prisons for 2009–2017. Map 2.1 displays the prison admission rates in Massachusetts cities and towns, including clusters within its three largest cities: Boston, Worcester, and Springfield. These cities account for 14 percent of the state's population but 32 percent of the state's prison admissions.[4] Prison admission rates are also high in the impoverished small cities around Boston, including Lawrence,

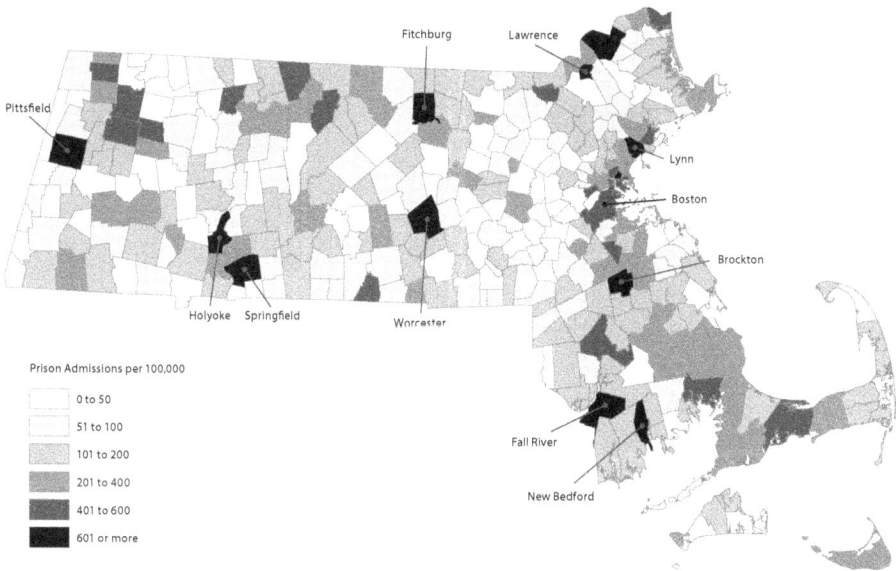

MAP 2.1. Prison admissions per 100,000 inhabitants in Massachusetts cities and towns, 2009–2017. *Source:* Author's compilation of data from Massachusetts Department of Correction prison records.

Brockton, Fall River, and New Bedford. This map describes a pattern of high prison admission rates within a wide range of local contexts, from large metropolitan cities outward to suburbs and more isolated small cities and remote towns. Moreover, it indicates the extreme spatial concentration of incarceration; there are few to no prison admissions from whole sections of the state. Certainly, while some places contain "million-dollar hoods," others are zero-dollar tracts.

The average prison admission rate across Massachusetts's census tracts in this dataset is approximately 4 people for every 1,000 residents, but in Boston, the average neighborhood rate is slightly elevated at 6 people per 1,000. The rates are even higher in the state's other large cities: in the same period, the average census tract in Springfield or Lawrence had a nine-year prison admission rate of 14 people per 1,000, more than three times the state average. On its own, this initial descriptive account shows the broad range of spatial contexts in which high incarceration rates may arise.

How do admission rates vary across localities? Table 2.1 displays low, medium, and high prison admission rates in Massachusetts census tracts within the ten cities with the highest prison admission rates. The admission rate is the number of people residing in a tract who were sentenced to state prison in 2009–2017 for a new criminal court commitment per 1,000 inhabitants. The state's prison system recorded 21,269 admissions to prison between 2009 and 2017. While the cities reported in table 2.1 account for 23 percent of the Massachusetts population, they account for 55 percent of total prison admissions (it is important to note that this necessarily means that 45 percent of the state's nine-year prison admissions came from cities and towns *not* included in table 2.1). Putting this in terms of the Think Tank's analysis of New York neighborhoods, disaggregating to the tract level shows that neighborhoods containing just 15 percent of the state's population account for over half (51 percent) of all prison admissions.

High prison admission rates are observed outside of Massachusetts's large cities. Overall, one-third of the state's census tracts have a prison admission rate in the highest tercile of the distribution. About twice the portion of Boston census tracts (62 percent) experienced this high rate of prison admission. However, in many other cities, high rates of admission are the norm. In the former manufacturing and mill towns of Fitchburg, Holyoke, New Bedford, and Pittsfield, 70–84 percent of census tracts fall in the highest tercile. At the tract level, we can see that *all* of Lawrence's eighteen census tracts and nearly

TABLE 2.1 Percentage Distribution of Prison Admission Rates for Massachusetts Selected Cities and Towns, 2009–2017

	Admission Rate (per 1,000)			Admission Count	N Tracts
	Low	Medium	High		
Massachusetts	33.0	33.0	34.0	21,269	1,461
Boston	16.8	21.6	61.6	3,602	167
Worcester	4.7	25.6	69.7	1,183	43
Springfield	—	8.1	91.9	1,931	37
New Bedford	6.5	9.7	83.8	776	31
Fall River	4.3	—	95.7	729	23
Lynn	—	9.1	98.9	771	22
Brockton	—	9.5	90.5	785	21
Lawrence	—	—	100.0	863	18
Pittsfield	9.1	18.2	72.7	370	11
Holyoke	9.1	9.1	81.8	370	11
Fitchburg	10.0	20.0	70.0	264	10

SOURCE: Author's compilation of data from Massachusetts Department of Correction prison records.

NOTE: The first three columns display the percentage distribution of tracts within each admission rate range. Low, medium, and high levels correspond to prison admission rate terciles for the state: low = 1.1 per 1,000 residents or fewer; medium = 1.1 to 3.3 per 1,000 residents; high = more than 3.3 per 1,000. The fourth column is the total prison admission count for the given geographical area, and the fifth column is the number of census tracts in the geographic area.

all of the tracts in Fall River, Brockton, Lynn, and Springfield experience the highest rates of prison admission in the state.

The top 1 percent of prison admission rates by tract has rates of 23 to 77 per 1,000 in the nine-year study period. Of these fifteen census tracts, just two are in Boston. The remaining thirteen are found in small cities and suburbs. One partial explanation for this finding in the ninety-ninth percentile is that the average population is smaller in these census tracts (2,338, compared to an average of 4,433 for the entire sample), a fact that may account for very high prison admission rates.

Cities with populations at or below 90,000 (as displayed in table 2.1: Brockton, Fall River, Fitchburg, Holyoke, Lawrence, Lynn, New Bedford, and Pittsfield) have experienced dramatic shifts in economic conditions since 1960, including growing poverty rates. As noted in chapter 1, the Massachusetts legislature officially named these places "Gateway Cities" in an effort to draw attention to small and medium-sized cities experiencing severe economic decline.[5] Compounding economic decline with consistently low educational attainment

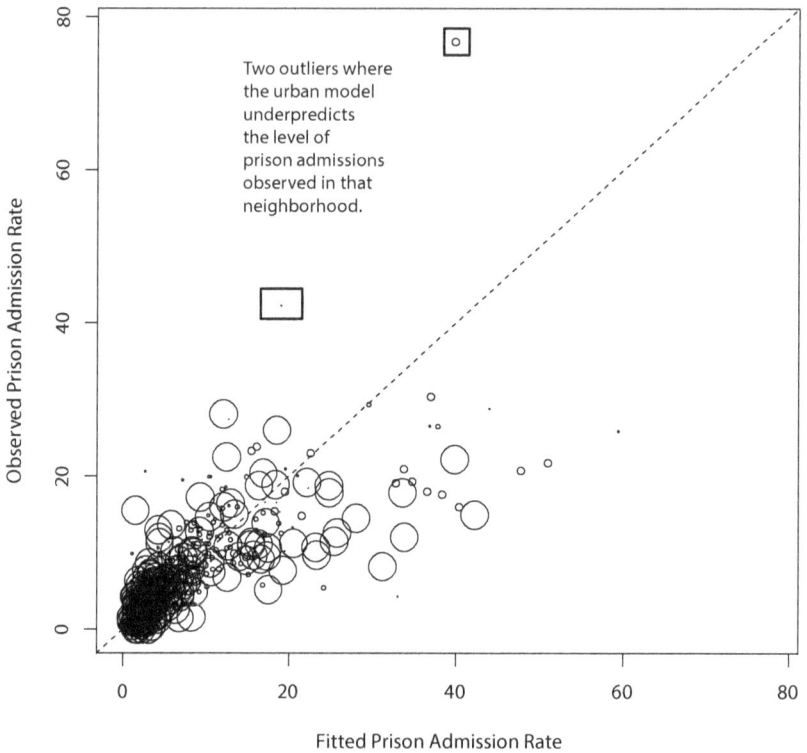

Two outliers where
the urban model
underpredicts
the level of
prison admissions
observed in that
neighborhood.

FIGURE 2.1. Observed prison admission rates against fitted prison admission rates from regression results of log prison admissions in Massachusetts census tracts, 2009–2017. Circles drawn in proportion to the population size of the city where the tract resides. *Source:* Author's compilation of data from Massachusetts Department of Correction prison records.

among residents and high rates of population turnover, these small towns in many ways typify urban decline, yet they are geographically isolated, resource deprived, and demographically distinct from major metropolitan cities. A regression analysis shows prison admissions are closely related to conditions of urban inequality and social control in a statewide analysis (see the appendix for full regression results). In a regression model that excludes the broader spatial context of places (place-based fixed effects), we can learn more about the applicability of the urban model across geographic space by studying outliers. In statistical terms, outlier analysis allows us to study how well theories linking urbanicity to punishment explain contemporary patterns of prison admissions in a qualitative way. Here, I examine the regression residuals. Figure 2.1 displays a plot of observed and predicted prison admission rates with each unit (census tract) indicated by circles drawn in proportion to the size of the city population in which the tract resides.

The residual plot shows two small-city neighborhoods with large positive residuals (in which the model grossly underpredicts the admission rate in places where we know the admission rates are actually very high). Notably, negative residuals, where imprisonment is *over*predicted, tend to cluster in Boston (the largest circles in the plot). In other words, some census tracts with social conditions theorized to be associated with prison admissions—criminalized violence, large Black populations, and concentrated disadvantage—have prison admission rates much lower than expected. However, if we only considered Boston tracts, this study would not observe the highest rates of incarceration in the state. From observations in this residual analysis and findings in the regression analysis, it's clear that *punishing places* exist in a diverse set of communities, many of which have not been studied. From this diagnostic plot, we can observe that indeed the model motivated by the theoretical discussion fits prison admissions well in many areas. The surprise, in fact, is just how absent small cities are from discussions of place and punishment.

The outlier tracts with large positive residuals—where the model grossly underpredicts the prison admission rate—are located in Springfield and Lawrence. Both of these neighborhoods are surrounded by neighborhoods with much lower admission rates (hence the lower predicted rate in the focal tract). These majority-minority census tracts have higher than average reported violent crime, drug arrest, and poverty rates—much like the other places in the state that have sustained but not recovered from significant mid-twentieth-century economic collapse.[6]

A final regression analysis (see figure 2.2) reports results from a similar analysis, but includes indicators for the spatial context of the census tracts: Greater Boston cities, small cities beyond Greater Boston, and suburbs and rural towns beyond Greater Boston (tracts in the city of Boston are the reference category). These regional spatial controls estimate how much of the variation in prison admissions is associated with unmeasured differences in the community area in which the census tract resides, net conditions of urban inequality and social control. These results suggest that small cities have a 22 percent higher prison admission rate than Boston census tracts, even after accounting for neighborhood-level conditions

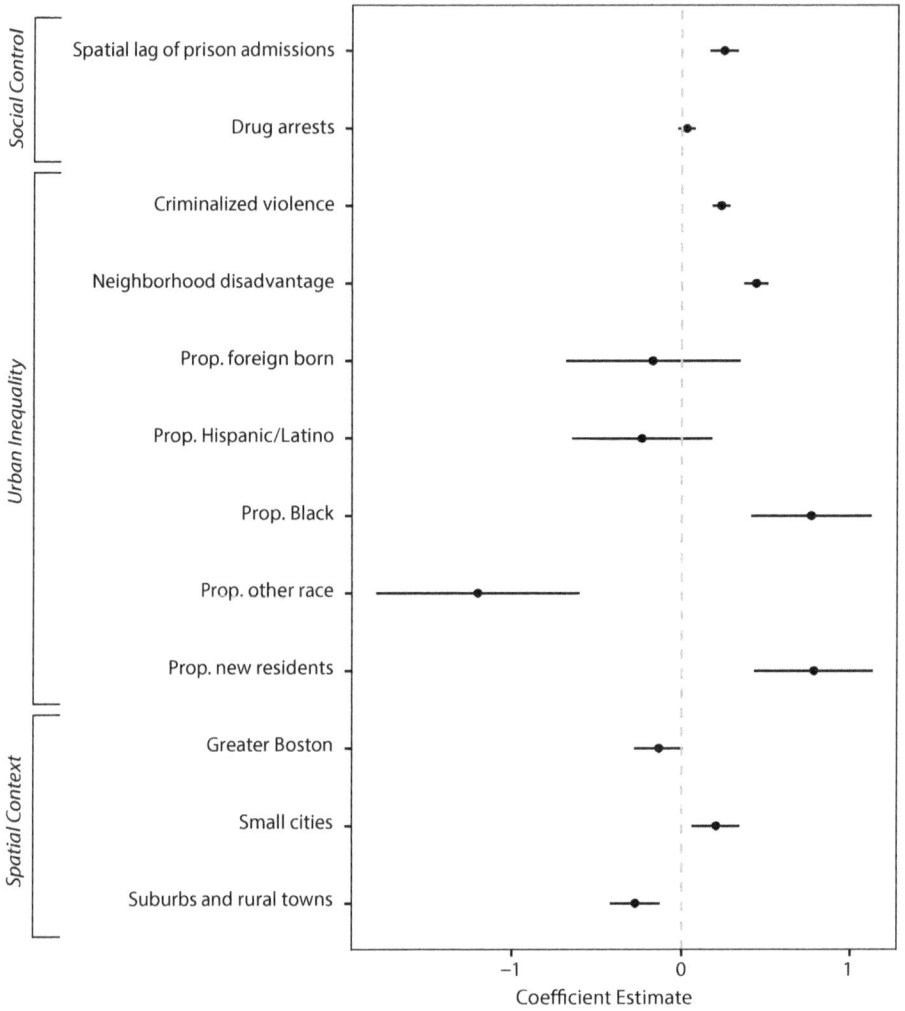

FIGURE 2.2. Estimated associations among prison admissions and urban inequality, social control, and spatial context of mass incarceration in Massachusetts census tracts, 2009–2017 (95% confidence intervals). For spatial context estimates, the reference category is Boston neighborhoods. *Source:* Author's compilation of data from US Census, Massachusetts Department of Correction prison records, and crime reports.

theorized by the urban inequality and social control perspectives on place and punishment.

Research on the spatial pattern of incarceration has mainly focused on a narrow set of neighborhoods, has provided largely descriptive analysis, and has rarely strayed beyond case studies of metropolitan cities. A statewide analysis of the spatial distribution of prison admissions in Massachusetts extends earlier research in three ways. First, I find evidence that prison admissions are profoundly spatially concentrated—far beyond what a single analysis of Boston neighborhoods would indicate. Eleven cities, which together contain less than a quarter of the total state population, accounted for over half of prison admissions during the study period. The regression analyses indicate a significant, localized spatial structure of prison admissions across Massachusetts. Drilling down from cities to census tracts reveals an even more stark concentration: over half of all prison admissions were drawn from neighborhoods that account for just 15 percent of the state's population.

Second, my analysis indicates prison admissions are concentrated in communities characterized by concentrated disadvantage and a greater share of the population that is Black, even after controlling for different measures of reported crime, drug arrest, and spatial clustering. The main empirical expectation—that imprisonment clusters in poor non-White communities—is largely supported. Neighborhood criminalized violence and prison admissions were consistently associated after controlling for arrest rates, race, socioeconomic, and spatial factors. The analysis offers strong evidence of community-level punishment, in which a small number of poor neighborhoods across the state experience very high rates of imprisonment that are not fully explained by their reported crime rates. In this analysis, suburban and rural communities do not experience significantly higher levels of prison admissions than do cities; rather, small cities throughout the state and poor suburbs of Boston have the highest rates of imprisonment. The current theoretical model presented by urban and social control scholars does not account for patterns of incarceration in these areas. Analyses such as these are rare and contribute to a growing body of research that analyzes social disadvantage and social control with geographic variation.[7]

The third innovation or extension of current research comes from my outlier analysis, which provides further evidence of high prison admission rates in small cities and suburbs. Smaller cities may be experiencing concentrated disadvantage like that of their large urban counterparts. They may also be experiencing entirely different social conditions. The outlier analysis suggests that in order to account for the highest incarceration areas in this state, which are found in isolated suburbs and small cities, a theory of the spatial context of incarceration must broaden from deep inner-city poverty to include disadvantaged urban and suburban areas.

In returning to the Think Tank's original results in the Seven Neighborhoods Study, I see a strong pattern in my data that mirrors theirs. What they called "crime generative factors" describes a social ecology of racism, racial profiling, redlining and racial segregation, profoundly underresourced schools, fragmented family structures, high rates of unemployment, deep poverty, and substance use problems.[8] The correlations among these conditions with incarceration rates remain significant decades later. What has changed significantly is the overall spatial distribution of high incarceration rates. While 75 percent of prison admissions came from seven neighborhoods in New York City in the earlier periods of mass incarceration, this pattern has changed dramatically in subsequent years.[9] Indeed, the Million Dollar Hoods project, which uses jail admissions data (as opposed to prison) in Los Angeles County, now reports that cities far beyond LA proper boast some of the county's highest jail incarceration rates—and experience deep levels of community loss to time behind bars.[10]

The effects of mass incarceration, after statistical modeling across an entire state's nine-year carceral admissions data, stretch well beyond the bounds of poor inner-city neighborhoods nested within large metro areas. If the concentration of incarceration among the most marginal members of society represents a type of social exclusion from full membership in American community life, analyzing various forms of social disadvantage and formal social control entirely within metropolitan areas underestimates the inequalities associated with incarceration. An urban bias mistakenly suggests that deep social inequalities emerge only in major cities, and that incarceration only really affects large cities. Instead, imprisonment closely follows the contours of race, poverty, and other forms of disadvantage in both large cities and the surrounding cities and towns that have become centers of regional economic decline, untreated health conditions, unaddressed social problems, and punitive policy responses. Digging into case studies of such high-rate small cities helps me, in the following two chapters, to trace histories of race, social control, and inequality in locations more commonly theorized than empirically studied in sociology.

THREE

Small Cities and Mass Incarceration

If policing in New York under Giuliani and Bloomberg was crime prevention tainted by racist presumptions, in other areas of the country ostensible crime prevention has mutated into little more than open pillage.

—COATES (2015)

ON AUGUST 9, 2014, MICHAEL BROWN, an unarmed teenager, was killed by police officer Darren Wilson in Ferguson, Missouri. Shot six times, his body was left lying on the ground for four hours in the middle of an apartment complex on Canfield Drive. The viral videos and images of this gruesome slaying and Michael Brown's desecrated body, coupled with the delay in medical attention, fueled worldwide outrage about the tactics of police officers in American cities and the utter indifference they displayed toward Michael Brown and his family. Darren Wilson was never indicted for this killing, and the community continues to seek justice for Michael Brown and others who came before and after. Indeed, Michael Brown's tragic death became an important symbol of the long-standing, unresolved abuses of state power in poor communities of color and a devaluing of Black people's humanity.

The vigils and protests that followed Michael Brown's death were fueled by long-standing community grief. Unresolved matters of racial injustice and the legacies of state violence had inflected the relationship between residents and police officers, and Brown's killing seemed to be a breaking point. And while spontaneous protests and news media focused on St. Louis, the epicenter of the movement on the ground, Ferguson, was a small suburb of just 21,000 residents. Soon its dynamics of poverty, race, and policing were laid bare to the world.[1]

The Civil Rights Division of the Department of Justice conducts what are known as "pattern-or-practice" investigations under a federal statute passed in 1994. That statute was a partial response to the six days of devastating conflict that roiled Los Angeles following the acquittal of LAPD officers in the brutal, on-camera beating of unarmed motorist Rodney King. Under this statute, the DOJ is allowed to investigate almost any report of police action that suggests patterns or practices of excessive force, biased or discriminatory policing, and/or other unconstitutional practices. When the allegations are upheld, the DOJ can seek agreement with local governments on policing reforms or—as it did more aggressively under the Obama administration— go to the federal courts to force changes under closely monitored consent decrees. Since 1997, the DOJ has conducted at least forty investigations of policing practices in cities across the United States. Only fourteen, including the Ferguson investigation following Michael Brown's death, were in places with populations under 100,000.

What is now called the Ferguson Report was released to the public by the DOJ in March 2015. It uncovered a community completely overrun with policing and punishment. The Justice Department identified a coordinated law enforcement practice of extracting fines to raise city revenue alongside a consistent pattern of excessive use of force, racially discriminatory traffic stops, and racist email exchanges among police and court officials. Perhaps most staggeringly, the DOJ report indicated that at the time of the report's publication, 16,000 people had outstanding arrest warrants in Ferguson, a city of 21,000.[2] Not all of the people with warrants necessarily lived in Ferguson, but the figure nonetheless indicated the colossal role of criminal legal institutions in just one small, impoverished suburb. Prior to the summer of 2014, few outside of St. Louis had ever heard of Ferguson. Without Michael Brown's tragic death, they may never have heard of it at all.

Less than two years later, the *New York Times* ran a story about Dearborn County, Indiana, which sends more people to jail per capita than nearly any other county in the United States. Indiana's overall jail admissions remained steady at a rate of 25 per 10,000 residents between 2003 and 2016, but in the same period, Dearborn County more than quadrupled its contribution to the carceral population. By 2016, it was sending about 114 people per 10,000 to jail, an increase of 141 percent over its 2006 admissions. By comparison, the county-level jail admission rate including New York City is 21.9, Chicago's Cook County is 27.4, and Boston's Suffolk County is 5.9 per 10,000. The authors of the *Times* article attributed Dearborn County's outsized growth in prison admissions to "rural resistance to lighter penalties."[3]

What can we learn about mass incarceration and criminalization from Ferguson, Missouri, and Dearborn County, Indiana? As the last two chapters emphasized, social scientific theories have not fully evaluated the preponderance of extreme levels of social control and high levels of harshly punitive policy and enforcement in these lesser-known places. These two places captured the public's attention, yet they are characteristic of a larger set of places that rarely gain scholarly interest. Ferguson and Dearborn County should generate deep curiosity, compelling us to explore the world of small cities and nonmetropolitan areas and the conditions of social disadvantage, criminalized behavior, and social control within them. More precisely, they urge us to ask: *Where are today's punishing places? What are the conditions of small cities and towns that give rise to high levels of punishment, and what mechanisms help explain these conditions?*

Chapter 2 focused on theories pertaining to the urban account of mass incarceration, while this chapter aims to train a deep focus on places that have been too often forgotten, ignored, or hidden from public view, scholarly attention, and government oversight. In this chapter, I explore historical trends in Massachusetts and in US counties, demonstrating the geographic variability of the spatial pattern of American incarceration since at least 1990, or as early as halfway through the period associated with mass incarceration, from about 1990 onward.

CENTERING SMALL CITIES IN STUDIES OF MASS INCARCERATION

From the earliest discussions of mass incarceration, the understanding was that imprisonment was spatially concentrated in the poorest neighborhoods of the largest metropolitan areas. More specifically, as discussed in earlier chapters, research on the spatial pattern of mass incarceration argues that the pattern is highly concentrated in areas of severe urban disadvantage.[4] Though chapter 2 explored the inextricable link between the conditions of urban decline, racial segregation, and social control efforts, this relationship can be observed in a diverse collection of cities and towns.

Recently, the public opposition to the racist presumptions of big-city policing strategies such as New York's infamous stop-and-frisk policy—referred to by Coates at the outset of this chapter—came to haunt those policies' supporters. In his failed campaign for the 2020 democratic nomination for president, former New York City mayor Michael Bloomberg was daunted by intense scrutiny of his prior statements and his administration about targeted neighborhood policing practices. In an audio-recorded discussion of his program at the 2015 Aspen Ideas Festival, for example, Bloomberg had stated: "Put the cops where the crime is, which means in minority neighborhoods. So, one of the unintended consequences is, 'Oh my god, you're arresting kids for marijuana that are all minorities.' Yes, that's true. Why? Because we put all the cops in minority neighborhoods. Yes, that's true. Why do we do it? Because that's where all the crime is. And the way you get the guns out of the kids' hands is to throw them up against the walls and frisk them." Neighborhoods experiencing the greatest exposure to violence and deprivation were included by researchers and policy makers among the places considered "at-risk" and in need of additional surveillance and intensive intervention, including stop-and-frisk. This "new penology," a term coined by Malcolm M. Feeley and Jonathan Simon, included a rising set of practices that involved the identification and management of unruly groups, deploying techniques as an "aggregate in place of traditional techniques for individualizing or creating equity."[5] Through the language of probability and risk, the new penology was directed at neighborhoods. Criminologists and geographers developed what are called crime heat maps and directed law enforcement to focus their efforts on hot spots. Around the country, using crime prediction (including, increasingly, the use of proprietary algorithms to direct control efforts) and quality-of-life policing became a way for police to focus their resources and efforts and for courts to estimate the levels of risk (including the chances that a given individual is involved in gang-related activities).[6] In studying jail, John Irwin, like Feeley and Simon, points to the social control of the rabble through a managerial, actuarial system that is not itself concerned with either punishment or rehabilitation.[7] This same practice was applied to whole neighborhoods.

If the goal of prior literature was to focus our attention on crucial matters of racist urban policing practices in cities like New York and Chicago, my work seeks to expand our scope beyond those places. Specifically, the practice of targeting neighborhoods for policing, surveillance, arrests, harsh sentences, and removals to jail and prison have never been limited to the boundaries of major cities now at the forefront of the national conversation on public safety and jail reform. Small cities' systems of policing, court processing, and incarceration look much like those found in New York, Boston, or Chicago. And the disadvantaged neighborhoods within large cities simply do not account for the majority of imprisonments today.

To be sure, individual studies are bringing much-needed attention to geographies beyond the urban. For instance, a growing body of research has begun to attend to fatal police violence in suburban contexts.[8] A study on the probability of prosecutors seeking the death penalty in Maryland found a thirteen-times-higher appetite for it in suburban Baltimore County than in Baltimore City, noting that prosecutors in other suburban and exurban counties seek it three to five times more than those in Baltimore City.[9] Mine is not the first study to consider county-level incarceration rates (though it is the first to access and analyze an entire state's longitudinal data in full) beyond large cities.[10] John Eason has demonstrated the social order common to rural communities where a prison may be a major employer, source of revenue, and lockup to removed residents all at once.[11]

The importance of surburban and rural policing and court processing, spread across scattered studies—no matter how rigorous and relevant—remains subordinate to urban research. Not only are these community areas *spatially* marginalized, they are *academically* marginalized. Research agendas on place, criminalization, and punishment in noncentral cities have remained on the fringes of social scientific work on place disadvantage, even though decades of evidence suggest that poverty, racial segregation, and policing practices are fundamental to understanding the proliferation of penal responses to a host of social problems. The powerful dichotomy of the White suburb and Black urban neighborhood that dominates so much political rhetoric comes at great cost: philanthropy, scholarly attention, and policy all underscrutinize the range of places in which many people live and come face to face with state violence and policing, and indeed, harsh punishment.

If what appears to be a nascent pattern of decarceration continues in the years to come, small cities, poor suburbs, and rural towns risk being left behind. How can reform efforts come to these places unless research, policy, and advocacy take the conditions in them seriously? Small cities and rural places have experienced jail and prison system population growth, yet rural relationships with incarceration are usually only discussed in terms of being receiving sites for prison building.[12]

The issues of small cities have largely been taken up by urban planners and geographers who have sought to draw attention to the importance of revitalization in these forgotten and satellite communities. For example, in 2007 the Massachusetts Institute of Technology held a symposium on what it termed "forgotten cities," which were defined as *old* (more than 5,000 inhabitants by 1880), *small* (between 15,000 and 150,000 residents as of the year 2000), and *poor* (median household income of less than $35,000). The symposium and report identified 150 US cities, home to 7.4 million people, that met these criteria, and 7 were in Massachusetts.[13] The final report of this symposium concluded: "For a host of reasons, revitalizing these cities is especially difficult. The perennial challenges facing forgotten cities tend to be implicitly understood but rarely articulated. They are: a lack of civic engagement and institutions, inadequate governing capacity, and a chronically negative collective mindset. Together, these factors undermine the ability of local stakeholders to forge collective schemes of cooperation."[14]

One of the cities listed in the "Forgotten Cities" report is Flint, Michigan, a city with a population of just under 100,000 residents located about an hour northwest of Detroit. National attention came to Flint in 2014 when a state-appointed emergency manager disconnected Flint residents from the Detroit water supply, and the city began drawing water from the Flint River for eighteen months.[15] As early as March 2015, public officials knew that the water contained E. coli and carcinogens; by fall of that year, it became public knowledge that Flint's drinking water contained high levels of lead and copper, contributing to significant reported health problems, particularly related to the lead plumbing in the Flint public schools.[16] Katrinell Davis writes in *Tainted Tap* that small cities like Flint suffer from policy neglect and a struggle for self-advocacy, as demonstrated by the long and troubled history of delivering basic services in a context of persistent economic decline.[17] In January 2021, the Michigan Attorney General's Office charged eight former state officials with forty-two criminal counts, including former governor Rick Snyder, for their roles in the Flint water crisis.[18] Holding these individual to account for poisoning the people of Flint, and in particular their children, while powerful and unprecedented, does little to address larger systemic inequities that make small cities vulnerable to similar crises. Racial segregation across the region—and really the structural advantages in accessing clean water (and other goods and services) that Flint's neighboring White communities have—explains much of the preventable water crisis in Flint.[19]

MASSACHUSETTS'S FORGOTTEN CITIES

This chapter focuses on six "forgotten" cities in Massachusetts: from west to east, Holyoke, Springfield, Fall River, Lawrence, Brockton, and Lynn. Each once boasted a thriving manufacturing economy, and many were left

TABLE 3.1 Socioeconomic and Social Control Conditions
of Selected Cities in Massachusetts

	Poverty Rate[a]	Violent Crime Rate[b]	Uniformed Officers Per Capita[b]	Prison Admission Rate[b]
Largest city				
Boston	15.3	725.7	320.6	533.0
Small cities				
Brockton	13.2	1,051.6	192.0	822.6
Fall River	16.5	1,167.4	253.4	859.6
Holyoke	26.0	966.9	277.8	1,074.9
Lawrence	21.9	1,093.8	158.3	1,080.9
Lynn	13.9	777.2	200.1	823.6
Springfield	24.5	1,091.3	295.4	1,249.1

SOURCE: American Community Survey five-year estimates (2014–2018), Massachusetts Department of Correction prison records, and the FBI Uniform Crime Reports (2016).

a. Poverty rate calculated as a percentage of all residents.

b. Rates of reported violent crime, prison admissions, and number of uniformed officers calculated per 100,000 residents.

disadvantaged and destitute by deindustrialization in the latter part of the twentieth century. Old factories and towering red brick mills now stand empty, or sometimes have been converted into loft apartments and offices meant to attract Greater Boston commuters seeking relief from Boston rents. Main streets through once-thriving downtowns and strip malls along major thoroughfares stand vacant.

Table 3.1 displays key measures used for the quantitative analysis presented in this chapter, showing that these small cities have higher levels of reported violence and prison admission rates than the state's urban center, Boston, and with the exception of Brockton and Lynn, they have higher poverty rates, too. Their police forces are overshadowed by Boston's, yet their prison admission rates are all higher (sometimes much, much higher).

I estimate how these levels have changed over time, and how differences in social control, social and economic inequality, and the broader spatial context of cities in Massachusetts play a role in shaping levels of prison admissions in places that, like these, have been variously dubbed forgotten, declining, and in Massachusetts, "Gateway Cities." The terms both signify the decline (and thus the need for attention) in these places and contain a hopeful note that any could potentially be turned around. To some extent, theories can help to explain how mass incarceration came to places outside of the view of sociology and social policy. But what would it take for urban sociologists and sociologists of punishment to consider these places just as important to the story of mass incarceration as their larger counterparts? In "The Black Family in the Age of Mass Incarceration," Ta-Nehisi Coates describes an unbridled system of social control permeating places that have escaped scrutiny. The rest of this chapter offers a look into small cities so that we may explore patterns of imprisonment across the era of mass incarceration and across the vast geography of US jurisdictions. Rather than examine one city, we will visit several cities and look into their trajectories of racism, economic deprivation, and mass incarceration.

There are two ways a study of small cities could expand current theories of place and punishment. First, these cities share key demographic and social patterns that provide important background information and point to potential explanations for the rates of prison admissions found in these areas. These cities were nearly 100 percent White in 1970 (see figure 3.1), but since then they have experienced a dramatic transformation in racial and ethnic composition via immigration and economically based displacement from Boston toward relatively more affordable small cities. Increases in reported crime and social control practices by law enforcement may correspond to this demographic shift; they may also simply reflect local social services' inability to adequately address poverty in these communities.[20] Where poverty and decline have decreased other government revenue streams, such as property taxes, this can mean raising money to pay for public services, including law enforcement, through a brutal system of fines and fees levied against the poor themselves (as was revealed in the Ferguson Report).[21] In short, scholarship framing mass incarceration as an urban problem (through the lens of either social control or inequality) is largely correct, but incomplete because it has not been in conversation with recent poverty scholarship showing that the centers of disadvantage have moved away from the "inner city" to small cities and suburbs. Taking the movement and concentration of poor people and people of color out of cities and the high rates of prison admission in tandem supports the theory that mass incarceration is the handmaiden to neoliberalism, functioning as a force for the control of dispossessed and impoverished communities that have suffered in a time of mass retrenchment. Thus, any increases in White incarceration in these areas are collateral to the movement of population and changes to punishment regimes in areas outside major cities.[22]

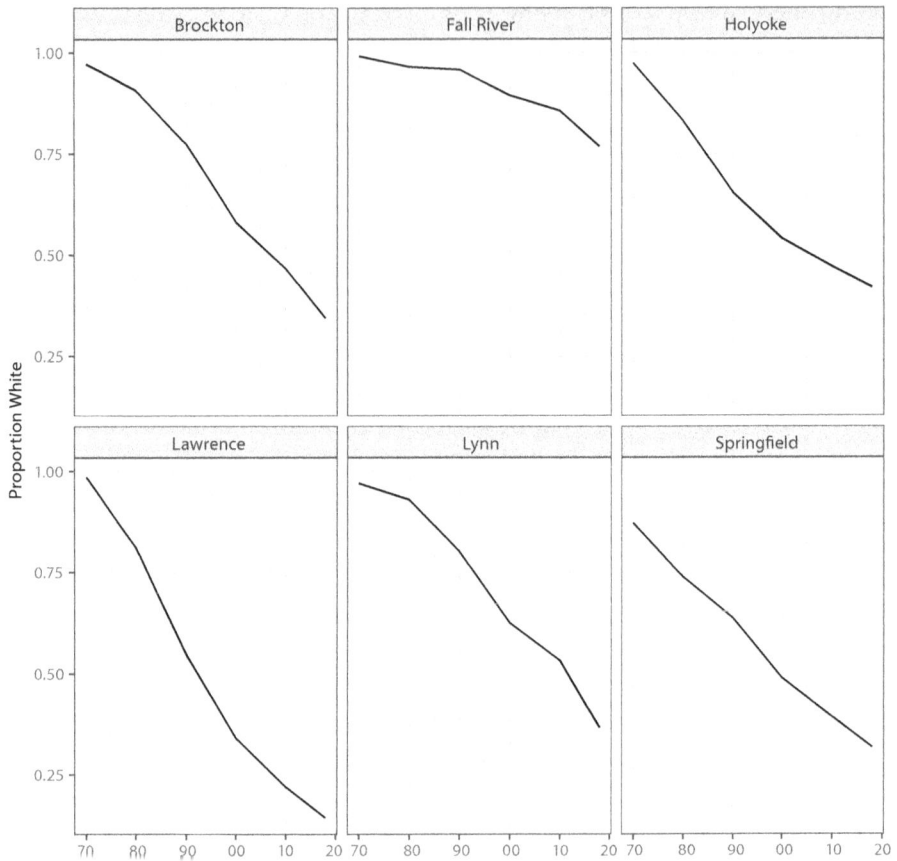

FIGURE 3.1. Changes in demographics: White population 1970–2018. *Source:* Author's compilation of data from US Census and American Community Survey.

A second theoretical expansion could result from a close examination of the social control infrastructure in these areas. As impoverished and racially marginalized groups moved in (see figure 3.2), small cities (often already struggling) experienced intensifying concentrated disadvantage and criminalized violence. These cities have fortified their capacity to police and prosecute at the same time that larger cities have begun to decrease prison admissions, with their deeper resources and research-informed advocacy aimed at keeping more people out of jail and prison. Scholarship on mass incarceration has missed these places as valuable sources of comparative data. The patterns of policing, court processing, and incarceration may be much more widespread in these small cities and rural areas than in large cities today.[23]

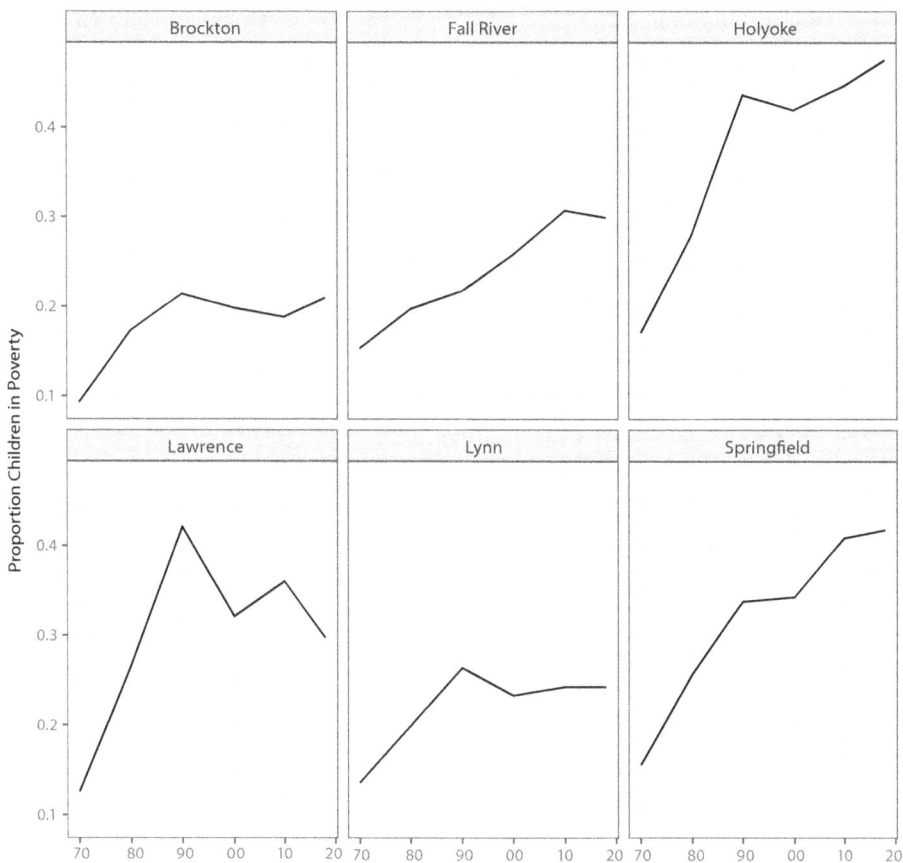

FIGURE 3.2. Changes in demographics: child poverty 1970–2018. *Source:* Author's compilation of data from US Census and American Community Survey.

A TOUR OF SIX MASSACHUSETTS SMALL CITIES

Brockton, much like other New England towns, owed its late-nineteenth- and twentieth-century prosperity to manufacturing, mostly shoes and their component parts, such as leather goods and tools. Known as "The Shoe City" in the early 1900s, Brockton was among the biggest and most successful towns in the Northeast and boasted up to ninety-seven shoe factories and an additional one hundred component factories at its industrial height.[24] As deindustrialization walloped the Rust Belt and the Northeast, Brockton's industry gave way to global pressures. Its last factory closed in 2009.

Racial integration and social justice issues have been contentious here. During the Great Migration (approx. 1916–1970) of Black populations out of the American South, only two of Brockton's churches openly accepted Black parishioners. Factories systematically discriminated against Black job seekers, and redlining and restrictive covenants deeply segregated the city. The Brockton area branch of the NAACP was chartered in 1954 and fought mightily against civil rights violations in education, housing, and labor.

In this Gateway City, poverty, joblessness, and high rates of reported violent crime exceed state averages and concentrate in the poorest neighborhoods. In 2016, one in every one hundred people could expect to be the victim of violence (murder, rape, robbery, and aggravated assault) in Brockton. In 2017, Brockton received state aid to respond to spikes in gun violence, and it used the funding to increase the number of detectives and state troopers "focus[ed] on high-visibility traffic stops and patrolling areas prone to crime" in order to make people "think twice about carrying a gun on the streets."[25] District Attorney Timothy Cruz commented: "When we do that, we are able to get a significant number of individuals off the street, which will drive down the gun violence and will take the bad guys and put them where they belong, which is in jail."[26]

Brockton is a Gateway City for reasons beyond its need for economic justice. Once nicknamed the City of Champions in honor of hometown athlete Rocky Marciano, it is also an important new destination for Haitian and Cape Verdean immigrants. New civic institutions, churches, and other social supports have brought renewed community engagement. In 2019, the city council appointed its first-ever Black mayor (indeed, its first *non-White* mayor).

Just to the southwest of Brockton is Fall River, a historic textile town. Cotton mills producing printed cloth, including, at one point, the headquarters of global leader American Printing Company, employed thousands of residents in Fall River at its peak. In an already familiar story, dozens of these mills were closed down or destroyed by fire in the latter half of the twentieth century. Today, the poverty rate in Fall River is twice the state average. There are few programs to address homelessness, substance use problems, and emergency food needs, though Catholic Social Services offers support for hunger, legal services, housing, and disability.

Fall River also has the second highest reported violent crime rate of any city in Massachusetts, 1,167 per 100,000, compared to 726 per 100,000 in Boston. Much of the disorder is attributed to the fact that this town is plagued by opioid addiction. In some neighborhoods, heroin and other opioids are regularly sold openly and used in vacant buildings.[27] Fall River admitted 3,652 residents to substance use treatment facilities in 2013, a rate of 397 per 10,000 residents, compared to a statewide rate of 153 per 10,000; worse yet, it has one of the highest rates of opioid-related overdose deaths in the country.[28] In a city with about 90,000 residents, 64 people died of an overdose in 2016, a rate of 7.1 per 10,000 (in comparison, Boston, with a population 685,000, had 195 overdose deaths in 2016, or a rate of 2.8 per 10,000).

To the north of Brockton and Fall River are the cities of Lawrence and Lynn. Lynn, another city powered in the early twentieth century by shoe production, is closer to Boston (ten miles north); like Brockton, it saw manufacturing dwindle by the century's close. Its last shoe factory shut down in 1981. Lynn, however, is currently in the midst of a rapid revitalization. A rebranding campaign to replace its notorious Prohibition-era nickname—City of Sin—with the more positive City of Firsts, reflects a sort of civic optimism, even as drug use, poverty, and infant mortality remain stubborn problems. In 2017, 61 people died of an overdose in Lynn, or 6.5 per 10,000 residents, and its poverty and infant mortality rates are both double the state's averages.[29]

Approximately twenty-five minutes northeast of Lynn is Lawrence, Massachusetts. Lawrence's textile industry collapsed earlier, just after World War II, and the city never fully recovered. After the mills left, the middle followed. The resulting declines in population and revenue eroded the social infrastructure available to Lawrence's residents. *Boston Magazine* dubbed it the City of the Damned and "the most godforsaken place in Massachusetts" in 2012, and reporters from the *New York Times* noted widespread city government corruption and the state takeover of Lawrence's public school system.[30] Today it has high unemployment (18 percent), high poverty (nearly 30 percent), and the fourth-highest reported violent crime rate in the state (1,094 violent crimes per 100,000 residents). For many years a drive down Lawrence's main streets led to the hulking, mostly vacant former mills now being renovated into mixed-use and mixed-income apartments.

A city that is over three-quarters Latino, Lawrence did not elect its first Latino mayor until 2009. Former Mayor Dan Rivera worked to implement a number of reforms, and he commented specifically about the urgency to diversify the Lawrence Police Department as soon as he took office: "We needed more people of color, more bilingual folks because there was an 80 percent chance that if you called for help in Lawrence, 911, the police officer that came to your door was not going to speak your language. An 80 percent chance that you are not going to be able to communicate to the person that you called to save you."[31] Lawrence has aimed to tie revitalization to public safety, as a new public art works project demonstrates.[32] Iluminacíon Lawrence is a citywide project begun in 2019 that creates an immersive public art experience using LED lighting and projections. "The mission of ILUMINACIÓN LAWRENCE," its website reads, "is to celebrate the city's diverse history and peoples by lighting public spaces to enhance the public realm, engage community, *improve public safety*, and make the city a more vibrant and accessible place."[33]

Springfield and its neighboring suburb, Holyoke, are in western Massachusetts, just north of the Connecticut border. Springfield has seventeen neighborhoods, including the North End and Brightwood, which are featured prominently in Tim Black's book *When a Heart Turns Rock Solid*. In describing the loss of manufacturing jobs characteristic of these cities of Massachusetts, Black notes that the intense racial and ethnic segregation, coupled with an all-White political leadership, exacerbated social tensions and the concentration of deprivation found within the Puerto Rican neighborhoods to which many families moved seeking generational mobility—the hope that living here would mean a better life for their children.[34] Today, Springfield city leaders are focusing on transportation redevelopment to better connect New Haven, Connecticut and western Massachusetts cities to Springfield, encouraging business and housing development as it refurbishes its transit system and presents itself as a bedroom community for commuters.

Holyoke, in past days the Paper City, is another that lost its manufacturing industry and was never the same; with little economic redevelopment, it remains extremely underresourced.[35] Amid the long-term decline in manufacturing, the area addressed the demand for cheap, unskilled agricultural labor by recruiting Puerto Rican families into agriculture, many through the Department of Labor of the Commonwealth of Puerto Rico.[36]

Thousands of Puerto Rican people thus sought refuge in Holyoke in the aftermath of Hurricane Maria, a Category 5 storm that devastated Puerto Rico and other Caribbean islands in 2017.[37] Holyoke already boasted one of the largest mainland *boricua* communities in the county, and it registered two hundred new enrollments in public schools in the year following the hurricane.[38] Civic leaders are now pushing for early childhood education reforms. A promising innovation district was established in Holyoke's city center to promote economic development, public art projects, affordable housing, and clean energy initiatives.

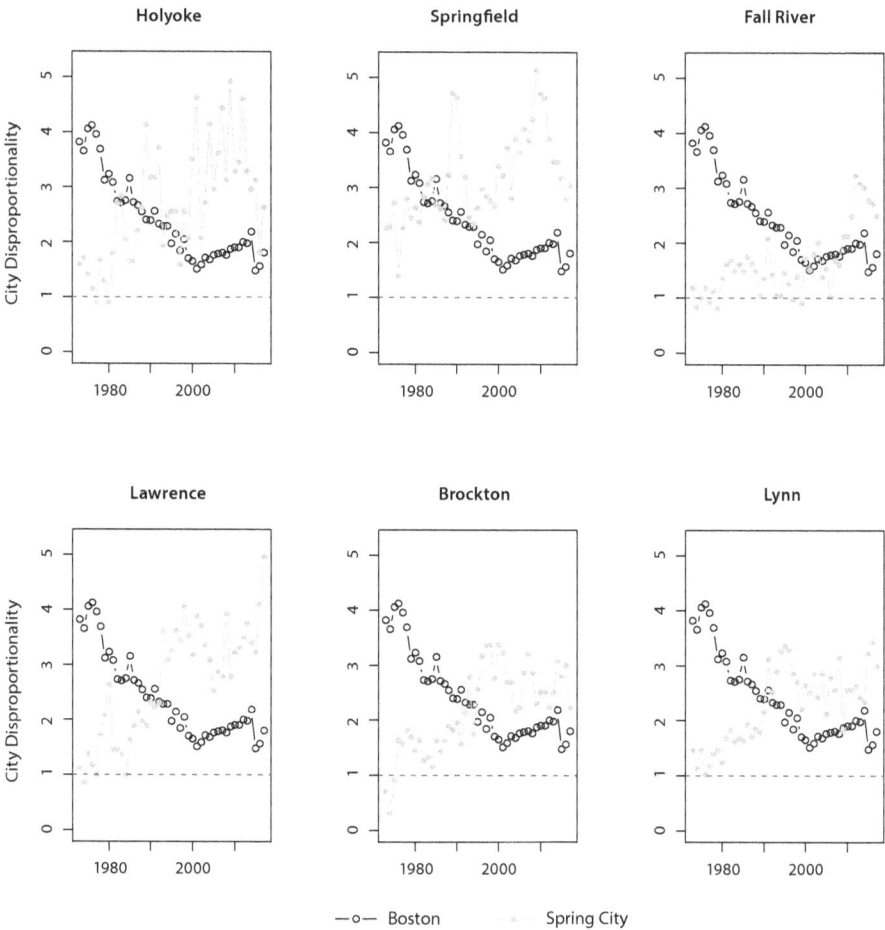

FIGURE 3.3. Prison admission disproportionalities by cities and regions in Massachusetts, 1973–2017. *Source:* Author's compilation of data from Massachusetts Department of Correction prison records.

These legacies of industrial decline, combined with contemporary conditions since the Great Recession, population decline, and the arrival of new populations in more recent years, could all help explain the rise of imprisonment in these small cities in first two decades of the twenty-first century. Figure 3.3 displays six time-series plots. The plots have two lines: for all six, Boston is represented across time by the black line. Figure 3.3 plots the level of disproportionality of imprisonment experienced by each of these six focal cities and how it changed over the forty-four-year period from 1973 to 2017

(1973 is the first year geographic data on prison admissions are available in Massachusetts). By disproportionality I mean: What is the ratio of prison population to community population? Are a city's residents overrepresented or underrepresented in the prison admission population? The dashed line indicates a 1:1 ratio, in which the population is directly proportional to the proportion of people who are sent to prison from that same geographic area. In 1973, Boston accounted for nearly half of all admissions to prison, despite only having about 18 percent of the state's population—the incarceration rate for Bostonians, in other words, was about 4 times higher than the proportional baseline. A steep decline lowered that to 1.5–2 times higher incarceration in the period from 2012 to 2017, all while Boston's population size remained stable for several decades. Today, only about 20 percent of the state's prison population hails from Boston each year, nearly proportional to the city's population size.

The pattern has been the opposite in the Gateway Cities. Since 1973, all now disproportionately contribute to the state's prison admissions, though this wasn't the case in earlier years of historic rise in imprisonment. Holyoke, Springfield, Lawrence, and Lynn have roughly doubled the expected prison admission population share, while the increase came a little later to Fall River, the majority White city bordering Rhode Island. As figure 3.3 shows, each of these cities has a prison admission rates that is three times its presence in the Massachusetts state population since around 2000 (except Fall River, where this level of disproportionality came around 2010). Just as the prominence of the Boston population in prison admissions steadily declined, disproportionate prison admissions from small cities became commonplace.

Figure 3.4 reports the rates of prison admissions in each city from 1973 to 2017 (with Boston, again in black, reported for comparison). The rates in Lawrence, Holyoke, and Springfield have all exceeded the rates in Boston, while the other three cities have closely tracked or only slightly exceeded Boston's rates. Overall, it should be noted, Massachusetts's state incarceration rate is low compared to other states and to the nation; what stands out is that the rates of incarceration in small cities are among the state's highest, and at the very least should be as much of a concern as the rates in the state's largest metropolitan city. These historical data point to understudied trends in where people are living before they go to prison; at least since 2000, the people of small cities have been deeply impacted by imprisonment, though few researchers have thought to examine these data until very recently.

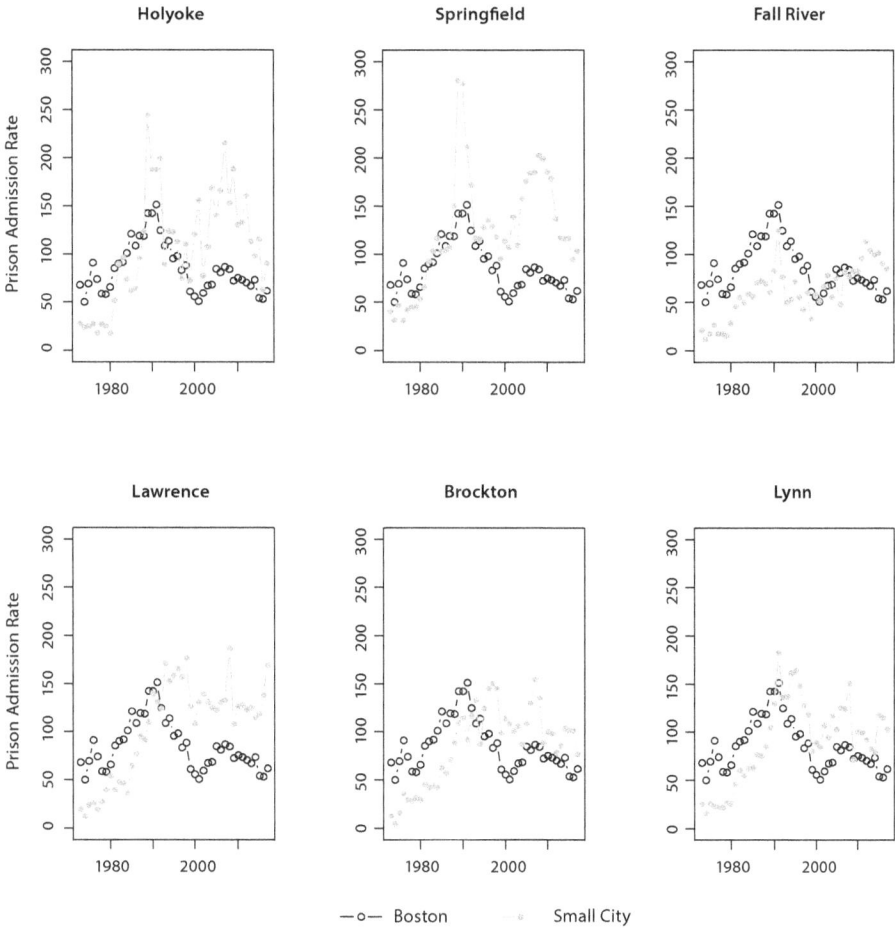

FIGURE 3.4. Prison admissions rates by cities and regions in Massachusetts, 1973–2017. *Source:* Author's compilation of data from Massachusetts Department of Correction prison records.

ANALYZING MASSACHUSETTS SMALL CITIES AS PUNISHING PLACES

Small cities are sites of mass incarceration, but what are some of the drivers of city-level incarceration rates in a statewide analysis? What conditions of these cities help explain their high rates? The theoretical framework of place and punishment discussed in chapter 1 points to several explanations for the spatial pattern of incarceration. We would expect city-level imprisonment rates to be driven primarily by three main conditions: urban inequality, social control, and the spatial context. Here, urban inequality can be defined as the multifaceted and highly correlated adversity of segregation, concentrated socioeconomic disadvantage and abandonment, and violence (concentrated disadvantage refers to the correlations of poverty, public assistance receipt, unemployment, and other socioeconomic measures that together form a pattern of disadvantage). One way to measure social control is to estimate a city's policing capacity by assessing the number of uniformed officers per capita. And the spatial context of Massachusetts includes Greater Boston, small cities, and outlying suburbs and rural towns.

My unique data source is the Massachusetts Department of Corrections, which has kept records on prison admissions and geographic data on the city of commitment from 1997 to the present day. (For more information on the data used for this analysis, see the appendix.) Figure 3.5 reports the results of my analysis of two periods of data spanning 20 years: from 1997 to 2006 and from 2008 to 2017. The first includes the years in which prison admissions peaked, while the more recent period has been a time of consistent decline in prison admissions. Within each, I explore the associations between urban inequality, social control, and the spatial context to understand how each factor may (or may not) have changed in relationship to prison admissions.

In both time periods, two hypothetical cities that differ by 20 percent in their Black population as a portion of their total population would have 30–44 percent higher prison admissions. For the share of the Latino population, prison admissions in the earlier period would be 23 percent higher in the city with the greater number of Latino residents. About the same difference in the level of prison admissions (22 percent) would be associated with a standard deviation increase in the concentrated disadvantage score and a 20 percent increase in the amount of vacant housing in the city, but this is *only* true in the later period (2008–2017), indicating a shift from earlier periods. Reported violent crime is significantly associated with prison admissions, but hewing to the findings of prior research, the size of the effect is small. A 1 percent increase in the reported violent crime rate is associated with a .08 percent increase in the prison admission rate in the earlier period, but that association grows significantly in the later period. After 2008, a 1 percent increase in reported violent crime is associated with about a .23 percent increase in prison admissions.

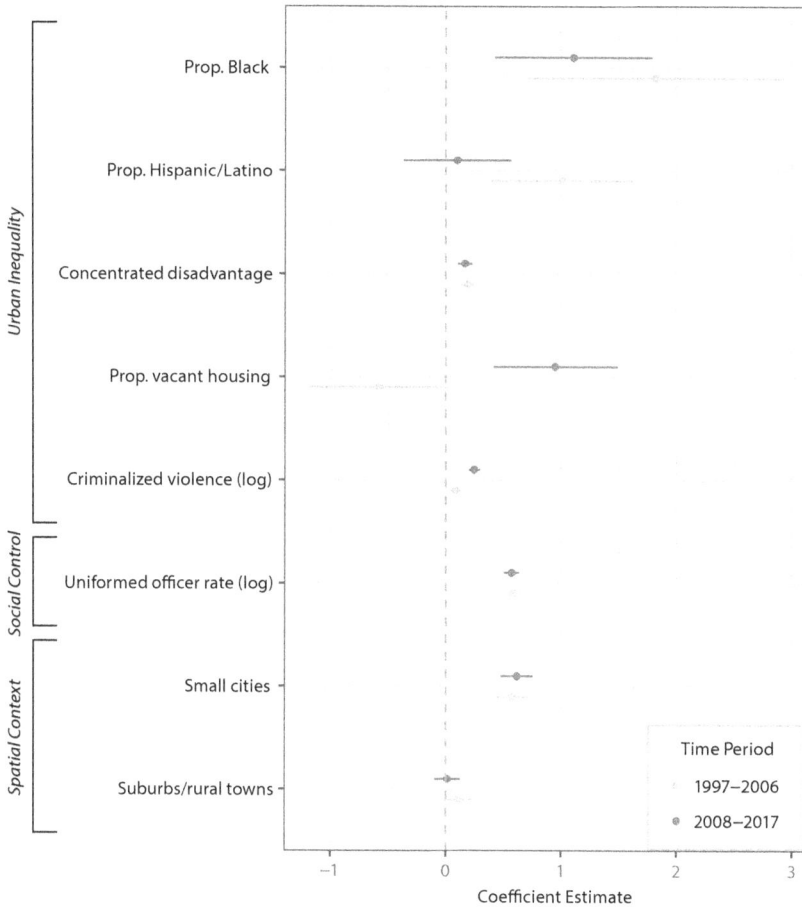

FIGURE 3.5. Estimated associations among city prison admissions and urban inequality, social control, and spatial context of mass incarceration in 1997–2006 and 2008–2017 (95% confidence intervals). For spatial context estimates, the reference category is Greater Boston cities and towns. *Source:* Author's compilation of data from US Census, Massachusetts Department of Correction prison records, and FBI Uniform Crime Reports.

Strikingly, the number of uniformed officers per 100,000 is strongly related to the prison admission rate in both periods, holding urban inequality measures constant. According to these results, in both periods, an additional 10 officers per 10,000 residents is associated with a 10 percent increase in the prison admission rate.

The differences by spatial context drive home the significance of studying places beyond the biggest metropolitan areas. Using Greater Boston (Boston and its surrounding cities and suburbs) as the reference category, small cities had, on average, 78 percent higher prison admissions in the earlier period (1997–2006) and 87 percent higher prison admissions in the later period (2008–2017), holding constant the urban inequality and social control environment across these different types of cities.

These results demonstrate the enduring importance of urban inequality, social control, and spatial context in twenty years of mass incarceration data. Significantly, the relationship between reported violent crime rates and prison admissions has grown stronger in more recent years. Compared to Boston and its surrounding cities and suburbs, small cities show significantly greater levels of prison admissions as early as 1997 and continuing into 2017.

Taken together, these models describe a multifaceted social ecology of economic disadvantage, racial composition, criminalized violence, and social control that accounts for the patterns of imprisonment in Massachusetts cities. Small cities have significantly higher incarceration rates than Boston and its suburbs, as well as suburbs and rural towns in the rest of the state. My six focal cities, particularly Fall River, Lawrence, Brockton, and Springfield, are embedded in a context of significant social and economic inequality, and they are meaningfully isolated from the public goods concentrated in the Greater Boston region, including transportation and a thriving labor force.

EXPLORING MASS INCARCERATION BY URBANICITY AND REGION IN US COUNTIES

To what extent are very high small city imprisonment rates limited to or generalizable from Massachusetts? This is a key question in any case study, so I turn to jail population and prison admissions data provided by the Vera Institute of Justice for a large sample of US counties, dividing the data into two categories: (1) counties centered on a large urban city and (2) counties centered on small/midsized cities, suburban areas, and rural counties (see the appendix for detailed information on the data sources and years for this analysis). The small-city trend in Massachusetts is not limited to the Northeast region of the United States. In some areas, it is even more pronounced.

First, let's take a moment to note that the *jail* is a different kind of institution than the *prison*. There are a number of important distinctions, starting with the scale of population and the frequency of admissions and releases. A jail is a county or city facility that incarcerates pretrial defendants unable to make bail and people who are serving short sentences. Prisons, by contrast, are state or federal facilities that imprison people serving longer sentences. As such, an important difference is the general function of jails versus prisons. Jails are treated as the "front door" to the criminal justice system, incarcerating people as they await trial or serve relatively short sentences (anywhere from a few days to a few years). Prisons represent the deep end of a criminal justice process, where individuals are serving sentences for typically more serious violations. Another major difference between the two forms of incarceration is population flow. In 2020, approximately 631,000 men and women were locked up in local jails, compared to nearly 1.3 million people in state prisons.[39] On the other hand, people go to jail more than 10 million times each year, compared to about 600,000 prison admissions per year. There are many more jails than prisons, and jails may be closer to home than prisons, which are often sited and clustered in remote and rural areas.[40] Because these institutions are distinctive institutionally and demographically, we might not expect similar trends in the spatial patterns of jail and prison admissions. I present data on these two institutions separately in order to explore the patterns of both forms of incarceration as they relate to the county-level spatial context.

Figure 3.6 plots these data separately for jail population rates and prison admissions per 100,000 population from 1983 to 2016. A gray dashed line marks the year in which the average rate of jail population or prison admissions in large urban counties fell below non-large urban counties. In the top graph, we see that in 2003 the average jail admission rate in urban counties fell below rates in non-large urban counties and has persistently declined over time, while jail admission rates in non-large urban counties, on average, increased over time.

The bottom panel shows a similar story, but slightly later: while prison admissions have been declining overall since the mid-2000s, that decline has been limited to large urban counties. Smaller urban, suburban, and rural counties have either maintained or increased the rate of prison admissions during large counties' period of rapid decline.

Thus, by 2016 (in states for which there is reliable county-level data), there was an almost nationwide shift in individuals' residences prior to incarceration or imprisonment.[41] Given the data from both Massachusetts and US counties, mass incarceration is better characterized as a *broad mode of governance affecting communities beyond large metropolitan cities.* Small urban cities, suburban areas, and rural towns experience extreme levels of

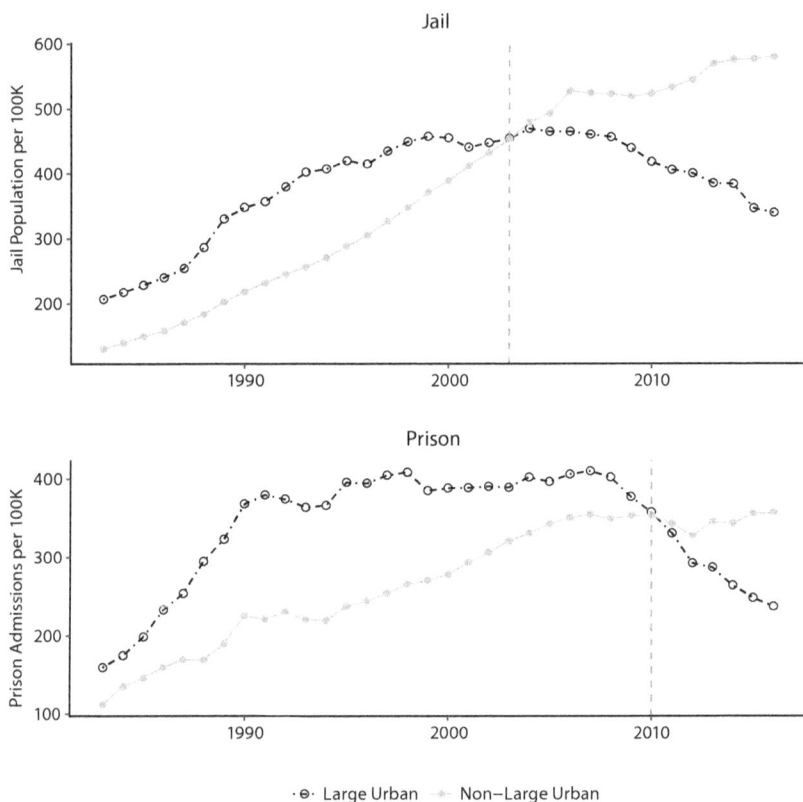

FIGURE 3.6. Jail population and prison admission rates by urbanicity in US counties, 1983–2016 (in thousands). *Source:* Author's compilation of data from Vera Institute of Justice (n.d.).

disadvantage, including poverty, opioid epidemics, and criminalized violence, and these areas are now the places where the experience of incarceration is most common. It is a dramatic inversion of the relationship between place and punishment, though few have observed this shift before now.

Figures 3.7 and 3.8 plot jail population rates and prison admission rates, respectively. These plots of the four main regions of the United States reveal significant differences in the spatial context of mass incarceration. In the plot of jail population (figure 3.7), the time-series graphs demonstrate that, in 1983, the rate of jail population was highest in large urban counties across all regions of the United States. By 2016, the jail population rate was highest in areas beyond large metro areas in all regions except the Northeast (the shift is particularly pronounced in the West and South, but can also be seen in the

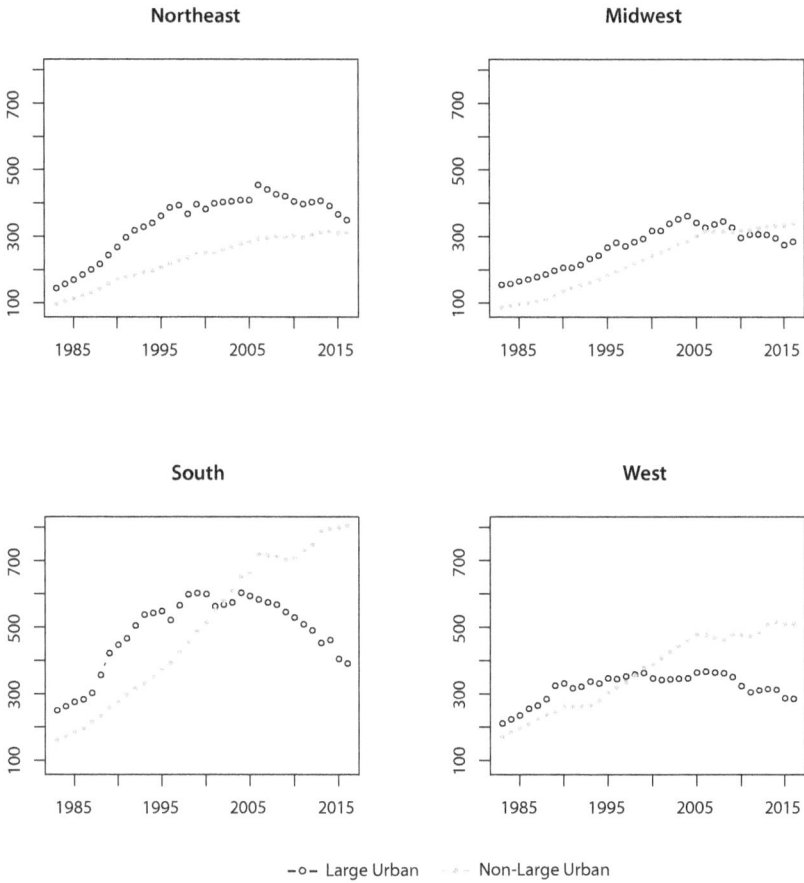

FIGURE 3.7. Jail population rate by urbanicity and region in US counties, 1983–2016 (in thousands). *Source:* Author's compilation of data from Vera Institute of Justice (n.d.).

Midwest, alongside a narrowing of the difference between large city counties and their counterparts in the Northeast).

Figure 3.8 plots county-level prison admission rates by region for 1983–2016. These data suggest a similar trend: in all four regions of the United States, which have remarkably different punishing regimes, histories, and overall rates, prison admissions show significant decline only in counties centered on large metropolitan cities. This is true in the Northeast (as with Massachusetts), as well as in the South.

The striking reality is that the pattern of decarceration in American prisons is mainly limited to populations hailing from large city counties. Small

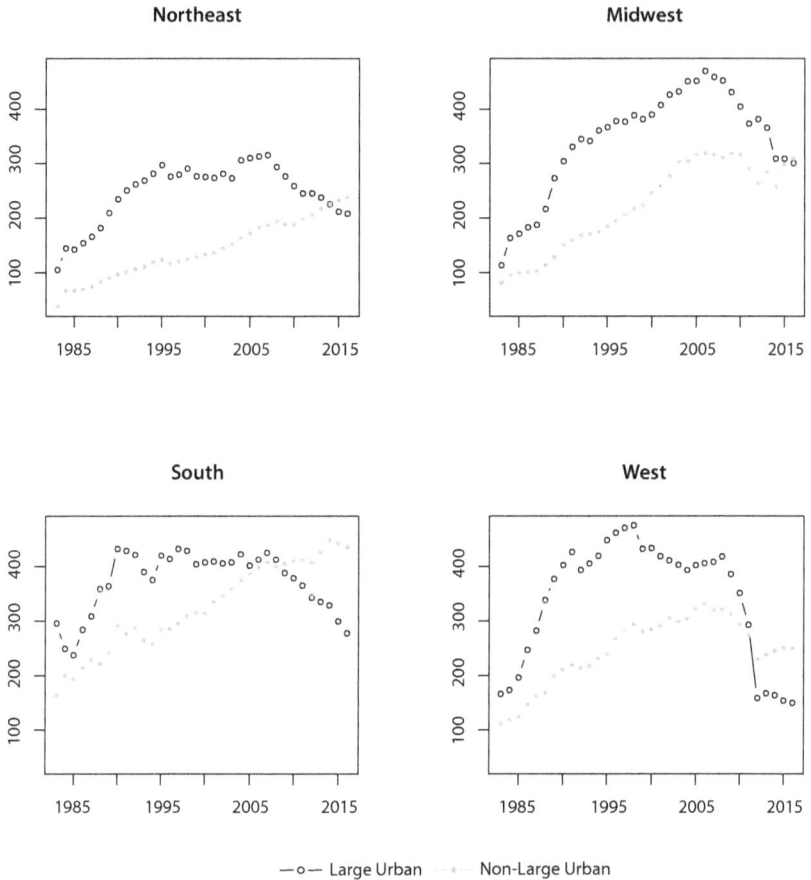

FIGURE 3.8. Prison admission rates by urbanicity and region in United States counties, 1983–2016 (in thousands). *Source:* Author's compilation of data from Vera Institute of Justice (n.d.).

counties are being left behind in the reform efforts to reduce incarceration rates and in some cases continue to rise.[42] The dramatic drop in the West tracks the 2011 California Realignment Initiative, which led to a 41 percent reduction in new prison admissions and a drop of nearly 30,000 people incarcerated in state prisons, but most of these declines were among people from large-city counties. Little consideration has ever been given to the possibility that decarceration (the steady decline in imprisonment rates since the mid-2000s) may itself have a spatial context. This pattern of incarceration decline could be explained in part by shifts in policies and practices, as well as by larger regional shifts in place stratification throughout the United States. The graphs presented demonstrate a shifting spatial and geographic landscape of punishing places for *both* jails and prisons since the mid-2000s.

What is remarkable is the similarity in prison admission patterns across very different cities and regions of the United States. But the historical trajectory of the spatial patterns I have examined lends new insight into the evolution of American mass incarceration. In this chapter, I have presented spatial data across a long time horizon in order to provide a broad, demographic approach to the study of cities, poverty and inequality, and punishment. The decline in incarceration rates in Boston and large urban counties was consistent with the same cities' steep declines in violence. Examining places across the era of mass incarceration shows us that for a variety of reasons, mass incarceration may have become the policy instrument for responding to social problems associated with the social and economic conditions of small cities and towns. However, we have only now begun to understand how these places have become intimately linked with the prison system.

Ninety-six percent of cities in the United States have a population of fewer than 50,000 residents.[43] These places have been absent from research on punishment and neighborhood inequality. Small communities, which often experience high rates of population turnover and joblessness, have been hard hit by the worsening effects of the opioid epidemic. Frequently geographically isolated and resource deprived, these suburban and satellite cities have driven the recent growth in both mass imprisonment and racial segregation.[44]

THEORIZING THE EMERGENCE OF PUNISHING PLACES IN SMALL CITIES

We punishment scholars miss so much when we focus analysis on only a subset of places. The level and conditions of criminalization and police violence found within Ferguson, Missouri, following the death of Michael Brown provided a crucial window into the possibility that small cities are under the radar for both research and criminal justice reform efforts. The result is a fundamentally skewed view of both urban social processes and punishment regimes. As I discussed in chapter 1, this kind of thinking allows researchers to make sweeping claims about the origins of patterns within the criminal justice system (e.g., urban policing, harsh rural prosecutors, retributive state politics), when in reality a multitudinous array of institutional arrangements, in a diversity of places with varying degrees of poverty, racial segregation, and violence, has produced very high incarceration rates.

In sum, I have laid out four key findings in this chapter. First, small cities have seen a rise in punitive social control, leading to a rise in prison admissions and jail incarceration at least since the 1990s in Massachusetts and since the 2000s in US counties. Second, mass incarceration is part of the local ecology, alongside concentrated disadvantage and violence, in these cities. Third, punishing places are found not only in the core of inner-city neighborhoods in major urban centers. Small, midsized, and rural counties have some of the highest jail and prison admission rates in my samples. Finally, these trends are the result of large demographic shifts, decline, and the political conditions and policing infrastructure in small and midsized cities.

The data presented in this chapter describe a general trend of metropolitan decline in prison admissions and a steady or increasing rate of prison admissions in nonmetropolitan areas. Thus, declines in the prison population (or jails) have been largely limited to large metro areas. The *growth* in nonmetropolitan carceral populations seems to be more attributable to jail populations than to prison populations. These differences can point us toward community conditions and jail incarceration—often considered the front door of criminal justice—versus prison admissions, often considered the end of a longer criminal justice process. However, the main focus on nonmetropolitan trends has been on jail growth (e.g., the Vera Institute of Justice has illuminated the trends in jail populations in recent years), not prison admission rates, but both trends deserve deep attention as scholars and policy makers alike attend to the necessary reforms addressing the consequences of mass incarceration for communities.

To answer the questions posed at the outset of this chapter, punishing places have emerged in forgotten and ignored cities, where a dearth of services and conditions of neglect have led to steady and ever-growing jail and prison populations. I offer here hypotheses that could help explain why rates of imprisonment are highest, especially in the case of Massachusetts, in small cities:

1. *All criminalization and punishment is local.* Prison admissions are highly dependent on local policing and prosecutorial practices, as well as the capacity for criminal justice processing. On the one hand, prosecutors got tougher (or have always been tougher) in small cities and rural counties than in their urban counterparts. On the other hand, prosecutors and police departments became reformist in big cities.

From misdemeanors to capital cases, today there are few places in the United States where nonmetropolitan jurisdictions are more lenient than urban jurisdictions.[45]

2. *The political atmosphere, local struggles for dominance, and institutional structures within small cities were ripe for harsh punishment.* National politics surrounding law and order created incentives and a policy feedback loop that established remarkable consistency in the rise of mass incarceration across a very diverse set of places. Thus, the extent to which there were early adopters and late adopters and degrees of punitiveness had to do with how partisan politics either impeded or enhanced punitive policy and practice. In this way, geographic variation in prison admissions stems from struggles within the penal state. Geographic variation is caused by the outcome of local struggles and intersecting fields populated by criminal justice actors vying for dominance. This may explain why we might see greater decline in large urban centers, where there is a much stronger contingent of powerful figures (including reformers and lawyers) and more resources.[46]

3. *Socioeconomic conditions and the social policy environment make small cities particularly vulnerable to harsh punishment in later periods of mass incarceration.* Social and economic disadvantage, changing demography, and conditions of remoteness and isolation interacted to create extreme levels of marginality in contexts where jails and prisons became the policy response as larger, metropolitan counties and cities sought alternatives. In an absence of robust welfare and social services, and with overwhelming policy neglect, these places are the most vulnerable to punishment.

4. *Racial social control is remarkably consistent.* The criminal justice system has been used to enact racial social control since the end of slavery. From policing to prison, the criminal justice system follows dispossessed groups and populations. Variations are based on variation in the presence of racially and ethnically marginalized populations.

The first two hypotheses have been put forth by scholars of law and politics, who focus on the influential actors, institutional capacity, and political conditions of particularly rural police, courts, prisons, and the larger community. I build on these theories by exploring the social and spatial conditions of small cities, combining insights from both social control and ecological theories of punishment. The next chapter focuses on the third hypothesis above, relating to the social service environment of small cities, and chapter 5 explores the theoretical frameworks of race and racism producing the current spatial pattern of incarceration.

In chapter 4, I explore some of the mechanisms explaining these spatial patterns of punishment in an interview study of sixty-four social services providers in cities throughout Massachusetts. In these semistructured interviews, several mechanisms emerged describing how isolation, remoteness, and the conditions of small towns that give rise to persistent poverty, drug use, and incarceration deepen marginality and expose people to greater risk of criminalization. These conditions contrast with the *concentration effects* of so-called inner-city neighborhoods and point to a different set of conditions of isolation, policy neglect, and stigma that are underexplored by the larger literature on place and punishment.

FOUR

Social Services Beyond the City

ISOLATION AND REGIONAL INEQUITY

WHAT EXPLAINS HIGH RATES OF INCARCERATION in small cities and counties? What determines variation in these punishing places? Up to this point, I have presented only quantitative analyses of Massachusetts's highest imprisonment rates, underlining that imprisonment is concentrated in the state's small cities and suburbs. This pattern can be observed in all four regions of the United States, and the shift in imprisonment and jail incarceration rates from large urban counties to smaller counties has so far been undertheorized by the larger literature on social control and ecological theories of punishment, though this is a relatively recent shift (since the early 2000s).

To better grasp the socioeconomic conditions and the ways incarceration may or may not be mitigated by social services, I conducted a qualitative study of the social service environment in small cities statewide. During the summer of 2019, I traveled to a number of Massachusetts cities (including all those discussed in chapter 3) to conduct fieldwork and interview social service providers. Along with a research assistant, I reached out to 365 organizations using contact information from a statewide reentry services handbook. My resulting sample of 64 providers represents a diversity of fields, from working directly with formerly incarcerated people to working broadly to address poverty, mental illness, substance use, joblessness, and housing insecurity in their communities. Each provider works with people affected by mass incarceration (including arrest and incarceration histories). Our interviews included focus groups of two to six people interviewed together, along with one-on-one interviews conducted in person or over the phone. Some interviews included field site visits to shelter facilities, service offices, and community centers. In total, these semistructured interviews uncover some of the unique challenges prisoner reentry and social service providers navigate in small cities in an era of mass incarceration. The interview questions and other details are available in the appendix.

Prisoner reentry—a term used by researchers and policy makers to describe the transition from prison back to communities—is a significant part of an understanding of mass incarceration. But so far this book has focused on prison *admissions*, not releases. About 600,000 people leave prison and return to communities across the United States each year.[1] When people leave prison, they face enormous challenges, including extreme poverty. Especially if someone has unpaid fines or fees, it can be difficult to reinstate a driver's license or ID, a critical first step to accessing housing, employment, and transportation.[2] People may search for work, only to experience discrimination or paltry wages.[3] Housing is perhaps among one of the most difficult aspects of life after prison; many people live unstably housed, relying on arrangements with family or friends, or in shelters.[4] People leaving prison, especially those with histories of substance use problems, face astronomical overdose risk.[5] Moreover, about 2 in every 3 individuals who are incarcerated will be arrested again within three years of release.[6] Given the fact that a group of people the size of Boston's population (about 600,000) leave prison each year and face these challenges, it is no wonder that social services have become focused on the unique challenges of prisoner reentry and intervene in the cycle of reincarceration. In this study, I keyed in on social service providers who work directly with formerly incarcerated people to understand the challenges and risks that people face in their communities, and how their services aim to interrupt incarceration in a context of very high rates of imprisonment.

The interviews sought to understand (1) the types of services available to people returning from prison and (2) the challenges to reentry in suburban areas and small cities with high rates of imprisonment. What types of programs and resources are available in these towns, and how accessible are they? How do practitioners in underresourced areas describe the conditions of poverty and the social policy response? What barriers stymie practitioners in supporting formerly incarcerated people and preventing recidivism in their regions? In this chapter I present several key themes that demonstrate how the social conditions of small cities could give rise to very high rates of incarceration.

"Regional inequity," in the words of my participants, was among the strongest themes in my interview data. In general, the research, policy, and funding for social services, in particular reentry, focused so heavily on Boston that the small cities felt left behind. And because Boston is the center of gravity for services and social policy, the spatial challenges of distance *from* Boston meant that many of the interviewees' clients struggled to access services, such as substance treatment and mental health services, or jobs, which are more plentiful outside of small cities. Part of their work often required providing transportation to population centers such as Boston in order to access any services for their clients. This had numerous implications for the delivery of care, access to services, and sustainable employment.

For people leaving prison, there are several often paradoxical conditions that make it extremely difficult to access services.[7] They may have court-ordered financial obligations such as fines, fees, or child support but very little to no income. Job applications (let alone commutes) frequently require a driver's license or other form of identification, but to have their driver's licenses reinstated, many former inmates must pay the entirety of these fines and fees (and any interest that has accrued). This paradox is particularly vexing when returning to a city where jobs may be far away in Boston or in other, wealthier cities and suburbs.

A social worker from Lowell, Massachusetts, a city of about 100,000 north of Boston, describes the difficulty of accessing transportation and work in her city:

> People aren't able to get cars usually, especially when they are first coming out of incarceration. So that's a big one for people. I would say we're constantly looking for jobs that are more accessible for people. Honestly, a lot of our members won't take those jobs just because they know they're not going to be able to get there unless they have their own car. Some people will try to do the Uber thing, but that gets expensive too. It's tough. Some of the providers will give them rides. Sometimes they'll be willing to give people rides if they're convenient, but that's a big one that makes it really difficult for people with the jobs if they don't have the access to a car. That's a big difference to Boston. Boston has obviously a much more robust public transportation system than we do up here.

Joblessness—already a major hurdle for individuals with a criminal record in any city—is exacerbated by transportation troubles. Over half ($N = 37$) of participants discussed this problem, and it was mentioned at least 244 times in my 64 interviews. Lowell is only about an hour's drive from Boston, and the two cities are connected by a commuter rail line—which means Lowell is arguably a best-case scenario for transportation access among this sample's represented cities.

In areas farther away from Boston, local bus systems are the only viable form of transportation. An employee at a job training center in Holyoke described a hypothetical public transport commute to access a job in a nearby city involving a four-hour trek, demonstrating the challenges that remoteness brings to stable employment:

> [To get to] Greenfield on a bus requires taking a bus from Holyoke to Northampton, which would take about an hour and a half. And then in Northampton, switch over in Northampton, you switch off of the Pioneer Valley Transit and then you move over to a different transit, which will bring you up to Greenfield—I want to say almost 4 hours total on a bus, and it's cost prohibitive for people. You can take a [chartered bus] and spend the $12 to get there. A monthly bus pass will only work in the Pioneer Valley. Once you leave the Springfield area, if I wanted to go to Northampton or Greenfield, it's a different bus system, so my bus pass doesn't work. You guys have your T and your pass [in Boston] and it works there, but wouldn't work down here. That can be cost prohibitive and a barrier to employment because if you're relying on the buses and they want you to work second shift and the last bus leaves at 10:55 and you have to work at 11 o'clock, you can't take that job.

This sense of transportation inequity was echoed by an addiction recovery counselor in Holyoke, Massachusetts:

> I think we're limited by our bus transportation system. There's a lot of great jobs that are on the outskirts. It's not high ridership because people in those areas have cars. It's like a self-fulfilling prophecy, nobody's riding, but then nobody's investing in it. Right? Boston—ha. The Boston [recovery] program is bigger and they have a very advanced transportation system—they can get anywhere in the city 24 hours a day.

The spatial mismatch of jobs and population, coupled with an inadequate transportation system, provides important context for the high rates of incarceration in these areas. Poverty and persistent joblessness are strongly associated with the chance of incarceration; living in an area with so little transportation deepens the social disadvantage in ways that make someone have to choose between losing out on a job opportunity or driving without a license—either of which exposes them to possible arrest and reincarceration. While many scholars of reentry and social service delivery have noted these challenges in urban settings, remoteness and isolation deepen preexisting marginality in these small cities and towns.[8] As jobs become fewer and fewer, the vulnerability of remoteness and isolation will only worsen.

In *The Truly Disadvantaged*, William Julius Wilson famously argued that large-scale structural changes to society and the economy in the twentieth century generated a similar spatial mismatch between poor families and job centers, and he suggested it had given way to a rise in concentrated poverty. This mismatch has been documented in later periods and different regions. Individuals travel hours to work minimum-wage jobs in far-off communities. America's regional inequality compounds the problem, pushing workers farther and farther away from job centers. National news has described intense spatial mismatches in regions such as California's Silicon Valley and around New York City, where a demographic inversion has shifted population, jobs, and capital; young professionals now prefer to make their homes in the big city than in small cities and suburbs.[9] Once the preferred neighborhoods of wealthy city commuters (who drove or took trains to earn healthy wages), small cities are now mostly inhabited by poor and working-class commuters, who travel great distances for work. Social service providers told me in an assortment of ways that the lack of public transportation exacerbates joblessness and even leads to greater chances that some of their clients will end up in (or be returned to) the criminal justice system.

Spatial mismatch goes beyond the available economic opportunities and can affect health-care access. The opioid crisis has laid bare other regional inequalities in the state not directly related to employment. Even in a wealthy, well-resourced state with expanded Medicaid, the opioid crisis has been devastating, particularly in small cities.[10] According to CDC WONDER data, since 2012 the rate of opioid-related death in Massachusetts has risen to more than two times the national average.[11] The places with the highest rates of opioid-related deaths are all small cities (Fall River, Carver, Quincy, Everett, and New Bedford), and they also have some of the highest unemployment rates in the state.[12] Thus, many participants I spoke with recognize that supporting people in their recovery often involves multiple services, including housing and employment support. One substance recovery coach commented about trying to help clients get jobs in small cities, "Western Mass has fewer jobs in general. Fewer employers. It's a little bit more of a rural environment . . . there's just less access out there. And then there is Boston."

Part of their recovery program connects people with substance use problems to job training, but the spatial distribution of job training programs creates hardship for people in small cities:

> Boston has a ton of different job training providers out there. So people who are in Boston, they can choose from up to 10 different job training programs to go through. Whereas in Springfield they have two or three. And then Worcester and New Bedford—it's been very hard for us to build up our [recovery] program out there because there's just very few job training programs out there.

Bruce Western and Catherine Sirois analyzed employment and earnings data from the Boston Reentry Study, a longitudinal survey of men and women leaving state prison and returning to the Boston area. Panel data from a sample of men and women released from prison to the Boston area showed unemployment rates between 40 and 60 percent over the course of a year; earnings averaged around $1,000 a month, about the federal poverty line for an individual.[13] But in the view of the social workers and providers I talked to who work in small cities, Boston is a best case for people leaving prison or struggling with addiction. According to my participants, the collective understanding is that jobs are still more plentiful, and transportation to these opportunities more accessible, in Boston than in the communities they serve.

Beyond employment support for people with substance use problems, currently the distribution of treatment services for opioid and other substance use disorders means that individuals may have to travel hundreds of miles for daily treatments. A substance use counselor in Western Massachusetts who specializes in supporting families lamented how little treatment capacity was available in her area:

> Probably the first thing that comes to mind is treatment slots or beds. It's so difficult, we just don't have enough slots. For example, many people with opioid use disorder that choose to go on Methadone have to travel to Vermont or down to Springfield to try to get their methadone treatment. And that's an enormous ride, and it's a daily ride. So that's an enormous burden on families because typically, it's the family member who has to drive them.

Traveling long distances for treatment can be a major barrier to sobriety for individuals with substance use problems. But there are also *collateral consequences* when individuals and family members must try to access services but find themselves in low-resourced environments. In other words, individuals may need to burden family and friends with helping them access services, even sometimes driving hundreds of miles per day for resources that simply do not exist where they live. Moreover, spatial restrictions on post-release supervision (e.g., individuals must remain in particular jurisdictions while under the surveillance of parole or probation) further limit access if a person must reside in a certain place after their release from prison. For example, individuals who are barred from leaving the state as a condition of their parole status could not go to Vermont for treatment without violating their post-release conditions and potentially facing reincarceration or, if they cannot get services, relapse.

In the context of an opioid crisis, spatial mismatch can be fatal. A harrowing vignette from one interview with a reentry services social worker detailed the final hours of a woman's life, which ended en route to Boston because she did not have access to a court-ordered treatment facility in the Springfield area:

> So here's a woman waiting in some court. I don't remember which county court. You have to wait all day. You're detoxing. There's no medical care. We, because we do the transportation for all of Western Massachusetts, we're waiting to see how many [civil commitments] we have that you grab all those people and then you drive two and a half hours that way [to Boston]. So she waited all day. She had a cardiac event while in our van, our officers did a great job, brought her back with basic life CPR and everything. They brought her back once, maybe even twice, but then they got her to the hospital where she expired. That didn't have to happen. And it happened because of the wait. And because the resources are all the way over that way. And we can't provide care for women.

According to one participant, this tragedy was the direct result of *regional inequity*. Women in her area must travel long distances to receive court-mandated treatment and services. Every day, providers run the risk that someone who is detoxing and awaiting transfer could go into cardiac arrest or experience another life-threatening medical event.

Transportation, spatial distance, and the dearth of resources allocated to small cities presented numerous challenges for providers and their clients. Participants often reported feeling forgotten by state initiatives, particularly in relation to funding for reentry and treatment services. At a minimum, inadequate public transportation made accessing employment and substance use treatment extremely difficult; at worst, it was deadly. Placing treatment and other resources in the places where the opioid crisis hits hardest, for example, could save lives and reduce the chances that individuals end up arrested or back in jail.

POLICY NEGLECT: LIMITED FUNDING
AND STATE SUPPORT FOR SMALL CITIES

Whether talking about state, federal, or philanthropic funding, a common theme among participants was that Boston received the lion's share of funding and support for reentry, substance use, mental health, and other services.[14] Mirroring this sentiment, Viviana Chui-Sik Wu found in a national sample that community foundations tend to emerge in urban communities, whereas rural and more vulnerable communities with high proportions of residents who are unemployed and thus have large service gaps experience a rarity of philanthropic activities.[15]

Shelters receive funding from a number of sources, but in Massachusetts one of the funders is the Massachusetts Department of Mental Health. One participant who works in Holyoke's substance support services talked about the challenges of opening a much-needed homeless shelter in the community:

> They had applied to do [a shelter] in Holyoke and got denied because they said, "oh—there's already one in Springfield." It's kind of close. We hear that frequently—"well, Springfield and Holyoke are not that far away." But the thing is they are very different communities, and a lot of people from Springfield don't want to go to Holyoke. People from Holyoke don't want to go to Springfield. And also the fact that we are predominantly Hispanic here in Holyoke. Something that would respond to them and be a little more culturally sensitive would be ideal.

State policy makers in this instance did not consider the distance between Springfield and Holyoke that might make shelter housing access, particularly in the winter, impossible. Moreover, the population needs of each city, for example language and cultural barriers to social service access in Holyoke, and the size of the need in both communities, have not been accounted for in the decision to place only one shelter for both cities.

In the context of state and federal funding, providers commented on feeling forgotten by funding initiatives. In the case of prisoner reentry, one provider in Worcester described feeling left behind in the rollout of the Second Chance Act, federal legislation that gives grants to states and nonprofit organizations to support reentry services. The participant reflected on how funding for reentry in cities and in Massachusetts has been unequal:

> There isn't really a municipal response to prisoner reentry at all. And often in Worcester we feel like Boston gets all the funding when new things come out. So a few years ago there was this Second Chance Act, it created all these new beds for prisoner reentry, but they went to Springfield, Boston, not Worcester. So we noticed those things. It gets frustrating because the second largest city in New England [Worcester] should have been allocated resources to deal with these issues.

As we saw in chapter 3, Worcester had one of the highest rates of incarceration in the state well before the passage of the Second Chance Act in 2007. I was also struck by the point that there isn't a municipal response to prisoner reentry. While I largely agree with this view, in 2017, Boston mayor Martin J. Walsh launched the city's first Office of Returning Citizens, a signal of how larger cities have recently shown an orientation toward a city-level response to mass incarceration.

THE DOUBLE DISADVANTAGE OF HOUSING AND WORK

The word *housing* came up 700 times in my 64 participants' comments. Typically, housing scholars have focused on how unequal cities like Boston, experiencing rising rents and neighborhood gentrification, have pushed populations out to suburbs and exurbs.[16] As a result, housing research adequately establishes that housing is unaffordable in major metropolitan areas, without illuminating much at all about the housing crisis in small cities. The very weak job market in small cities makes even the lower rents of nearby small cities (compared to Boston) completely unaffordable, and commuters pushed out of those higher-rent markets often lock up the available stock anyway. Multiple providers described housing as the first and most fundamental challenge facing their formerly incarcerated clients. In central Massachusetts, for example, I heard:

> Finding housing has to be the most challenging thing for anyone in this industry for folks. And it's not just because of criminal records, but the criminal records certainly exacerbate that issue. But affordable housing in Massachusetts is at a crisis level. So that's a problem certainly for people who've not had jobs and may not have a whole lot of money saved up to pay the rent.

One participant, a reentry and substance coach, was among those displaced from Boston due to its rising cost of housing. She had lived in one neighborhood her whole life, and a smaller city offered respite. But in talking to providers from small cities, the lower rents do little when a crippling job shortage leaves many without any income at all.

Farther to the west, providers in Springfield described housing challenges and noted that even emergency shelter housing was hard to access without identification:

> Housing is a tough, tough, part of the equation. And so we do have good relationships with all our local shelters. Sometimes our function is really just to verify to the shelter that this is the person that they say they are. Because so often they lose their ID, don't have proper identification—you can't even get into a shelter.

Homeless shelters and transitional housing are heavily impacted in these small city areas. Providers from more remote towns described homeless encampments set up in local campgrounds and forests. I interviewed the directors of the only housing shelter in one small city north of Boston, where they reported that every day they are providing shelter above capacity (usually around 70 additional people per night). The city, fearing it might "attract" homeless populations from nearby Boston and other cities, has no plans to expand shelter beds in fear that "if you build it, they will come." During my visit, a young woman slept on a yoga mat spread out in a shelter hallway, and I was shown utility closets stacked with floor mats that are brought out each night to accommodate some of those who need shelter but cannot be provided a bed due to capacity constraints.

Participants from the Gateway Cities of Lowell and Lawrence characterized their cities as undergoing intense affordable housing crises:

> Affordable housing is a huge crisis [in Lowell]. There is not enough affordable housing for people at all. People keep getting their rents raised and different things and they're just really struggling with that.

Majority-Latino Lawrence, just sixteen miles east of Lowell, is home to a large population of recent immigrants. The combination of two forms of precarity—undocumented status and housing insecurity—results in vulnerable, stressful lives, said one social worker:

I think rent's huge, that's something that I want to say is the top of the list. Because obviously an immigrant—his or her main concern will be the immigration status. The rent and Lawrence, with limited housing and increased rent make it very difficult for families to maintain their way of life.

Like the crisis of mass incarceration, the crisis of affordable housing is a feature of small cities and towns, too. For people living on the extreme margins, such as the men and women leaving jails and prisons and returning to these cities, the scramble for adequate housing compounds the already-high barriers of daily life with a criminal record. Unstable housing and homelessness can lead to criminalization and interactions with police, making housing insecurity both a cause and consequence of criminal justice intervention. Joblessness in these areas makes even more "affordable" rents unaffordable.

STIGMA AND THE OPIOID CRISIS

A final theme from my conversations with small city social service providers is the stigma associated with substance use. Nearly two-thirds of participants ($N = 47$) discussed opioids, heroin, or fentanyl in their interviews. Opioids were mentioned 180 times, and stigma was raised 75 times. Many recalled the early years of the opioid crisis and the elected officials who actively opposed the siting of treatment services, safe syringe exchanges, and sober housing in their communities. The stigma has not abated, according to one group therapy coordinator:

In terms of sober homes, the whole idea of stigma is really crippling. Nobody thinks we should have them. "That's a great idea. Just don't do it in my yard."

This "Not in My Backyard" backlash against sober housing may explain the way that substance use and homelessness actually lead to incarceration in small cities. Without access to transitional sober housing, individuals are more likely to relapse, and relapse is a significant predictor of arrest, technical violations of community-based correctional rules, and incarceration. "Wet housing" is fought even more vigorously, though it can be a way to stabilize those who are not yet ready for sobriety, putting them on that path by getting them housed and able to seek treatment and employment, regardless of whether they ever choose to get sober.

The judgment surrounding substance use problems affects not only those dealing with addiction but also their families. The substance use family therapy coordinator mentioned previously told me:

> We also try to do drop-in centers and other things to reach out to families. One of the struggles period though, is that for a lot of people, the shame and the stigma prevent them from reaching out for help.

Substance use stigma, of course, is not limited to small city areas. But to the degree that the community is aware of individuals' difficulties due to the city's size and capacity for informal surveillance, and in the context of self-described "close-knit" communities, stigma can have an outsized impact. A mental health services provider discussed this stigma, extending its chilling effect to sex offenders and other people with criminal records:

> Not only just the stigma of somebody who might have to register [as a sex offender], but I think also the stigma of coming from incarceration. There are some programs that we've worked with that don't want to take anyone right out of incarceration or are not willing to work with us.

More than two dozen social workers cited stigma as a major barrier to providing services and getting people to show up. I interviewed an employee of a syringe access and exchange in Western Massachusetts, asking about some of the barriers faced by people with substance use problems in their community:

> There's quite a few [barriers]. And the main one is the stigma. There's stigma on individuals that are actively using, especially for someone that's chronically homeless, they don't have the means to get clean clothes and shower. Their appearance is a little off. They might smell a little differently than other people, and the fact that somebody might know that they're an active drug user, as soon as they walked into the door, they're again looked at differently. That's what they're telling us—just the mistreatment that they get at some places, like they're less than human. Who wants to be treated like that when you're going out to go seek some help, some assistance? And they're treating you a different way because of the way you look, your appearance, the fact that you're an active drug user. If I was to go in somewhere and I got treated that way, I probably won't be going back.

Substance use, criminal records, and homelessness are all highly stigmatized, for both individuals and their families. Research has focused on drugs and stigma in rural areas, finding that the conditions of rurality lead to greater stigma and harsher punishment of people with substance use problems.[17] In small cities, providers emphasized how the stigma surrounding their clients became a significant additional barrier to getting a job or housing, or accessing basic services.

MECHANISMS OF EXCLUSION AND MARGINALITY IN SMALL CITIES

Qualitative data are vital if we are to uncover the mechanisms underlying the quantitative analyses presented in this book—in particular, what conditions of small cities are salient in explaining their high rates of incarceration. My interview data reveal particular issues facing these areas in providing reentry support services. Addressing more gaps in research on social control and punishment outside of urban centers, this qualitative study sheds light on several elements of the social policy environment in the neglected cities contributing outsized populations to Massachusetts's prisons. These findings were summed up by a director of reentry services in Western Massachusetts:

> Housing is a huge barrier for us. There's only one shelter, not that many beds. We have not a huge robust industry out here. Right? There's not a lot of jobs. And it's a small area, so everyone knows everyone. So there's not a lot of opportunity to reinvent yourself.

The inadequacy of affordable housing and shelters, combined with profound social closure and stigma, a very weak labor market, and an intense opioid crisis, renders these areas particularly vulnerable to criminal justice intervention. Moreover, interview data suggested that police departments and sheriffs play a significant role in the provision of social services in small cities. This could also contribute to higher rates of incarceration, as individuals are forced to interface with law enforcement in order to access services.

One of the largest reentry providers in Springfield, for example, is run out of the county sheriff's department. As I entered the field site, ready to tour the location and conduct my staff interviews, I noted how much it was like entering jail or prison. Individuals entered through metal detectors and signed in as if entering a secure facility. A staff member explained this was by design, while another's office was decorated with dozens of mug shots of people who had either died from violence or overdose—a foreboding message to all who entered. Coupling social service provision and law enforcement in small cities makes it harder to avoid arrest, technical violations, and going back to jail.

. . .

In this chapter, I have presented several themes that emerged from interviews with 64 people who work to support those who are most vulnerable to criminalization. These individuals are close to both the populations affected most by mass incarceration and the realities of the social policy environment of these cities. In chapter 3 I hypothesized that socioeconomic conditions and the social policy environment make small cities particularly vulnerable to harsh punishment in today's era of mass incarceration. The interviews with social service providers revealed a bleak picture: conditions of remoteness and isolation interact with deep economic marginalization and policy neglect to create extreme levels of marginality. These providers feel left behind in a state that drives much of its attention toward Boston, the capital city and largest metropolitan area in the region. Collectively, the participants described a troubling reality that without addressing regional inequities in transportation, housing, substance use treatment, jobs and training, and access to funding and resources, marginalized people will continue to face great risk of extreme poverty, relapse into substance use, and criminalization.

In chapters 3 and 4, I have focused on large-scale spatial patterns of incarceration and emphasized the new and surprising role that small cities, suburbs, and other nonmetropolitan areas play in patterns of mass incarceration. Now I ask directly: What happens to the pattern of racial inequality and mass incarceration when we undertake this broad spatial analysis? Does including more places amplify or deviate from the central importance of race in the story of mass incarceration? In the following chapter, I explore the racial context of punishing places, demonstrating that even in a sample of places that includes many majority-White areas, racial segregation significantly contributes to ongoing inequities in imprisonment.

FIVE

Race and Communities of Pervasive Incarceration

> One thing we must of course expect to find, and that is a much higher death rate at present among Negroes than among whites: this is one measure of the difference in their social advancement. They have in the past lived under vastly different conditions and they still live under different conditions: to assume that, in discussing the inhabitants of Philadelphia, one is discussing people living under the same conditions of life, is to assume what is not true.
>
> —DU BOIS (1899)

AMONG THE FIRST MAJOR EMPIRICAL WORKS IN AMERICAN SOCIOLOGY, W. E. B. Du Bois's *The Philadelphia Negro* triangulated across qualitative interviews, administrative records, and survey data to provide an account of Black life in a large urban city from the perspective of Black people. It was a project of unparalleled scope, in which Du Bois conducted interviews in twenty-five hundred households and recorded the life histories of ten thousand men, women and children.[1] At the tail end of the nineteenth century, Philadelphia's population was undergoing rapid social transformation. International and domestic migration, with African Americans beginning the Great Migration between 1900 and 1970 from the American South to the neighborhoods of the North, had resulted in Philadelphia having the largest Black population of any US northern city. In 1870, about 22,000 African Americans had been living in Philadelphia. By the 1900 Census, there were about 63,000 Black Philadelphians.[2]

In this work and others, Du Bois offered a sociological framework for analyzing differences in the worlds of White and Black people in the United States. The eminent scholar's analysis of mortality divergences across race, for instance, pointed to social environments as an underlying explanation. To White academics and scholars who traditionally proposed racial inferiority as a driver of yawning gaps in the life chances of Black and White people, this idea was revolutionary.

In fact, throughout the late nineteenth and well into the twentieth centuries, prominent scholars would attribute a host of Black-White differences in mortality, morbidity, and other health conditions to the supposed racial inferiority of the former.[3] Historian Khalil Gibran Muhammad has traced the legacy of racial inferiority claims in early federal crime statistics, too, noting that when the Federal Bureau of Investigation began its first official record keeping (during Jim Crow), crime statistics were presented as obvious "proof" of Black people's higher propensity for crime.[4] Muhammad explains the pathways from biological to cultural claims of racial inferiority: "The statistical evidence of Black criminality remained rooted in the concept of Black inferiority or Black pathology despite a shift in the social scientific discourse on the origins of race and crime. The shift from a racial biological frame to a racial cultural frame kept race at the heart of the discourse. Although racist notions of (permanent) biological inferiority gave way to liberal notions of (temporary) cultural inferiority, racial liberals continued to distinguish Black criminality from white and ethnic criminality. *In effect, they incriminated Black culture.*"[5]

This racism persists in contemporary discussions about the disproportionate rates of incarceration among Black men, such that just the fact that Black men are incarcerated at higher rates than Whites, if not carefully interpreted, frequently reinforces harmful stereotypes, like the myth that Black men are inherently more violent and criminal than White men. The causal misattribution that relates Blackness to criminality, however subtle or explicit, can have lasting harmful effects.[6] Rejecting this idea, if we follow Du Bois's framework, means we can empirically analyze the differences in social environments that lead to differences in particular groups' well-being on any number of measures. Incarceration could be analyzed as a metric of social well-being in communities, along with other more common measures of community well-being, both because it is so often used as a response to social problems (as discussed in chapter 3), and because it results in large-scale community harms.[7]

When it comes to debates surrounding American punishment, mass incarceration, and racial disparity's roles in both, research has mainly explained disparities as resulting either from macro-historical forces or micro-interactional racial bias and discrimination in individual decision-making. Macro-level arguments propose that punitive policies heaped the harshest penalties on the most vulnerable and racially dispossessed populations, and that tendency continues. The individual bias perspective argues that carceral disparities follow from discrimination and racial bias that emerge at the discretionary stages of criminal justice encounters, such as stops, arrests, charges, convictions, and sentencing decisions.

Only a few key studies have addressed the spatial context of extreme racial segregation in their analyses.[8] Following her study of block groups—and in a direct corrective to the scholar Michelle Alexander's characterization of mass incarceration as the *new* Jim Crow, a system of racial oppression and racial caste in which policies were assembled to fight the War on Drugs and sent Black people to prison at astronomical rates—Traci Burch has argued

> that racial residential segregation also shapes imprisonment outcomes suggests that scholars should continue to pay attention to the traditional elements of racial hierarchy that continue to structure the life chances of African Americans. The theoretical contribution is a subtle one: to call mass imprisonment the "new" Jim Crow because it isolates (to a large degree) black males from society is to ignore the continuing importance of racial isolation outside of prisons for shaping outcomes for poor black people. In other words, many African American prisoners were isolated even before they were convicted and sentenced because of the "old" Jim Crow.[9]

Foregrounding extreme racial segregation, as Burch argues, as a contributing factor in the extreme racial segregation of mass incarceration constitutes a subtle but important reframing.[10] This perspective on the racist origins of the criminal justice system provides a critical link between macro-level structural conditions and racially biased state-citizen interactions influencing later disparities in punishment.

In this chapter, I argue that race is a master status, organizing racial segregation and a broad array of punitive racial projects aimed at marginalized communities.[11] The spatial pattern of incarceration can be viewed, in this perspective, as the summation of multiple, spatially contingent criminal justice encounters, fundamentally driven by patterns of residential and activity-space segregation.

The social and spatial context associated with high levels of incarceration must be empirically grounded and clearly articulated as the result of racialized place disadvantage. If mass incarceration *is* the new Jim Crow, the link between these two racial projects is the hypersegregation of populations by race, ethnicity, and socioeconomic disadvantage, which remains the hallmark of American social organization to this day.

While the term *mass imprisonment* has become commonplace, its original meaning deserves revisiting. David Garland defined mass imprisonment as a mode of governance characterized by two distinct empirical realities: (1) historically unprecedented high rates of imprisonment and (2) the demographic concentration of incarceration.[12] These two conditions mean that whole groups, rather than individual criminals, experience the effects of punishment by removal.

The most prominent and convincing case for the centrality of race in understanding mass imprisonment is articulated by Michelle Alexander in *The New Jim Crow: Mass Incarceration in the Age of Colorblindness*. By targeting Black men and decimating communities of color through the War on Drugs, the US criminal justice system functions as a contemporary system of racial control, even as it formally adheres to the principle of colorblindness.[13]

Some scholars, however, have criticized what they see as an overemphasis on racial disparity in the research program on mass incarceration.[14] Keying in on race, they argue, can mean limiting our grasp of the implications of overall rates of incarceration, the conditions of imprisonment, and the rates of imprisonment in majority-White states, where the War on Drugs has produced an increase in Whites' incarceration rates.[15] Provocatively, Marie Gottschalk states at the outset of *Caught: The Prison State and the Lockdown of American Politics* that "the United States would still have an incarceration crisis even if African Americans were sent to prison and jail at 'only' the rate at which Whites in the United States are currently locked up."[16] Taking on Alexander's framing, Gottschalk warns that reformers' and researchers' conflating of racial disparity and very high rates of incarceration obscures key social and political features of the prison system that are in desperate need of scrutiny and policy prescriptives.

Similar arguments have been raised more recently by John Clegg and Adaner Usmani in an article published in the journal *Catalyst*, "The Economic Origins of Mass Incarceration." Clegg and Usmani similarly argue that the overemphasis on race as the driving force behind mass incarceration, what they call "the standard account," has obscured the true class origins of the rise in imprisonment.[17] They summarize their argument thus: "In reaction to soaring crime rates, the American public, white and black alike, demanded redress from the state. Politicians, white and black, pivoted to respond. But the weakness of the American working-class prohibited meaningful social reform. Moreover, due to the persistent incapacity of the American state to redistribute from rich taxpayers to impoverished cities, no sustained, significant effort to fight crime at its roots was feasible. As a consequence, state and local governments were left to fight violence on the cheap, with only the inexpensive and punitive tools at their disposal."[18] The sheer scale of the prison system is a result of paltry social policy investments, particularly, they argue, at the federal level. Then what accounts for the stubborn levels of racial disparity, which have remained high despite recent declines in disparity? Clegg and Usmani point to research showing that after accounting for bias at each stage of arrest, conviction, and sentencing, nearly three-quarters of the Black-White disparity "is explained by the fact that black Americans are more likely to commit criminal offenses."[19] They do attribute this "fact" to the social environments of Black Americans, and argue that one can simultaneously take seriously crime as an antecedent to mass incarceration while not blaming or stereotyping Black individuals for a criminal propensity.

The arguments made by Clegg and Usmani share similarities to prior debates and points raised by Gottschalk and James Foreman Jr. in his critique of *The New Jim Crow,* published in the *New York University Law Review.* Clegg and Usmani rely on national statistics related to educational attainment and imprisonment rates to make their point about the relative salience of class (as opposed to race) in the run-up to mass incarceration. However, this perspective treats *place* as merely a backdrop for mass incarceration, not a key driver of disparities that they attribute to class differences. For them, the disparity is measured at the point at which people have been imprisoned, not the gulf in neighborhood resources that drives both criminalized behaviors and the punitive response from the state. Moreover, the salience of race in understanding mass incarceration is not simply about who goes to prison, but also who else is harmed in mass incarceration's wake. While the disparity in Black-White incarceration has remained relatively constant, critiques of the racial disparity perspective miss the important interaction between scale *and* disparity, which has affected communities of color for generations. It takes a certain pervasive racism for the state to incarcerate 33 percent of Black men since the mid-twentieth century in jails or prison.

This *pervasiveness* of incarceration among subsets of the population is historically unique to the era of mass incarceration, even if the disparity itself is not historically new.[20] The combination of scale and disparity has created *communities of pervasive incarceration,* which I define as places with extreme rates of imprisonment, embedded within the spatial fabric of high rates of imprisonment. Racial disparities *are* a defining feature of the American system of punishment, persistent across historical periods, but they never before reached the scale we have seen in recent years. The fact of pervasive incarceration must be a central empirical problem for social scientists of punishment and criminal justice, which fundamentally requires an understanding of incarceration in the United States as an instrument of racial disadvantage. Moreover, studies that aim to divide "warranted" and "unwarranted" components of racial disparity, meaning the differential involvement in crime and bias, respectively, almost never take into account the social environment prior to criminal justice contact. It's as if *bias* is only introduced at the moment of arrest and is not present in the structure of American communities, making them more vulnerable to criminalization in the first place. Studies that examine single stages of criminal justice contact often ignore social context, and thus the Du Boisian imperative to never assume that White and Black people have equal conditions of social life.

But what explains the racial disparities, and why are they so stubbornly persistent over time? I turn to two main arguments used to explain the striking demographic concentration of incarceration. First are theories of the emergence of policies that transformed the social realities of impoverished communities of color, and second are theories of racial discrimination and bias.

Broad structural arguments point to state and federal policy, the transformation of welfare, and other political shifts in American public and political pushes to heap punitive policies on the marginalized Black poor.[21] Population-level analyses powerfully demonstrate the intense demographic concentration of imprisonment. For example, 60 percent of Black men without a high school diploma will go to prison in their lifetimes.[22] Staggering figures describe a prison system fundamentally linked to and resulting from social inequality; a combination of social welfare neglect and retrenchment have opened space for policies that actively punish Black poverty, including behaviors and activities associated with it (recall the criminalization of Black culture), and produce a racial caste system in which African Americans remain dispossessed.[23] State policy and historical modes of racial oppression, in which a population is punished at the same time that it is estranged from prosocial institutions, are a potent mix that, in this view, creates racial disparity.[24]

Another prominent view of racial disparity in punishment follows from research on discrimination, specifically how individual-level bias can produce harmful outcomes for Black men in and beyond the criminal justice system. Individual decision-making, such as the decisions to arrest, convict, and punish, is inarguably a prime contributing factor in disparity patterns. A large research literature has examined how bias generates racial disparity at different points of the criminal justice process. Research on police encounters finds, for instance, that Black and Latino men in the United States are at the highest risk for arrest, use of force, and death.[25] Minority defendants are regularly found to endure especially harsh treatment in the courts, and they are incarcerated at rates disproportionate to their involvement in criminalized behavior.[26] The late sociologist Devah Pager's landmark studies demonstrated how race and the stigma of criminal records significantly impact life chances and labor market outcomes.[27] If individual bias, inserted throughout the process of escalating criminal justice contact, causes racial disparities in all these outcomes, it makes sense to aim policy reforms and interventions at individual state actors; thus reformers call for implicit bias training of prosecutors and police officers, the installation of cameras on patrol units and officer uniforms, and diversity and equity training for frontline bureaucrats.[28]

Neither of these theoretical perspectives adequately considers how *place* shapes the practice of policing and criminal justice processing, let alone how it shapes racial disparity in imprisonment rates. Drawing from Du Bois's insights, I argue that racialized neighborhood patterns produce communities of pervasive incarceration, in which incarceration has become a facet of spatially differentiated patterns of instability, violence, and poor health. We can no longer underemphasize extreme residential segregation as an element in sociological theories of race, disparity, and incarceration.[29] The racial-spatial divide that has characterized residential patterns in the United States for over a century, coupled with spatially organized criminal justice (including policing and court processing) in the era of mass incarceration, means that vulnerable neighborhoods with distinct ethnoracial compositions are intentionally exposed to the greatest surveillance by and harshest treatment from criminal justice authorities.

Racial disparities in incarceration must be conceptualized as both contextual (at the local, community level) and cumulative (across the life course and across criminal justice contact). Segregation—and the fundamental differences in social environments—is the missing stage in explaining the persistence of racial disparity in incarceration.

This theoretical gap has significant empirical implications. The literature's focus on racial disparities resulting from either state policy or individual bias has so far relied on national and state-level data, or data on bias from a single point in the criminal justice process. This approach obscures how incarceration is experienced within neighborhoods, especially when large-scale analysis means eliding the very small number of places that contribute the lion's share of this country's incarcerated population.[30] Incorporating a spatial analysis of neighborhoods contextualizes criminal justice policies and shows how they are enacted across and within communities. It also allows researchers to consider the prior neighborhood environments of those behind bars, revealing the severity of racial inequality *prior* to arrest, conviction, sentencing, and confinement to prison.

Another problem is that some studies of racial bias in decisions made by line officers, prosecutors, and sentencing judges have found little evidence of racial animus, leading to the erroneous conclusion that racial bias is *not* a fundamental feature of the US criminal justice system.[31] Incorporating spatial analysis of prior neighborhood environments provides greater insight into how racial disparities accumulate across different stages of the criminal justice process, beginning with the choice to surveil particular neighborhoods. Policy reform that has focused on individual-level interventions to reduce bias among actors in the system is all but certain to have little impact on the overall racial disparities; it is even less likely to be effective if most of the racial bias in the system actually comes from the pattern of residential life preceding criminal justice contact.

. . .

Black neighborhoods have received significant scholarly attention as sites of intense social control and the concentration of socioeconomic disadvantage. Black Americans' experience of concentrated neighborhood disadvantage is altogether different from that of any other racial group in the United States. Here I introduce the idea of incarceration as a facet of concentrated disadvantage, exploring it at different scales of place (neighborhoods, cities, and counties) and across geographies (large cities, suburbs, small cities, and rural towns).

Importantly, neighborhoods are spatial contexts to which people are connected and derive meaning. Yet many discussions of disadvantage at the neighborhood level have led to policy reforms that aim to move people away from those places, in large part due to evidence that doing so improves people's health, well-being, and economic outcomes.[32] In some neighborhoods, the conditions of social control are so extreme that other community structures—such as informal social control, social trust, and residential stability—may be impaired.[33] But we should also consider the possibility that moving people out of these neighborhoods undermines the bonds that people have with those places and people within them. For some, leaving may never be an option. By focusing on neighborhood social contexts, we should begin to envision place-conscious interventions that reduce and, ideally, put an end to harsh relationships between the state and community.[34]

In what follows, I used geocoded prison admissions data to uncover the neighborhoods experiencing the highest imprisonment rates, how local prison admission rates cluster with other neighborhood-level conditions such as reported crime and poverty, how different racial groups experience the concentration of imprisonment, and what types of localities experience the greatest racial disparities and disproportionalities. As in chapter 3 of this book, I draw on county-level data for the entire United States as well as a comprehensive nine-year dataset of all Massachusetts prison admissions. Sociologists have described a social mapping of neighborhood poverty and violence that is categorically different by race.[35] To what extent is this true for the experience of imprisonment?

DIVERGENT SOCIAL WORLDS:
POVERTY, VIOLENCE, AND IMPRISONMENT

The idea that White and Black people live in *divergent social worlds* can be traced through the works of Du Bois, William Julius Wilson, Robert J. Sampson, Ruth Peterson and Lauren Krivo, and Patrick Sharkey.[36] In their work on the racial differences in exposure to violence, Peterson and Krivo have carried forward a methodological discussion regarding the relevant and appropriate comparison groups in studies of local community experiences of social disadvantages across racial groups—and they report that it is actually impossible to find a large enough sample of White and Black neighborhoods with similar levels of reported violent crime to draw reliable conclusions about exposure to violence. While this methodological challenge remains unconquered, it stands on its own as a substantive finding about the conditions of place and inequality in exposure to violence in America. There is no comparison group when it comes to studies of neighborhood-level violence.

Wilson had presaged this finding in writing that there were not enough poor White neighborhoods to compare with poor Black neighborhoods, nor were there enough middle-class or well-off Black neighborhoods to compare them with the outsized sample of well-resourced White neighborhoods. In other words, the fundamental ways that race shapes and organizes American society make it challenging for us to compare community conditions of poverty. Wilson wrote, "Simple comparisons between poor whites and poor Blacks would be confounded with the fact that poor whites reside in areas which are ecologically and economically very different from poor Blacks. Any observed relationships involving race would reflect, to some unknown degree, the relatively superior ecological niche many poor whites occupy with respect to jobs, marriage opportunities, and exposure to conventional role models."[37] In comparing Black and White neighborhoods, community-level deprivations such as concentrated poverty, violence, or imprisonment rates do not vary in terms of degree or level, but in category or kind.[38]

My own empirical challenge in this vein is finding comparable neighborhoods for a study of racial and ethnic differences in neighborhood levels of imprisonment. Before I can even try, I must address a first-order empirical question: *To what extent does imprisonment follow the extreme and incomparable rates of poverty and violence across White and Black neighborhoods?*

Figure 5.1 replicates a figure from Wilson's *The Truly Disadvantaged*, replacing poverty rates with prison admission rates.[39] Wilson was interested in the contextual effects of living in high poverty areas for a person living below the poverty line. I draw a parallel to prison admissions in order to ask: What are the contextual effects of living in a neighborhood with a very high rate of incarceration for people who are sent to prison?

The graph shows that, prior to being admitted to prison, Black people overwhelmingly live in places with the highest rates of imprisonment; this is less likely for White people sent to prison. Specifically, 22 percent of White people, but just 7 percent of Black and 5 percent of Latino people, who went to prison in Massachusetts between 2009 and 2017 lived in areas with below-median prison admission rates. On the other end of the spectrum, 40 percent of White, 76 percent of Black, and 80 percent of Latino people who went to prison in this period had lived in neighborhoods in the top quartile (75th percentile or above) of the state's prison admission rates.

Building on the frameworks presented by Wilson and Peterson and Krivo, I compare disparities using three main metrics of differences in White and non-White social environments: rates of poverty, violence, and, from my study of Massachusetts neighborhoods, prison admissions.[40] I calculated a simple ratio of the means for each group on each measure, then divided the mean for Black or Latino neighborhoods in Massachusetts by the mean for

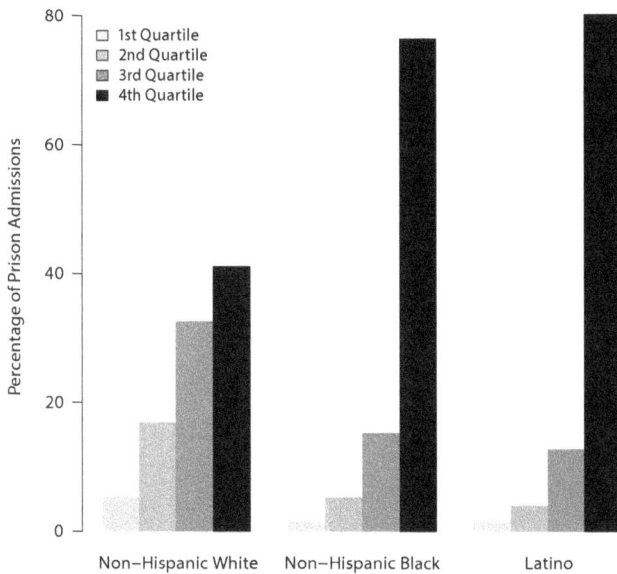

FIGURE 5.1. Concentration of prison admissions in nonincarceration and incarceration neighborhoods in Massachusetts, 2009–2017. *Source:* Author's compilation of data from Massachusetts Department of Correction prison records.

White neighborhoods (for each neighborhood, this means census tracts in which greater than 50 percent of the population is Black, Latino, or White).

Figure 5.2 (on which a value of 1 indicates no disparity) displays the results of my comparison, which indicate large racial disparities. On average, Black and Latino neighborhoods have a reported violent crime rate some 54 to 64 percent higher than the average White neighborhood. There are even greater disparities in child poverty: on average, Black neighborhoods have 2.7 times higher poverty and Latino neighborhoods have over 3 times higher child poverty than White neighborhoods. The greatest disparities are apparent in prison admissions, where we see that the nine-year imprisonment rate in Massachusetts's Black and Latino neighborhoods is 4.5 times higher than in the average White neighborhood.

· · ·

To understand how and to what extent imprisonment forms part of the social environment of marginalization, I conceptualize mass incarceration as an

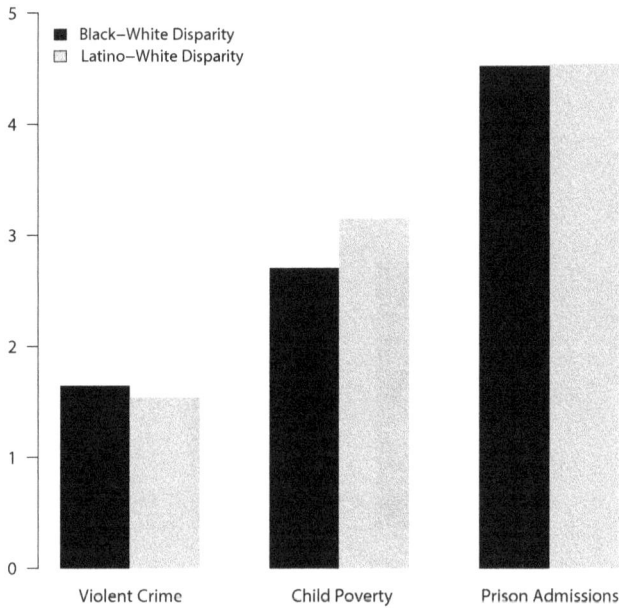

FIGURE 5.2. Comparing the Black-White and Latino-White ratios in reported violent crime, poverty, and prison admissions in Massachusetts census tracts, 2009–2017. A ratio of 1 suggests no racial disparity exists. *Source:* Author's tabulation of data from US Census, Massachusetts Department of Correction prison records, and crime reports.

ecological social problem that is mutually constitutive of many conditions of place. Conceptualizing incarceration as a community or even environmental condition has several implications for community members that may not be directly impacted by incarceration. Like poverty or violence, high neighborhood rates of imprisonment indicate an imbalance of social control, particularly an overreliance on the most extreme methods of crime control by place. Studying the relationship between race, socioeconomic disadvantage, and prison admissions at the place or neighborhood level demonstrates the social control perspective's analysis of "governing social marginality," but grounds it in local context.[41]

There are two ways I operationalize mass incarceration as an ecological social problem. First, I consider what *neighborhood conditions* Black, Latino, and White incarcerated people experience prior to incarceration. In other words, what preexisting neighborhood inequalities begin a cascading and cumulative disadvantage leading to imprisonment? Second, I assess what *levels of imprisonment* are found in majority-Black, -Latino, and -White neighborhoods? Or put another way, for whom has incarceration become a common, neighborhood event? These questions guide my analysis as I consider the spatial distribution of race, place, and punishment.

The term *disproportionality* implies that a group is represented in some system or social condition *out of proportion* to their prevalence in the general population. In technical terms, we can calculate this as a simple ratio between the percentage of persons in a particular racial group at a particular event (e.g., prison admission) compared to the percentage of the same racial or ethnic group in the overall population. This ratio could indicate underrepresentation, proportional representation, or overrepresentation. An examination of disproportionality in punishment in neighborhoods (as opposed to counties or entire states) brings attention to differences of local context and may reveal disparities in prison admissions obscured by state and national measures. Further, by comparing disproportionalities in incarceration at the tract level, this chapter adds to the urban inequality research that has previously examined the prevalence of violence and poverty in those marginalized communities.

How we operationalize neighborhood imprisonment can be relevant to the types of policy reforms we design. For example, consider two neighborhoods. From one neighborhood, say in a large city, several hundred people go to prison, but because of its large overall population, the rate of incarceration is comparatively lower. From a second, smaller neighborhood, fewer total people go to prison, but it has a very high *rate* of incarceration because of its population denominator. Which neighborhood condition matters most for ending mass incarceration? Rates, disparities, disproportionalities, and population totals each connect to different value commitments and policy reforms, including what various actors consider "appropriate" proportions in regard to incarceration. I focus here on measures that connect to questions of inequality in community life on the basis of (1) disproportionate imprisonment and (2) high rates of prison admissions, comparing White, Latino, and Black people and their respective majority neighborhoods.

Large racial disparities in the United States are starkly visible in patterns of health and mortality, exposure to violence and trauma, the accumulation of wealth, and incarceration. A significant body of research points to place-based disadvantage as explaining these disparities, much less for incarceration. Taking the example of wealth disparity, the persistently hefty wealth gap advantage of Whites over Black and Latino groups has been attributed to factors including policies surrounding social benefits and the real estate and lending markets, intergenerational socioeconomic disadvantage, and ongoing racial segregation in neighborhoods.[42] Research shows that places with less concentrated poverty, less income inequality, better-resourced schools, a greater share of two-parent families, and lower reported crime rates tend to produce better outcomes for children, and areas that generate better outcomes for kids tend to have higher home prices on average.[43] A recent study by the Federal Reserve Bank of Boston reported that Greater Boston's White households have a median wealth of $247,500, yet Black households have a median wealth close to zero.[44] Beyond the economy, wealth gaps produce intergenerational gaps in all aspects of life, from exposure to violence and environmental toxins to health and longevity. In what follows, I draw together two areas of research—place disadvantage and incarceration—into a single analysis of their implications for racial inequality. The first set of analyses considers disproportionality in cities and census tracts. The second models spatial patterns in prison admissions by race and ethnicity. And a final set of maps presents a spatial clustering analysis of *pervasive incarceration*, highlighting incarceration rate differences in Black, White, and Latino neighborhoods.

RACE, PLACE, AND DISPROPORTIONALITY IN PRISON ADMISSIONS

To study the relationship between race and ethnicity, neighborhood context, and imprisonment, I created a ratio comparing a given area's population to the prison admission population from 2009 to 2017 for two geographic units in Massachusetts (cities and census tracts). For data on US counties, I created the same ratio using prison admission data from 2008 to 2016 (see the appendix for details on these data and analyses). This is a very simple measure, developed by dividing the percentage of each race/ethnicity in the total population by the percentage of that same race or ethnicity in the prison admission population. A ratio of 1:1 may suggest a system that imprisons people *independently* of race. Any positive or negative change to that ratio would illuminate disparities indicating that rates of imprisonment may be *dependent* on race, with a measure of the likelihood of a person of the indicated race or ethnicity being present in the prison population as compared to their geographic area. For example, if the calculated ratio equals 2, the presence of people of that race in the prison admission population will be twice the size of that same racial or ethnic group residing in that geographic area.

Comparing Racial and Ethnic Disproportionality across Space: State, City, Neighborhood

At the state level, the total prison admissions in the data are as follows: of the 21,269 prison admissions between 2009 and 2017, 27 percent were non-Hispanic Black people (who account for 6 percent of the state's total population) and 29 percent were Latinos (a group that accounts for 10 percent of the state's population). Whites were underrepresented in prison admissions, at a 44 percent share of prison admissions but 75 percent of the state's population in the same period.

Table 5.1 displays ten cities with the highest number of prison admissions since 2009. With the exception of Fall River, New Bedford, and Worcester, these cities are majority-minority places, with large Black populations (e.g., Brockton), Latino populations (e.g., Springfield), or both. The only proportionate example of admissions appears in Lynn and Lawrence, but only for Latinos. Whether or not Whites are in the majority in these cities and towns, they are always underrepresented in the prison admission population, and whether or not Black or Latino groups together form the majority of the population, these groups are always overrepresented in the prison population.

With the exception of Fall River, these disproportionalities are actually lower than the state average in the cities contributing the state's highest prison admissions. In other words, there are enormous differences in disproportionality for Whites and non-Whites, but overall disproportionality fades when we limit analysis to the largest population centers where levels of imprisonment are highest.

Disaggregating from cities and into neighborhoods, without restricting by spatial or population markers, allows for an understanding of the ways imprisonment and disproportionality are locally experienced. Figure 5.3 plots Black and Latino disproportionality against White disproportionality at the neighborhood level. Each dot represents a census tract. Because a number of neighborhoods in Massachusetts record no Black population, only tracts with greater than 0 Black (or White) population and greater than 0 Black (or White) prison admissions are shown. Therefore, the analysis excludes those neighborhoods with zero population or zero prison admissions for any racial group from 2009 to 2017.

TABLE 5.1 Racial Disproportionality in Prison Admissions
in Massachusetts Cities, 2009–2017

	Ratio of Admissions to Population			Total Prison Admissions
	White	Black	Latino	
Population over 250,000				
Boston	0.42	2.51	1.29	3,476
Population 100–250,000				
Lowell	0.86	2.03	2.36	521
Springfield	0.31	1.86	1.29	1,891
Worcester	0.48	2.50	2.13	1,112
Population under 100,000				
Brockton	0.69	1.42	1.75	756
Fall River	0.79	5.41	1.95	745
Holyoke	0.23	1.30	1.79	421
Lawrence	0.79	2.00	1.08	812
Lynn	0.93	2.13	1.04	727
New Bedford	0.64	3.81	1.81	750

SOURCE: Author's compilation of data from Massachusetts Department of Correction prison records.

Figure 5.3 displays stark differences for Black versus White dispropor-tionality (top plot). For Whites, the 90th percentile of disproportionality in prison admissions and population is approximately 1.2, or just slightly over a proportionate level of incarceration. For the Black population, the ratio is astronomical, even at the median (14.4), where the disproportionality is twelve times Whites' 90th percentile (1.2). At the 90th percentile, Black dis-proportionality is 34.4; we are 34.4 times more likely to find a Black person entering prison than living in that census tract. This is nearly thirty times the 90th percentile for Whites. Another way to interpret this chart is that if Black disproportionality were the same as for White populations, all of the dots would be clustered together in the lower left corner.

Figure 5.3 (bottom plot) presents the same data for Latino versus White disproportionality. Latino prison admissions to population disproportion-ality is plotted against White admission to population disproportionality. In neighborhoods with a non-zero Latino population and non-zero prison admissions, the median ratio between the two populations is 7.2 for Latinos, over eight times the median for Whites (.87). For Latinos, the 90th percentile is 17.4, which means we are seventeen times more likely to see a Latino person entering state prison than living in a given neighborhood over the nine-year span of this data.

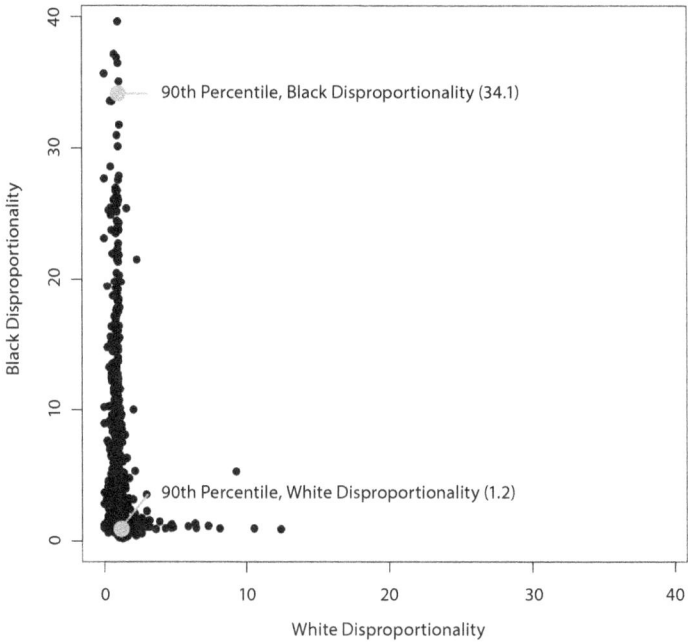

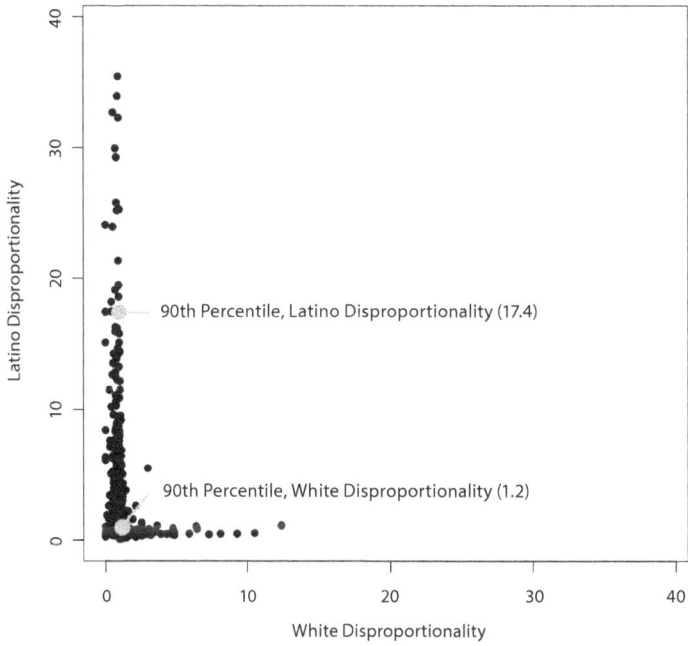

FIGURE 5.3. Black-White and Latino-White disproportionality in prison admissions in Massachusetts census tracts, 2009–2017. *Source:* Author's compilation of data from Massachusetts Department of Correction prison records.

How does this measure of racial and ethnic disproportionality in prison admissions vary in a sample of US counties? Figures 5.4 and 5.5 plot the distributions of racial disproportionality for White, Black, and Latino people admitted to prison from 2008 to 2016. Figure 5.4 breaks this pattern down into the four major regional categories of US Black disproportionality. The figure suggests a strong pattern of outliers, particularly in the Midwest,

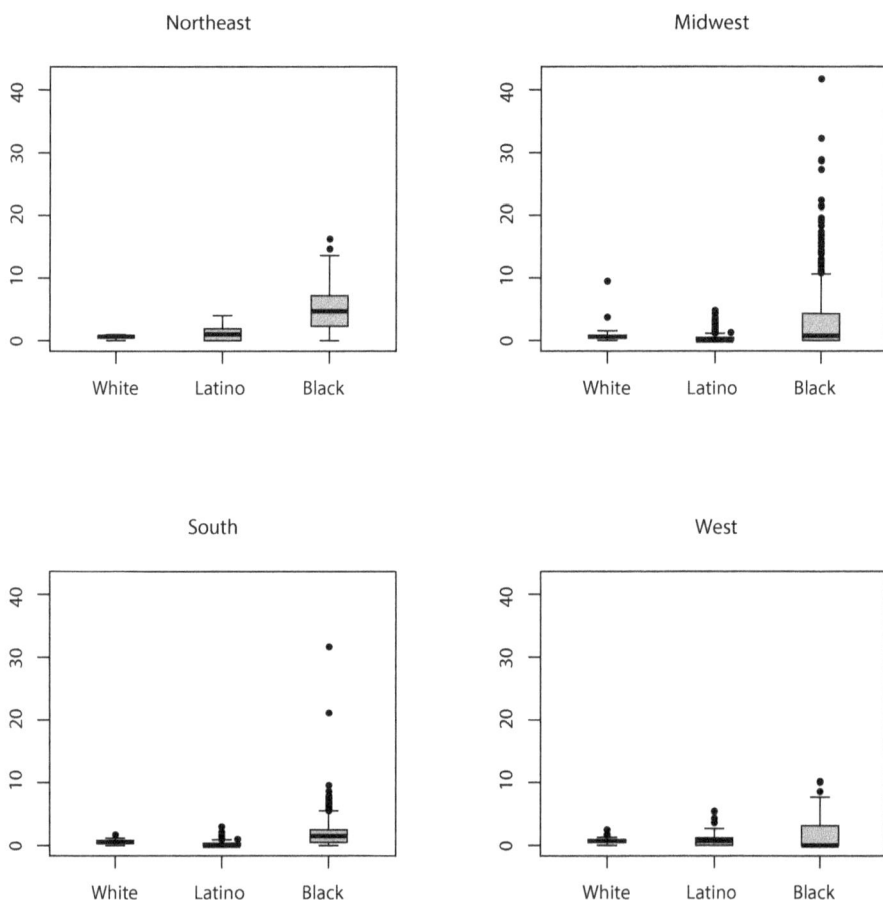

FIGURE 5.4. White, Latino, and Black disproportionality in prison admissions by region in US counties, 2008–2016. *Source:* Author's compilation of data from Vera Institute of Justice (n.d.).

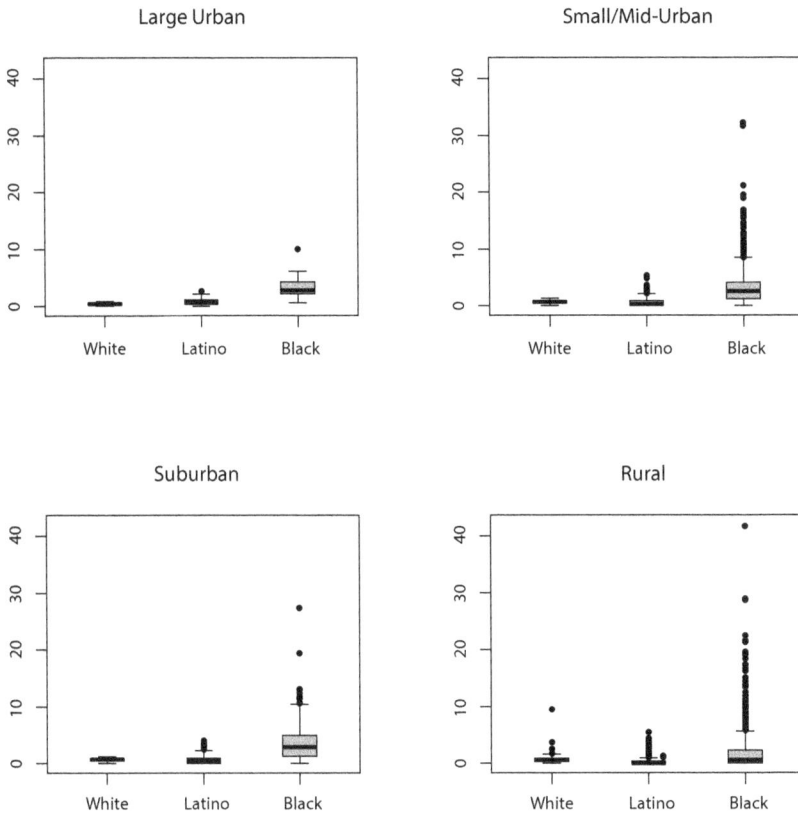

FIGURE 5.5. White, Latino, and Black disproportionality in prison admissions by urbanicity in US counties, 2008–2016. *Source:* Author's compilation of data from Vera Institute of Justice (n.d.).

whereas White disproportionality remains very low compared to Black and Latino populations. Disproportionality is most similar across groups in the West, but in all four regions, the average level of disproportionality for Whites is .6; for Black populations it varies from 1.6 in the West to 4.9 in the Northeast, and for Latinos it ranges from .2 in the South to 1.1 in the Northeast.

Figure 5.5 shows variations by urbanicity. Note that the proliferation of disproportionality outliers for Black populations is highest in small/mid-sized urban counties, suburban counties, and rural counties, where they are likely to represent a smaller portion of the overall population. The *average* level of disproportionality is highest for Black populations in suburban counties (3.2, meaning they are three times more represented in prison than in the community) and lowest in rural counties (1.6), though there are several outliers (indicated by dots in figures 5.4 and 5.5) in communities with very small Black populations but very high incarceration rates. For example, in Westmoreland County Pennsylvania, which has a border with Pittsburgh and Allegheny County, has a Black population of approximately 6,121, but sent 1,727 Black people to prison between 2008 and 2016 (eleven times their presence in the county's population). For Latinos, disproportionality is highest on average in the Northeast and urban counties. In Erie County, New York, with Buffalo as the county seat, Latinos are imprisoned at nearly three times the rate of their presence in the population. For Whites, the greatest underrepresentation is in large urban cities (.45), compared to small or mid-sized urban counties, where they are slightly less underrepresented (.63).

These graphs and figures reveal a startling national trend in racial disproportionality: for all regions and urbanicity types, on average and excepting outliers, White populations *are never overrepresented in prison populations*, and Black populations *are never underrepresented in prison admissions*. Indeed, there are only 3 counties (out of 3,139) where White imprisonment is overrepresented in relation to White population by a factor of 2 or more. There are 1,208 counties where imprisonment among Black Americans is two times or more their population share, and 80 counties where Latinos are imprisoned two times or more their population share. This analysis of US counties demonstrates the centrality of race in understanding the US prison population; this divided social world simply cannot be explained by economic differences among racial and ethnic groups alone.

. . .

Prominent arguments about the uniqueness of concentrated Black poverty are well-established, but scholars have only in passing or with limited data made a similar argument about neighborhood imprisonment rates.[45] By examining Black-, Latino-, and White-majority neighborhoods, we can visualize the distribution of imprisonment in each.

In Massachusetts, there are 36 census tracts with a Black population exceeding 50 percent; all but a trio in Brockton are located in Boston. These neighborhoods saw a minimum of 20 prison admissions from 2009 to 2017, and 1 majority-Black tract hit the high-water mark of 121. The mean and median are both approximately 13 prison admissions per 1,000 residents (see

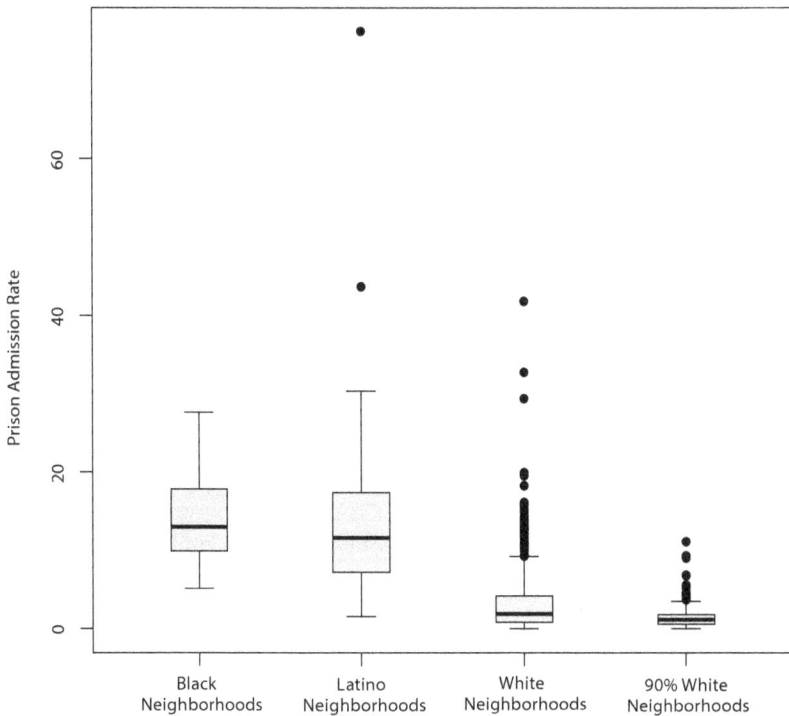

FIGURE 5.6. Prison admissions in Black, Latino, and White neighborhoods in Massachusetts, 2009–2017. *Source:* Author's compilation of data from Massachusetts Department of Correction prison records.

figure 5.6). Not a single majority-Black neighborhood had 0 prison admissions in the nine-year study period.

There are 53 majority-Latino neighborhoods in the state of Massachusetts, 7 of them in Boston. Still, unlike Black neighborhoods, the state's Latino neighborhoods concentrate in the smaller cities of Lawrence, Holyoke, Chelsea, Springfield, and Worcester. The total prison admissions in Latino neighborhoods range from 3 to 149 from 2009 to 2017. Like Black neighborhoods, not a single majority-Latino neighborhood had 0 prison admissions over these years. The mean is slightly higher (13.9) than the median (11.6; figure 5.6), due to the influence of outliers at the higher end of the distribution of prison admission rates (indicated by dots in figure 5.6).

Whites are in the vast majority in Massachusetts, and choosing a cutoff greater than 50 percent yields 1,232 tracts. Thus, figure 5.6 plots two boxplots for Whites: one that considers majority-White neighborhoods up to

90 percent, and a second for neighborhoods that are more than 90 percent White. The differences in rates for majority-White neighborhoods compared to minority neighborhoods are extraordinary. First off, the median for both cutoffs of White neighborhoods are well below the minimum for Black and Latino neighborhoods. The median prison admission rate in neighborhoods that are over 50 percent White but under 90 percent White is one-third the *minimum* rate found in Black neighborhoods. Recall that none of the Black or Latino neighborhoods saw 0 prison admissions in the nine-year period—here we see that 71 White neighborhoods went without sending a single resident to be incarcerated in the same years. There are several outliers in the White neighborhoods, but they track the second half of the distribution of Black and Latino neighborhoods, and excluding two outliers, prison admission rates in White neighborhoods never exceed a single Black or Latino neighborhood's rate.

Sample sizes are small for the total number of Black and Latino neighborhoods in Massachusetts, and as scholars of poverty and violence have found, this makes empirical comparisons challenging. But these results indicate a stark difference in the social environments of White and minority groups on the dimension of prison admissions.

PERVASIVE INCARCERATION

Up to this point, a series of analyses has shown that Black and Latino neighborhoods experience a different *kind* of punishment than White neighborhoods. These tracts are characterized by very high prison admission rates and significant disproportionalities when we account for corresponding population. Statistics can abstract social environments, while maps are powerful tools allowing us to visually engage with and interpret concepts like concentration, density, diffusion, and distance. I use them here to contextualize a social pattern of demographic concentration in prison admissions in places.[46] In this way, we can better imagine the scope of state power—particularly the power to remove people from community and into prison—in specific places and reveal the emergent pattern of incarceration by place.

I operationalize pervasive incarceration as a geographic concentration of incarceration (more formally, as a set of contiguous tracts that form a cluster of high rates of incarceration). This helps identify statistically significant clusters of prison admissions and allows me to categorize neighborhoods

TABLE 5.2 Percentage Distribution of Spatial Associations in White, Black,
and Latino Neighborhoods in Massachusetts, 2009–2017

Spatial Association	Black Neighborhoods	Latino Neighborhoods	50–90% White	Over 90% White	All Neighborhoods
High-high	94.4	45.3	6.1	0.5	10.8
Low-low	0.0	0.0	27.2	31.5	24.6
Low-high	0.0	0.0	0.9	0.0	0.7
High-low	0.0	0.0	0.3	0.2	0.3
Not significant	5.6	54.7	65.5	67.8	63.6
N neighborhoods	36	53	685	555	1,472

SOURCE: Author's compilation of data from Massachusetts Department of Correction prison records.

embedded in significant clusters as sites of pervasive incarceration. The contiguity of prison admission rates in neighborhood clusters, and thus the diffusion of imprisonment rates to neighboring areas, is key to theoretical arguments about the ecological structure of formal social control. Research on criminalized behavior and policing has found that such patterns spill over, influencing criminal justice contact independent of internal neighborhood context.

Table 5.2 displays the distribution of four types of spatial patterns of high or low prison admissions: spatial clusters (either high-high or low-low) and spatial outliers (high-low and low-high). The cluster is classified as such when the value at a location (in our case, the prison admission rate) is more similar to its neighbors (as summarized as the weighted average of the neighboring admission rates) than would be the case under spatial randomness.[47] Using the same breakdown of neighborhoods presented in figure 5.6, I present in table 5.2 the percentage distribution of spatial associations in White, Black, and Latino neighborhoods, as well as for all neighborhoods.

The result demonstrates the uniqueness of incarceration by racial neighborhood composition. Just 6 percent of majority-White neighborhoods have high-high spatial clustering, while all but 2 of the majority-Black census tracts reveal the same (high-high). In other words, *there is near perfect unity between Black neighborhoods and prison admission hot spots.* On the other hand, 361 majority-White census tracts—about 30 percent of all White neighborhoods—have significantly below-average prison admission rates and are surrounded by neighborhoods of low rates (low-low). Zero majority-Black or Latino neighborhoods can say the same. Empirically this is the very definition of *pervasive incarceration*: spatial clustering of prison admissions

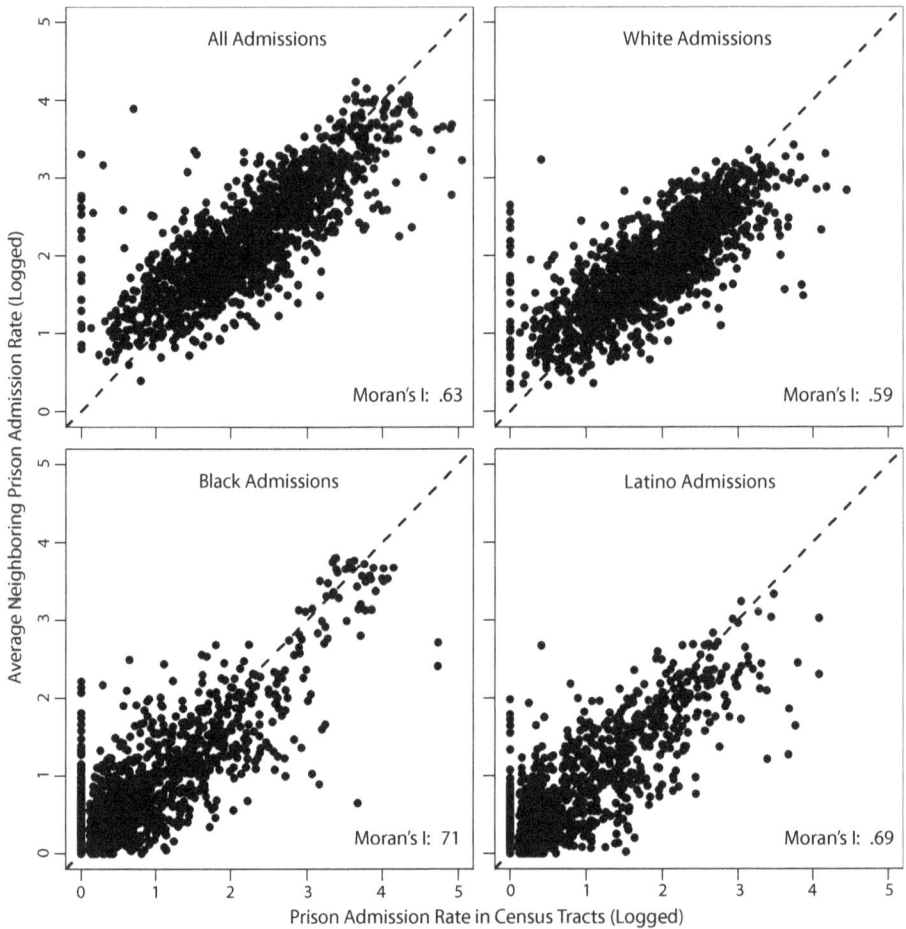

FIGURE 5.7. Plotting log prison admission rate by race/ethnicity against the average log admission rate of neighbors. *Source:* Author's compilation of data from Massachusetts Department of Correction prison records.

is a fundamental reality for all of Massachusetts's Black neighborhoods and slightly less than half of Latino neighborhoods, compared to about 1 in every 18 White neighborhoods.

We can quantify the level of spatial correlation in this area using a global indicator of spatial association (meaning a test for the existence of spatial clustering across the full dataset). Figure 5.7 plots the bivariate relationship between the admission rate in a census tract and the average admission rate in neighboring census tracts. The Moran's I statistic (a measure of the overall clustering of prison admissions) is reported in the bottom right corner of each graph (where a value of 1 means perfect spatial clustering, 0 is perfect randomness, and −1 is perfect dispersion).

Clockwise from top left, I present this bivariate plot for all prison admissions, then White, Latino, and Black admissions. There is significant spatial clustering for all three racial groups, but the clustering is significantly higher for Black admissions than for White admissions. These spatial analyses are an important step to measuring and capturing the concentration of incarceration in Black and Latino neighborhoods. But it is only a first step. Mapping these data is also key to understanding racial disparities in punishment.

Mapping Pervasive Incarceration

I now proceed to the more intuitive display of mapped data. In this section, each illustration presents the same geographic area three times, plotting Black, Latino, and White prison admissions separately overlaid on identical geographies. Map 5.1 shows the Greater Boston area, with a density of prison admissions plotted over the map by race and ethnicity. A striking feature of this comparison is the degree of spatial concentration for non-Hispanic Black incarcerated people against the relatively diffuse pattern for Whites. Latino prison admissions show more clustering than for Whites, but far less than for Black people.

In map 5.2 I turn to Springfield, Massachusetts, and its surrounding suburbs. Pulling Black, White, and Latino imprisonments apart to see how each group clusters in space shows that among Latino residents there is a strong

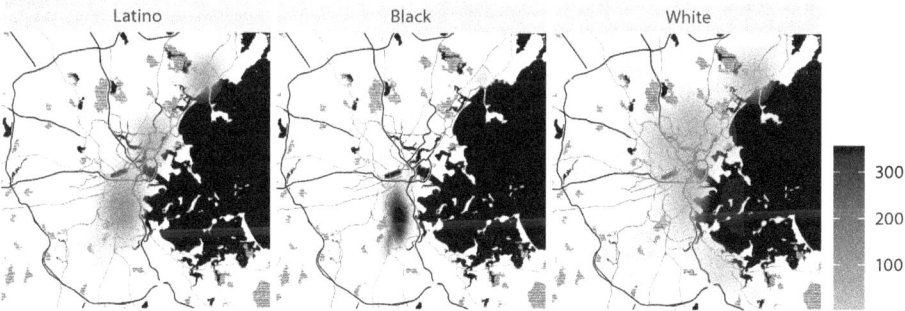

MAP 5.1. Prison admissions by race and ethnicity in Greater Boston, Massachusetts, 2009–2017 (counts in hundreds). *Source:* Author's compilation of data from Massachusetts Department of Correction prison records. Map tiles by Stamen Design, under CC BY 3.0. Data by OpenStreetMap, under ODbL.

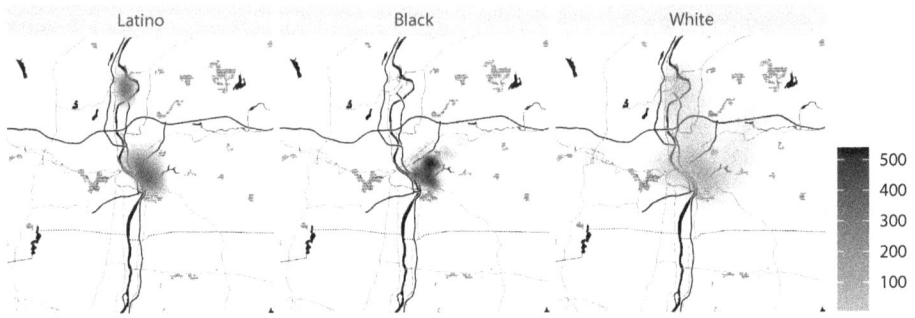

MAP 5.2. Prison admissions by race and ethnicity in Springfield, Massachusetts, 2009–2017 (counts in hundreds). *Source:* Author's compilation of data from Massachusetts Department of Correction prison records. Map tiles by Stamen Design, under CC BY 3.0. Data by OpenStreetMap, under ODbL.

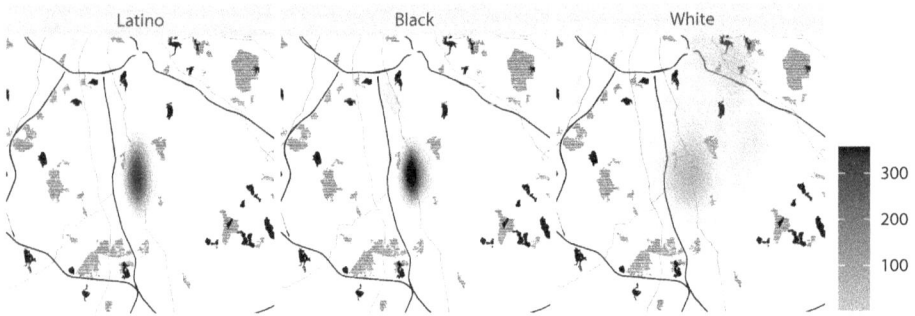

MAP 5.3. Prison admissions by race and ethnicity in Brockton, Massachusetts, 2009–2017 (counts in hundreds). *Source:* Author's compilation of data from Massachusetts Department of Correction prison records. Map tiles by Stamen Design, under CC BY 3.0. Data by OpenStreetMap, under ODbL.

spatial cluster of incarceration in the heart of Springfield and also in Holyoke, just to the north. For Black men and women, the pattern is, as in Boston, one of extreme spatial concentration even though Springfield's population is less than 200,000. And for non-Hispanic Whites, the pattern overall is spatially diffuse. There are no strong concentrations, which indicates that White people sent to prison almost never live in places marked by high levels of formal social control in Massachusetts, even exploring all places throughout a state with a large White majority.

Map 5.3 shows Brockton, Massachusetts, a small city near Greater Boston. Brockton is home to many Black and Latino residents, often displaced from

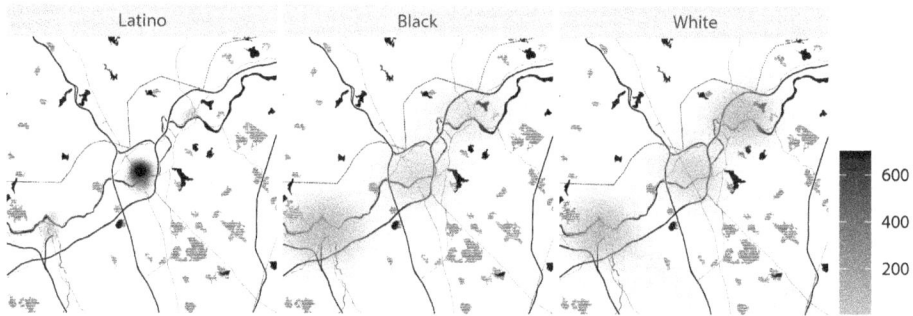

MAP 5.4. Prison admissions by race and ethnicity in Lowell, Lawrence, and Haverhill, Massachusetts, 2009–2017 (counts in hundreds). *Source:* Author's compilation of data from Massachusetts Department of Correction prison records. Map tiles by Stamen Design, under CC BY 3.0. Data by OpenStreetMap, under ODbL.

Boston due to the rising cost of housing there. Again, though, the spatial dynamics of incarceration patterns are similar to Boston's and Springfield's: people of color tend to live in very concentrated areas prior to incarceration, while Whites in any city type live their lives at much lower levels of concentration prior to incarceration.

Map 5.4 displays the northern part of Massachusetts, bordering New Hampshire. The cities of Lowell, Lawrence, and Haverhill are revealed by three clusters. This is the first map showing a slight deviation from the previous pattern: Latino men and women living in these areas prior to their imprisonment almost entirely cluster in the city of Lawrence, demonstrated by the deep cluster in the middle of the map on the far left. Black and White people are much less concentrated prior to imprisonment. Lawrence, like Brockton and several other cities named in chapter 3, is a declining postindustrial city that has experienced significant socioeconomic decline and the hypersegregation of Latinos since the 1970s.[48]

A final map offers an alternative story. Fall River (see map 5.5) has been hit hard by the opioid crisis, and joblessness and poverty are quite high among young White men. While it is true that there are virtually no places in Massachusetts where Whites are in the majority and the levels or rates of incarceration match those in Black or Latino neighborhoods, Fall River is a case in which White people admitted to state prison live in a context of pervasive incarceration. This is a type of concentrated criminal justice processing that tends to see very little coverage in the academic literature on incarceration and neighborhoods. Concentrated White incarceration is the exception, not

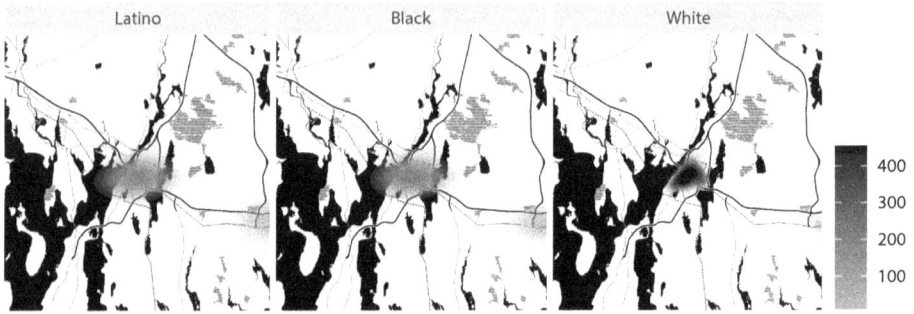

MAP 5.5. Prison admissions by race and ethnicity in Fall River, Massachusetts, 2009–2017 (counts in hundreds). *Source:* Author's compilation of data from Massachusetts Department of Correction prison records. Map tiles by Stamen Design, under CC BY 3.0. Data by OpenStreetMap, under ODbL.

the rule. Note that, in all of these maps, there are plenty of majority White census tracts and communities, but except in Fall River, we do not observe clustered or concentrated White prison admissions.

BRINGING SEGREGATION INTO ANALYSES OF MASS INCARCERATION

Incarceration and the durable inequality of neighborhood residence in the United States are both fundamentally patterned by race. In this chapter, I argue that *mass incarceration should be conceptualized as one of the legacies of racial residential segregation.* In this analysis of Massachusetts communities, we quickly learn that 70 White neighborhoods sent not a single person to state prison in nine years, but 0 majority-Black or -Latino neighborhoods can say the same. The national data tell a staggering racial story: except for 3 counties out of nearly 3,200, Whites are never overrepresented in prison admissions; for Black and Latino people, overrepresentation is a common experience. Indeed, more than 1,200 counties report an overrepresentation of Black people in the prison system of two times or more. We gain crucial insight into race, place, and justice by analyzing imprisonment not simply as an instrument for crime control, but as having an ecological structure that follows the racial-spatial divide characteristic of the structure of American communities. These conditions contribute to profound racial and ethnic divides in the concentration of well-being.

Previous chapters have brought attention to new trends in mass incarceration, while this chapter describes an important but long-standing pattern: the primacy of race as an organizing mechanism producing durable inequality in place *and* punishment. Spatial methods, neighborhood-level data, and a broad sample of places are central to uncovering this significant empirical reality. Previous ecological models of imprisonment have been limited to case studies of large urban cities. But variability and difference is best understood using the complete distribution of neighborhoods under the jurisdiction of a given prison system. With spatial methods and spatial data, we can describe the degree of inequality experienced in communities and consider how that inequality spreads to new places.

Like poverty and violence, incarceration is a uniquely racialized experience in US communities and neighborhoods. The gulf in prison experience for different racial groups could be explained by *ecological* differences in neighborhood quality, or by *social control* patterns of law enforcement targeting and hypervigilance. But these two theoretical perspectives fundamentally draw from an analysis of the spatial pattern and social context of place disadvantage. A spatial analysis of imprisonment provides a novel and unforgettable picture of the scale of racial and ethnic disparity. In Massachusetts, the difference in prison admission rates between White and Black or Latino neighborhoods, on average, is a factor of *four*, far higher than the differences in neighborhood conditions of poverty and violence.

The findings in this chapter point to the primacy of race in understanding mass incarceration and its persistence. For those that disagree with calling mass incarceration the new Jim Crow, one does not need to describe the system of punishment as a "caste" system per se in order to see that racial injustice has occurred. The hypersegregation of White advantage and Black and Latino disadvantage is inscribed in the prison system, a punitive and violent institution that grew exponentially following the spatially entrenched disadvantages and policing and court processing that drew human lives from the blocks and streets and communities of America and placed them in cages. The idea that class and race can be conceptualized as distinct drivers of mass incarceration denies the fundamentally racialized class system that cannot be simply operationalized by the educational attainment of those who end up in prison.[49] The dimension of socioeconomic status missing from prior analyses of racism and criminal justice is the *neighborhood*. We can say that for White people, even at this later stage of mass incarceration with ever-growing rural and nonmetropolitan prison populations, imprisonment is a rare event, never fully amounting to a community-level event. The advantages of Whiteness in neighborhood context must be fully considered in the analysis of mass incarceration.[50] For Black people across this country, mass incarceration, mass criminalization, and the lasting effects of contact with the criminal justice system are community conditions, affecting even those who are never placed in prison.

Putting these findings in the context of policy interventions aiming to end the cycle of incarceration, I view these results as suggesting that reintegration after incarceration could never truly be the goal of public policy overtures about individual redemption and the road to successful reentry. The catch-22 of incarceration and segregation makes a mockery of individual attempts at reinvention. If we want to build communities that reintegrate people after the trauma, isolation, and dehumanization of American incarceration, we have to seriously consider the unethical conditions in which people live both inside and outside those institutions. Through policy and practice, these conditions ensure that whole groups of people will suffer, no matter how hard they try to rebuild their lives after incarceration.

The reentry policy community wrings its hands over "what works" with regard to getting released people stable housing, employment, and health care and lowering recidivism. These are indeed important questions; providing individuals with a modicum of economic subsistence should be the first and foremost goal of any society, and the United States fails on this front in devastating ways, particularly for those coming out of prison. But the research presented here is much bleaker. The greatest intentions toward supporting individual self-improvement lead reformers astray from the question that should haunt all those concerned with American public policy: Why do some children, some men, some women, some people, remain the sole bearers of collective racial anguish?

W. E. B. Du Bois could not have foreseen the unprecedented social transformation of Black urban neighborhoods resulting from mass incarceration, but the legacy of his insight deeply informs an analysis of contemporary imprisonment rates in White, Latino, and Black neighborhoods. At the turn of the twentieth century, the scale of imprisonment was a small fraction of today's system, and I imagine if he were writing today, Du Bois might have included rates of incarceration as an important aspect of the social environment of disadvantaged Black communities.

In this way, I wish to promote a cautious interpretation of racial differences in neighborhood-level incarceration rates. Rather than assume that these places are intractably harmful for all people, we could reframe our concerns to the fact that policies of removal and abandonment—however well intentioned or evidence based—are unlikely to change the stratified neighborhood conditions of the United States. Rather than move people away or infuse neighborhoods with new programs that target "at-risk" youth or enhance job training, *what if we simply punished these places less?*

SIX

Punishing Places

The vision of justice embraced here is one in which the state recognizes collective and individual humanity and thus, through various means, aims to promote social inclusion and social solidarity.

—BELL (2019)

NEIGHBORHOOD INCARCERATION RATES are significantly tied to the social conditions of poverty, racial segregation, and violence. These conditions combine to produce an environment in which informal social control and collective efficacy are diminished, denying community's capacity to self-govern through informal channels. High levels of loss to the prison system and unmitigated vulnerability to the criminal justice system undermine full membership in American society. Under these conditions, individuals cannot access opportunity, fully engage in political participation, and enjoy the capacity to define and achieve their goals and dreams.

The US system of punishment is characterized by racial inequality and enormous social and economic costs to American communities, though most criminal justice reforms are aimed at individuals. Christy Visher described the traditional approach to ending the cycle of incarceration as fundamentally individual oriented, "where much attention is paid to an individual's personal characteristics—age, criminal record, substance use history—in assessing risk of future criminal behavior."[1] Reentry programs and reintegration initiatives typically deploy the model of individualized case management and stop short of incorporating family or community into the reintegration process.[2]

Conversely, a family- and community-centered approach would provide care, services, and financial support to family and community members surrounding incarcerated and formerly incarcerated people. Communities experiencing pervasive incarceration have been overlooked, and very few interventions, pilots, or initiatives have been implemented to reduce the harms of intense social control in those places. A spatial view of punishment fundamentally shifts our analysis to the punishing of whole places and communities. Policy interventions that transform communities and prevent the suffering caused by these community-level policies and practices must follow.

We face these realities with unprecedented knowledge. A National Academy of Sciences study on the causes and consequences of mass incarceration reports that the problems associated with mass incarceration cannot be solved with data analysis and empirical investigation alone: "In the domain of justice, empirical evidence by itself cannot point the way to policy, yet an explicit and transparent expression of normative principles has been notably missing as U.S. incarceration rates dramatically rose over the past four decades. Normative principles have deep roots in jurisprudence and theories of governance and are needed to supplement empirical evidence to guide future policy and research."[3] Normative questions regarding mass incarceration—and by that I mean moral and ethical inquiries—do not ask about causal or descriptive understandings (scientific, "positive" questions) of the people and places that were affected by the 500 percent increase in carceral population over just four decades. While I have tried to describe and explain *punishing places* throughout this book, there is an explicit normative goal within this project: to question and challenge the existence of places that harm all community through the conditions of mass incarceration. Thus, a normative question for this chapter is: Given what is already known about the origins and consequences of mass incarceration, particularly for Black people, how should we collectively respond to this historic injustice? Moreover, how can normative principles guide scientific inquiry, and can science be brought to bear on normative questions?

In practice, the social sciences divide scientific and normative inquiry into separate intellectual projects. The gold standard of randomized controlled trials (RCTs) must achieve what is called the "well-defined intervention" assumption: that exposures must be factors that can be conceptualized as treatments in an RCT.[4] Sharon Schwartz and colleagues call into question the conservativeness of this approach: "But if the valid estimation of causal effects requires well-defined interventions, then we seem to be stuck. There can be no evidence for structural changes, for social movements, for radically altering existing systems. Are there other approaches to causal inference that do not require well-defined interventions?"[5] Thus, the model of research that purports to be value free may itself have a built-in preference for incremental changes, sidestepping the harder, more complex, but potentially transformative solutions that respond to structural and systemic inequalities.

Moreover, unlike political science, law, and economics, the discipline of sociology has done little to formally carve out a subfield of normative theory. As a result, sociologists are often accused of being biased in their empirical endeavors due to some hidden or poorly articulated value commitment secreted in their ostensibly empirical projects.

The value-free ideal in science has long been evaluated and discussed. It stems from debates about the role of science in public policy, and it has created a value-science binary.[6] There is science that is *experimental*, in which we try to estimate causal effects by randomization or controlling for confounders. And there is science that is *observational*, in which we cannot ethically or practically manipulate most of the "variables." The best we can do is observe, record, and relate them to one another as reasonably and as meaningfully as possible.[7] Observational research is often necessarily more complicated and more debatable, but also arguably more important to us. While a scientific approach means being as observant and as logical as "humanly" possible in designing and conducting (and interpreting and sharing the results of) our inquiries, there is, at the very least, some *value* in being scientifically rigorous.[8] As scientists, our decisions over what to study, what variables to use in our analyses, and what interpretations to offer from our results all draw from value commitments.[9] The tension between value and science need not be an impediment to sociology. We display our values in the questions we ask, the methods we deploy, and the interpretations we offer. In fact, embracing our normative commitments presents new opportunities to harness knowledge and conduct moral investigations often relegated to the all too brief conclusions of our essays, journal articles, and books.

Racial equity, social welfare, full democratic membership, and justice are values that inform many empirical pursuits in sociology and are used to underline the sociological significance of our work. Landmark sociological research has sought to expand political power to the dispossessed, uncover institutional practices laden with consequences of racial disadvantage, and examine the ways that poverty is fundamentally charged with power relations.[10]

Punishing Places, at its core, is about community: community building, community-level political efficacy, and community bonds that can reduce—or in their absence, amplify—suffering and harm. A normative sociology could meaningfully outline key debates in these areas and propose research to better inform paths forward.

What if we placed the value statement at the center of the empirical project? What if there were ways to measure the values deficits in policy practices and outcomes? What if these became part of the central ways we measure social disadvantage in communities, similar to traditional measures of poverty and reported crime? For instance, could sociology define a set of value commitments and test the various ways social conditions violate (or adhere to) those commitments? Clearly defining and explicitly stating our values allows us to measure value deficits.

Part of the difficulty in synthesizing normative principles and empirical positivism (in its broadest definition, scientific study in which hypotheses are tested with systematically collected data) is actually a data problem. Deficits in our data produce significantly skewed portraits of inequality. This data poverty can be overcome by merging data and by gaining access to granular, community-level data on a host of subjects. Innovative data linkages—say, merging multiple criminal justice encounters with public health, voting, or employment data—could yield important insights into the vulnerability and resilience of communities in the face of social injustice. Special agreements for data sharing with prison systems or police departments are powerful, but extremely limited in what they can do. Most data are protected by special data use agreements (including data used in the pages of this book), and the timescales of approval processes mean that by the time data are available they are extremely stale. Moreover, the limited ways that crucial data are made available to the public prevents people in vulnerable communities from accessing this information for themselves. The lack of available data is not purely an accident, averting the possibility of state responsibility and accountability when data could lead to uncovering disparities, discrimination, or the prevalence of state violence.

In sociology our measures tend to describe particular conditions and social problems, in absolute numbers, rates, or ratios in a given geographic space. The often hidden implication of measures such as poverty, racial segregation, and violence are that each diminishes well-being and that living in such conditions reduces life chances for individuals and groups, net of individual and family characteristics. In this chapter, I propose a new set of measures for thinking about these conditions in a framework of vulnerability, in which measures of pervasive incarceration indicate *community loss* and *excess punishment* and social conditions describe a landscape of *vulnerability to intense formal social control*. These metrics allow for direct estimates of the community-level value deficits and effects of criminal justice policy.

Understanding and describing vulnerability to state violence and state social control opens up avenues for crafting policies that could ameliorate the consequences of mass incarceration by intervening in the vulnerability and harm resulting from state actions. In addition to mitigating these harms, I am advocating for policies that end harmful state policies and state violence. Rather than leaving the reader to do the work of imagining the grave social costs of mass incarceration for communities, I directly measure those costs in the following pages.

Note that there are still no consistent metrics for assessing community loss or vulnerability to excessive state presence. On the one hand, we could consider changing the research/empirical framework to directly address normative questions. On the other, we could change where/how studies of social control and marginalization are focused based on proven factors of vulnerability, rather than outdated or stereotyped notions of urban marginality. Reframing our questions and refining our measures should inform more effective policy interventions that address collective suffering, rather than perpetuating a narrow vision of controlling and punishing criminalized behaviors.

Drawing on the fields of environmental science, social service, and public health—fields that make explicit value commitments to ameliorating and eliminating environmental, social, and health hazards—I theorize incarceration as a social hazard to which racially segregated, high-violence and high-poverty neighborhoods are particularly vulnerable. In the following pages I explore neighborhood and community-based experiences of social control by looking at measures of excess incarceration, community loss, and punishment vulnerability. I also provide short data vignettes, opening paths for other scholars to replicate and expand upon these measures in studies of policing, court processing, and incarceration in communities.

EXCESS INCARCERATION

As shown throughout this book, incarceration is a population dynamic besetting the most vulnerable populations in the United States. Recent studies point to historically high rates of incarceration as an important indicator of the social well-being of communities and the quality of membership in American democratic institutions.[11] Incarceration is a common life event for Black men born in the 1970s, and the demographic consequences of mass incarceration will be felt for decades to come, even as incarcerated populations decline.[12] The life course effects and cumulative effects of incarceration in communities are analogous to demographic measures of mortality, which compare observed deaths with what would have been expected under a set of social conditions for the population. As such, demographic measures of mortality may be analogous to estimating the prevalence of punishment in communities. This conceptualization attends to the empirical question of modeling incarceration rates as a function of the stated normative goal of crime reduction, and it begins to respond to policy reform–related questions about soaring imprisonment.

Currently, criminal justice policy reform has reducing rates of incarceration as its foremost goal.[13] The United States incarcerates more than 2.2 million people in jails and prisons across the country, persistently the world's highest rate of incarceration (despite decarceration in recent years).[14] This stunning global primacy is paralleled only by its uniqueness within US history. Since 1970, after decades of relative stability in the overall rate of incarceration, this country has more than quadrupled its zeal for locking up its own.[15]

Most claims about the demographic concentration of incarceration, *when* they are based on research, are based on studies without sufficient geographic variation or using aggregated data (such as state-level information) to try to understand how context shapes demographic patterns in incarceration. Taking another tack, I examine rates of incarceration at the level of community and contribute to research on social inequality and mass incarceration using individual-level data from Massachusetts state prisons. Specifically, I import the concept of "excess mortality" from health research as a framework for examining a population's risk of incarceration.

In mortality research, the standardized mortality ratio (SMR) is used to calculate the observed number of deaths in relation to an expected number, based on a general mortality risk in the population. This is a way to suss out excess mortality and send researchers looking for its cause (a community with an abnormal SMR may, for instance, be dealing with a disease outbreak). This ratio has recently gained salience for Americans in learning about the true extent of COVID-19's mortality impacts.[16] Similarly, I use census data to calculate an expected rate of incarceration for gender groups, then examine variation in excess incarceration by race and ethnicity, where levels of punishment far exceed levels suggested by the overall historic average. After presenting the concept, I conduct a short analysis of Massachusetts prison admissions.

Two normative perspectives guide the concept and estimation of excess incarceration: an *abolitionist* view of incarceration and what I call a *crime warranted* perspective on incarceration. These two perspectives are most pertinent to the word *excess* in the concept of excess incarceration.[17]

Academics have tended to shudder at the idea of promoting the project of police or prison abolition. The idea rarely makes it into our work and publications. Thankfully, events in the summer of 2020 have prompted a shift; changes in the scholarly and policy dialogue have demonstrated serious renewed interest in abolition.[18] However, like reparations tied to historical injustices, this topic can be a political third rail. Recent nationally representative surveys indicate that Americans are very unsupportive of abolition, particularly White and conservative respondents.[19] If we conceptualize abolition not as the immediate closure and elimination of all police departments, prisons, and jails, but as a more gradual and contextual overhaul effort that systematically diverts resources from carceral institutions to communities, we immediately open the abolition discussion—and see its conspicuous absence in serious policy reform discussions. Allegra M. McLeod offers a more nuanced definition of and vision for abolition:

> But abolition may be understood instead as a gradual project of decarceration, in which radically different legal and institutional regulatory forms supplant criminal law enforcement. These institutional alternatives include meaningful justice reinvestment to strengthen the social arm of the state and improve human welfare; decriminalizing less serious infractions; improved design of spaces and products to reduce opportunities for offending; urban redevelopment and "greening" projects; proliferating restorative forms of redress; and creating both safe harbors for individuals at risk of or fleeing violence and alternative livelihoods for persons otherwise subject to criminal law enforcement. When abolition is conceptualized in these terms—as a transformative goal of gradual decarceration and positive regulatory substitution wherein penal regulation is recognized as morally unsustainable—then inattention to abolition in criminal law scholarship and reformist discourses comes into focus as a more troubling absence.[20]

As Angela Y. Davis writes in *Are Prisons Obsolete?*, "The most difficult and urgent challenge today is that of creatively exploring new terrains of justice, where the prison no longer serves as our major anchor."[21] Under an abolitionist framework, the inhumanity and ineffectiveness of incarceration as a crime control policy, especially in light of its collateral consequences, reveal that virtually all incarceration is excessive. Moreover, an abolitionist perspective views violence and other criminalized behaviors as preventable by meeting social needs, healing from trauma, decriminalizing behaviors, and employing transformative justice approaches to interpersonal harm.[22] In short, excess incarceration involves virtually all people in state custody today.

A crime-warranted perspective of excess incarceration takes a different view of the role of prisons in society. While abolitionists regard incarceration as a taken-for-granted institution in need of aggressive examination and gradual elimination, a crime-warranted perspective embraces the idea that crime, especially serious violence, represents a break in the social contract between person and state and suggests that under conditions of parsimony, imprisonment (particularly rehabilitative forms of incarceration) can be an appropriate response. Parsimony is key here: incarceration that is responsive to crime alone would indicate a justice system used sparingly and entirely for its capacity to punish criminals. The National Research Council's consensus report summarizes: "Punishments for crime, and especially lengths of sentences, should never be more severe than is necessary to achieve the retributive or preventative purposes for which they are imposed."[23] Further, parsimonious use of punishment minimizes unnecessary and extreme penal sanctions, possibly limiting their negative collateral consequences.[24] Under a crime warranted framework, excess incarceration could be conceived of as a failure of parsimony for two reasons. First, incarceration has been extended to noncriminal conduct, such as homelessness, crises caused by mental illness, relapse to substance use, and poverty. A second failure is in the increasingly harsh punishment of criminalized behaviors, leading to excessively long sentences, longer stays in prison, and placement in high-security facilities that enhance the harms associated with incarceration.

In either perspective—abolitionist or crime warranted—empirical evidence suggests that incarceration broadly responds to a set of social problems beyond crime (including mental illness, substance use, poverty, and homelessness) that nonetheless closely follow patterns of residential racial segregation and deep social marginality.[25] Incarceration and criminalized violence in the US context are bound up in a set of correlated conditions that have rendered punishment far outside the scope of crime control. In this way, incarceration spills over into nonjuridical areas and may be particularly intense in places where few other social policy levers exist. In short, where public health scholars argue that unnecessary death—excess mortality—cannot be just policy, so, too, must punishment scholars urge that excessive incarceration—to the tune of a globally and historically unprecedented surge in prison and jail populations—cannot be just policy.[26]

Excess punishment provides a direct measure of how value deficits harm communities. We can identify places that violate norms of parsimony or explore the level of excess under norms of abolition. And by combining imprisonment rates and disparities with the unusual harshness of American prisons, we can begin to theorize excess punishment as a community-level violation of the constitutional prohibition against cruel and unusual punishment.

Conceptualizing Excess Incarceration

Scholars of punishment have referred to the concept of "penal excess." Coined by David Garland in a comparative study of the expansive use of incarceration in the United States and New Zealand versus Scandinavian justice systems, *penal excess* describes a system of punishment that is retributive, sweeping, collaterally consequential, and disproportionately severe.[27] *Penal moderation*, in contrast, advances policies that express a commitment to "restraint, parsimony, and dignity."[28] Penal excess points to fundamental shifts in state responses to problems adjacent to—but still distinct from—crime.

Another body of work addresses the concept of "excessive force," particularly as wielded by police officers. Police are distinguished from citizens by the general right to use coercive force should they believe the situation calls for it.[29] However, this gives police officers an enormous range of discretion, which makes it hard to define excessive use of force. Broadly, excessive force is defined as more physical violence or the deployment of a more lethal weapon than a highly skilled police officer would find necessary in a given situation.[30] In the courts, two main levers have come to define and constrain police officers' ideas about reasonable and excessive force: criminal law and civil liability.[31] State criminal laws distinguishing criminal conduct from acceptable use of force attempt to operationalize the distinction, with admonitions to the effect that force should be used as a last resort and in no greater degree than is necessary or reasonable.[32] As we have seen in numerous high-profile cases in which police officers who have killed have not received indictments or convictions, or even charges, for those killings—this particular standard of excessive force has not proved enough to shift policing policy or practice. This points to the very weak instruments of justice that exist when state accountability is relegated to the existing courts.

Similarly, we might consider what constitutes reasonable use of incarceration. *Reasonable* seems to imply using confinement as a punishment of last resort. Instead, millions of people are confined to jails even though they have not been convicted; they stand accused and must await trial in confinement because they cannot post bail (a fact that, on its face, points to the disproportionate incarceration of disadvantaged people with less-resourced social networks).[33] Lengthy prison sentences rather than alternative means for economic security or community-based treatments are meted out to individuals for the possession and use of criminalized substances, for example. Communities lacking in strong social institutions such as a thriving workforce and available social policy interventions (job training, drug-related harm reduction programs, mental health services) may experience heavy police presence in the name of public order, which has led to abuses of authority, use of excessive force, and excessive incarceration at the community level.[34]

Another literature seeking to define "excess" empirically comes from health research examining patterns in excess mortality.[35] Excess mortality, sometimes referred to as mortality displacement, is a measure of premature death, from either natural or unnatural causes, and has been studied in research areas as diverse as schizophrenia, cancer, substance use, and war—and more recently, the COVID-19 pandemic. The geographic dimension of excess mortality has been studied to examine how local conditions of poverty and access to basic health care vary tremendously at the neighborhood level.[36] In addition, research has connected premature mortality and the experience of incarceration, finding that men who have been incarcerated are more than twice as likely to experience premature mortality as those who have never been incarcerated.[37] Mortality may be excessive relative to historic morality rates (for example, in the case of COVID-19), or it may be excessing relative to other places or populations.

Drawing on these concepts of penal excess, excessive force, and excess mortality, I present the concept of excess incarceration to describe the conditions in which incarceration rates either far exceed the purpose of crime control or far exceed norms regarding proportionate, parsimonious punishment (in terms of sentencing and length of prison stay); in the abolitionist perspective, excess incarceration accounts for all or most imprisonment. Excess incarceration describes conditions in which the observed rate of incarceration far exceeds levels that would indicate responsiveness to criminalized behavior. Under these conditions, vulnerable communities experience incarceration at levels that make it seem commonplace. Yet the profound consequences of criminal records and the experience of incarceration for labor market outcomes, family life, and the ability to participate in democratic institutions all indicate that excess incarceration represents the effects of the massive penal state on full membership in American society.

Operationalizing Excess Incarceration

The crime-warranted perspective has to assume that official measures of crime and violence account for *actual* crime, when it is commonly understood that crime statistics represent a combination of criminalized behaviors and social control efforts. With this limitation in mind, a simple model of crime and incarceration would model rates of incarceration as a function of crime, age, and gender. What a crime-warranted perspective might call "moderate punishment" would be areas in which crime predicts incarceration levels that are observed. On either side are excess punishment (more incarceration than crime would predict) and low punishment (the places that use punishment less than expected given levels of criminalized behavior). Each of these levels of punishment has a implications for how incarceration rates have increased, plateaued, or declined during an era of mass incarceration. Depending on regional and spatial conditions, such a measure provides important information about policy responses to historically high levels of incarceration.

Another way to consider mass incarceration in terms of "excess" is to construct what is called a mortality table, in which instead of death, we consider the rate of incarceration given an overall population rate.[38]

Excess Incarceration: A Data Vignette

In the following analysis I explore two years of data representing two different moments in Massachusetts's mass incarceration history: 1997, during the period of peak imprisonment rates in Massachusetts, and 2017, during the period of consistent decline in prison admissions in the state.[39] For the crime-warranted perspective, I use the total counts of prison admissions by gender from 1973 as the historic comparison to estimate excess incarceration; 1973 is the first year of available data from Massachusetts and represents a time just preceding the era of mass incarceration. Note that because the Massachusetts Department of Correction did not collect ethnicity data in 1973, table 6.1 only displays data for White and Black men and women.

A standardized imprisonment ratio of greater than 1 indicates there is excess imprisonment given prison admissions in the historical comparison.

TABLE 6.1 Excess Imprisonment among Adult Population by Race and Gender in Massachusetts, 1997–2017

Group	Comparison Rate	Total Population	Expected Imprisonment	Observed Imprisonment	Excess Imprisonment	Excess Imprisonment Ratio
Crime Warranted						
1997						
White men	37.8	2,590,239	979.7	649	-330.7	0.6
White women	1.6	2,815,135	45.5	43	-2.5	0.9
Black men	37.8	144,785	54.8	524	469.2	9.6
Black women	1.6	155,345	2.5	33	30.5	13.1
2017						
White men	37.8	2,396,930	906.5	670	-236.5	0.7
White women	1.6	2,555,437	41.3	49	7.7	1.2
Black men	37.8	241,782	91.4	478	386.6	5.2
Black women	1.6	257,992	4.2	13	8.8	3.1
Abolition						
1997						
White men	0	2,590,239	0	649	649	—
White women	0	2,815,135	0	43	43	—
Black men	0	144,785	0	524	524	—
Black women	0	155,345	0	33	33	—
2017						
White men	0	2,396,930	0	670	670	—
White women	0	2,555,437	0	49	49	—
Black men	0	241,782	0	478	478	—
Black women	0	257,992	0	13	13	—

SOURCE: Author's compilation of data from Massachusetts Department of Correction prison records and US Census. The comparison rate for the crime-warranted perspective is the rate of prison admissions by gender in 1973.

Conversely, a ratio of less than 1 indicates that contemporaneous data yield a lower imprisonment rate than the historic population levels would produce.

In the first period, we see excess imprisonment for Black men and women. In 1997, when prison admission rates were among the highest in Massachusetts, excess imprisonment disparities were widest. The Black male expected imprisonment count (based on historic levels) was 55, compared to the observed 524. Under historic norms, Black men were imprisoned in excess by a factor of nine and a factor of thirteen for Black women, while White men were incarcerated less than expected under historic norms (.6, or 331 fewer White men). The gap closes in the later period, owing to an increase in White men's and women's imprisonment rate and a decrease among Black men and women. Still, the overall rate of incarceration among Black men is over seven times the rate for White men in Massachusetts.

A second analysis reports a standardized imprisonment ratio from the abolitionist perspective. To calculate excess incarceration from the abolitionist perspective, I simply include 0 persons for each race and gender group. In a policy context of no imprisonment, excess imprisonment includes all people entering prison for each year. From the abolitionist perspective, these levels of excess punishment are akin to a major and devastating natural disaster, pandemic, or war. Excess punishment is affecting those most harshly punished, but from the abolitionist perspective, levels of punishment like this devastate society broadly.

In this section I have presented a conceptual framework and model for analyzing excess incarceration rates. I argue that excess incarceration is a way to understand rates of punishment that extend beyond the limited view of prisons as an instrument of crime control. Using two contrasting definitions of "excess" incarceration rates, even in Massachusetts, where rates are the lowest in the nation, excess incarceration is extraordinarily high, as are racial inequities, despite recent declines in both. Further, such an analysis makes justifications for incarceration as a crime deterrent irrational. The problem is not people committing crimes; the problem is policies that lock them up.

COMMUNITY LOSS

Incarceration is fundamentally segregative. By definition, incarceration deprives individuals of their liberty in a free society through a process of removal.[40] It extracts people from communities and denies them regular access to their families, friends, partners, children, and neighbors. Gresham Sykes writes on the deprivation of liberty: "What makes this pain of imprisonment bite most deeply is the fact that the confinement of the criminal represents a deliberate, moral rejection of the criminal by the free community."[41] In another classic text, *Asylums*, Erving Goffman defines the total institution (a category that includes highly regulated settings like the military and prison) in contrast to other social institutions: "Total institutions are also incompatible with another crucial element of our society: the family."[42] Under mass incarceration, the profound degree of removal and confinement has risen to a scale that presents the pains of imprisonment and its incompatibility with family life as a larger, societal condition and source of stress at the community level.

In the social sciences, our measures use counts of individuals caught up in the system (e.g., people stopped, arrested, convicted, incarcerated) to indicate the impact of incarceration on a larger community. This book is no exception; I frequently use counts of incarcerated populations or admissions to jail or prison in my calculations and arguments. And though these metrics help portray mass imprisonment and its demographic trends, they neglect to measure incarceration's other side: the communities from which incarcerated people have been extracted and the broad social and political costs that these removals represent.[43] Therefore, scholars have worked to carve out novel ways to measure population losses. For example, the concept of "missing men" describes how whole groups and subsets of population disappear via incarceration and premature death. Whole groups of people are missing from voter rolls and the labor force; in demographic studies of Black men, 1.5 million Black men have been counted as "missing" from communities across the country due to early death and being locked up.[44] The Million Dollar Hoods project (introduced in the preface and chapter 2) refers to the total time in jail for a given zip code as a measure of the *human cost* of mass incarceration.[45] Together, scholars in this vein have presented a framework for thinking about how our data infrastructure has distorted our basic understanding of the nature of social inequality in the United States. The fact that people lost to the criminal justice system are invisible to our nation's measures of educational attainment and labor force participation, among so many others, underscores just how deeply taken for granted it is that many in this country are prevented from sharing in the full membership afforded to others in the same society.[46] This research agenda ultimately presents measurements of the values of well-being and full membership in a democratic society, providing direct empirical evidence of deficits in those value commitments. The first step to full membership is being physically part of that broader community.

An indicator presented by Mimi Abramovitz and Jochen Albrecht, which they term the "Community Loss Index," highlights the understudied role of place as a source of stress and an aggregator of individual experiences of loss.[47] Their index captures *collective loss*, considering six types: the loss of work (unemployment), housing foreclosure, foster care placement, incarceration, long-term hospitalization, and untimely death. The authors argue that their scale is a response to the paucity of research on what happens to communities when large numbers of people living in close proximity suffer multiple and persistent losses. Using New York City as their research site, they find significant geographic variation in community loss and convincingly assert that community loss itself, net of socioeconomic and demographic factors, contributes to stress and hardship.[48] The Million Dollar Hoods project similarly measures the number of years people from a certain zip code in Los Angeles County spent in jail.

The idea that loss can be felt collectively, at the community level, has strong roots in the literature on grief and stress. Death of a loved one, natural disasters, and historic trauma have all been shown to create severe stress among individuals. The concept of ambiguous loss strongly applies to the case of incarceration; not knowing whether a missing person will ever come back creates *ambient stress*, a chronic condition in which torn-apart families become immobilized.[49] Ambiguous losses are compounded by hostile, disapproving, stigmatizing, or indifferent social attitudes pertaining to the loss of a family member through imprisonment.[50] The separation of having a parent incarcerated during one's childhood is highly traumatic and creates great uncertainty in the lives of children. Children experience the loss of a parent as a traumatic event, and they have greater difficulty coping in situations characterized by uncertainty.[51] Public health researchers include parental incarceration among key measures of adverse childhood experiences.[52] Joyce Arditti describes the experience of *disenfranchised grief* in her field notes from a project with family members of the incarcerated: "When someone goes to jail and you lose them from your daily life, almost like a death, you cannot grieve out loud, you have to grieve silently or else risk shame."[53] Disenfranchised grief envelops a loss that is not or cannot be openly acknowledged, publicly mourned, or socially supported, and it provides conceptual weight for understanding the inner lives of families who are disrupted by incarceration.[54] These hidden losses can complicate mourning and impede access to social supports during the separation of confinement. The emotional voids coincide with financial ones, further supporting the idea that mass imprisonment is a form of collectively experienced community loss.

Thus, community loss represents a fracturing of communities: a break in the bonds of society that creates additional hardships for those often most vulnerable to begin with. In this way, community loss violates a value commitment to full membership and social solidarity.

Conceptualizing Community Loss

Mass imprisonment creates a tremendous resource loss, removing individuals from work, family, and community roles.[55] Under historic conditions of mass incarceration, these waves of removal undermine a community's viability. Community loss thus involves both the loss of population, captured by the total number of people subject to incarceration, and potential time and life spent away from their community. The losses tied to environment—in which incarceration is one facet—are experienced by groups, in places, across generations. These losses may adhere to several other forms of toxic environments. Robert Manduca and Robert J. Sampson find that exposure to lead and neighborhood rates of violence and incarceration combine to independently predict poor Black boys' later incarceration as adults, Black boys' lower adult income ranking relative to their parents, and poor Black girls' teenage motherhood.[56] Mass incarceration as a community stressor has been conceptualized as a form of grief- or loss-related stress. In a series of studies, Jaquelyn Jahn finds that contact with the criminal justice system at the community level, including jail incarceration and police stops, affects a wide range of health outcomes, including births and mental health.[57]

Geography and community are important dimensions of grief and loss associated with incarceration. The distant location of prisons from population centers, particularly those most affected by high rates of incarceration, limits options for family and friends trying to communicate and connect with incarcerated people, exacerbating the feeling of social death for both groups. Incarcerated individuals can seem to have disappeared from community life.

Operationalizing Community Loss

Moving beyond population counts, one way to operationalize mass incarceration as community loss is to calculate the cumulative number of years individuals are sentenced to prison. Time spent in a prison and out of the community better captures the collective and cumulative experience of loss in communities. Personal loss of a family member can impact the children of the incarcerated and lead to foster care and removal; partners and loved ones and the well-being of the parents of the incarcerated are all affected by the loss of an individual to incarceration.[58] There are parallels to the public health metric of premature death, measured in the years of potential life lost, which is the difference between age at death and age- and sex-specific mortality. Loss in communities of pervasive incarceration could also impact social cohesion and engender a sense of legal estrangement, placing the police and courts, as well as social services, at a disadvantage because they operate best with strong community support and investment.[59] Finally, community losses yield significant economic and political costs, as large numbers of prime-age men and women cannot contribute to the neighborhood or community's economic viability (let alone their own family's), and political participation and power are suppressed by excluding most incarcerated people from democratic participation and even from population counts used for redistricting purposes (i.e., some incarcerated individuals are counted, for state purposes, as residents of their prison's community, not the one they were removed from).[60]

For this analysis, I use data for cities in Massachusetts. To calculate community loss due to mass incarceration, I add up the total years people were sentenced to prison from 1997 to 2009. This period includes the years in which the state's imprisonment rates were among the highest historically. I sum these years based on the recorded minimum and maximum sentence coinciding with each prison admission, and I include any time spent in jail immediately prior to imprisonment (often called "jail credits"). The resulting number is a very conservative estimate of community loss due to imprisonment, as it includes only those people admitted to prisons in a thirteen-year period and excludes those incarcerated in jails, juvenile facilities, and immigrant detention centers. For specific details on how community loss was measured, see the appendix.

Table 6.2 displays the average number of years lost and years lost per 10,000 residents. The city of Boston experienced 5,398 prison admissions between 1997 and 2009, for a minimum of at least 28,000 years lost (nearly 500 years for every 10,000 residents).

How do we make sense of this metric, bring it down to a legible scale? Well, if an average person works from age eighteen to age sixty-five, we are talking about the loss of 610 lifetimes of employment to prison in the city of

TABLE 6.2 Prison Admissions and Community Loss in Selected Cities in Massachusetts, 1997–2009

	Prison Admissions		Minimum Person-Years Lost		Maximum Person-Years Lost		Total Population
	Total	Rate	Total	Rate	Total	Rate	
Massachusetts	30,446	48.0	127,245	200.4	169,963	267.7	6,349,097
Largest city							
Boston	5,389	91.5	28,673	486.7	36,153	613.7	589,141
Small cities							
Brockton	1,310	138.9	5,785	613.4	7,446	789.5	94,304
Fall River	715	77.8	3,492	379.9	4,470	486.2	91,938
Holyoke	683	171.4	3,782	949.3	4,886	1,226.5	39,838
Lawrence	1,231	170.9	5,196	721.3	7,037	976.8	72,043
Lynn	1,137	127.7	4,398	493.9	5,977	671.2	89,050
Springfield	2,869	188.6	15,393	1,012.2	20,251	1,331.6	152,082
Worcester	2,557	148.1	6,788	393.2	10,533	610.1	172,648

SOURCE: Author's compilation of data from Massachusetts Department of Correction prison records. Population data from the 2000 US Decennial Census.

NOTE: Rates calculated per 10,000 residents in a given city. Prison admission counts and community loss are pooled (1997–2009).

Boston alone. It is the equivalent of voiding 7,000 students' four-year college educational experiences.

If chapters 3 and 4 identified key characteristics of the spatial inequalities in prison admissions, the astute reader will anticipate that these lost person-years are not evenly distributed. They are highly concentrated in the communities most heavily impacted by other forms of deprivation. Small cities, as chapter 3 showed, experienced some of the greatest per capita community losses. Springfield lost a minimum of 15,000 years to the prison system in just 13 years (see table 6.2); in a population of 150,000, this amounts to 1,000 years for every 10,000 residents. Brockton, Holyoke, Lawrence, Lynn, and Springfield all experienced greater community loss per capita than Boston. Inclusive of Boston, the cities in table 6.2 represent 20 percent of the state's population, but 57 percent of the state's community loss. Looking at community loss in years begins to allow us to imagine the true impacts of mass incarceration on community life, family life, and the economic well-being of communities.

The losses go from astounding to astronomical when we calculate using the maximum sentences and include recorded jail time. During this time period, Massachusetts saw arrests, charging, and convictions resulting in over 30,000 prison sentences. In total, the state sentenced people to maximum penalties totaling nearly 170,000 years in prison. Recall that Massachusetts has one of the lowest overall imprisonment rates in the country, yet this timescale is unfathomable by any population or historical standard.

We could deepen and expand the idea of community loss due to imprisonment. Rather than map Million Dollar Blocks, what if we map the number of months or years that individuals will spend away from their neighborhoods and communities? What if we map the total number of people who are no longer participating in the workforce due to incarceration and include them in our measures of unemployment down to the block level? These are just some of the ways that these metrics could further change public opinion and policy directives related to the costs and impacts of incarceration.

Map 6.1 maps community loss onto cities and towns in Massachusetts from 1997 to 2009 as the number of years per 10,000 residents. Comparing this map to others presented throughout this book, we can see that loss is highly spatially concentrated. Specifically, years of loss are concentrated in disadvantaged small cities and contiguous suburbs, but also in places like Plymouth, just at the start of Cape Cod (the large tract shaded black on the eastern side of the state). As community loss is the summation of all criminal justice processing—from arrest to sentencing—numerous communities in

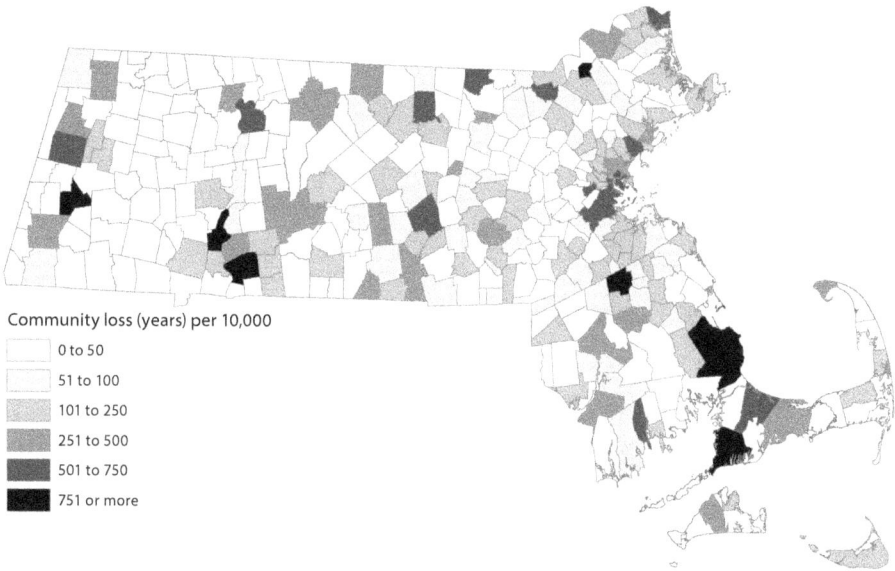

MAP 6.1. Community loss (years) per 10,000 residents in Massachusetts cities and towns, 1997–2009. *Source:* Author's compilation of data from Massachusetts Department of Correction prison records.

this state lost more than 750 years for every 10,000 residents, while others saw very little loss to the prison system.

Figure 6.1 presents results from a regression analysis of the minimum and maximum number of years lost, as well as the prison admission rate, considering the associations between community loss and racial composition, concentrated disadvantage, vacancy/abandonment, and the spatial context of cities in Massachusetts. The results suggest that cities with a greater proportion of the overall population that is Black, are socioeconomically disadvantaged, and have high levels of vacant housing have greater levels of community loss, and these relationships are all statistically significant. Loss is particularly felt in small cities (compared to Greater Boston), and for many of these metrics, the relationship is stronger for levels of community loss than for the overall admission rate (see the appendix for a detailed discussion of the regression results).

So far we have considered community loss at the level of cities and towns. How do rates of community loss vary with conditions of neighborhoods? Next I examine levels of community loss in neighborhoods for different racial compositions of neighborhoods in a later period, 2009–2017 (see the

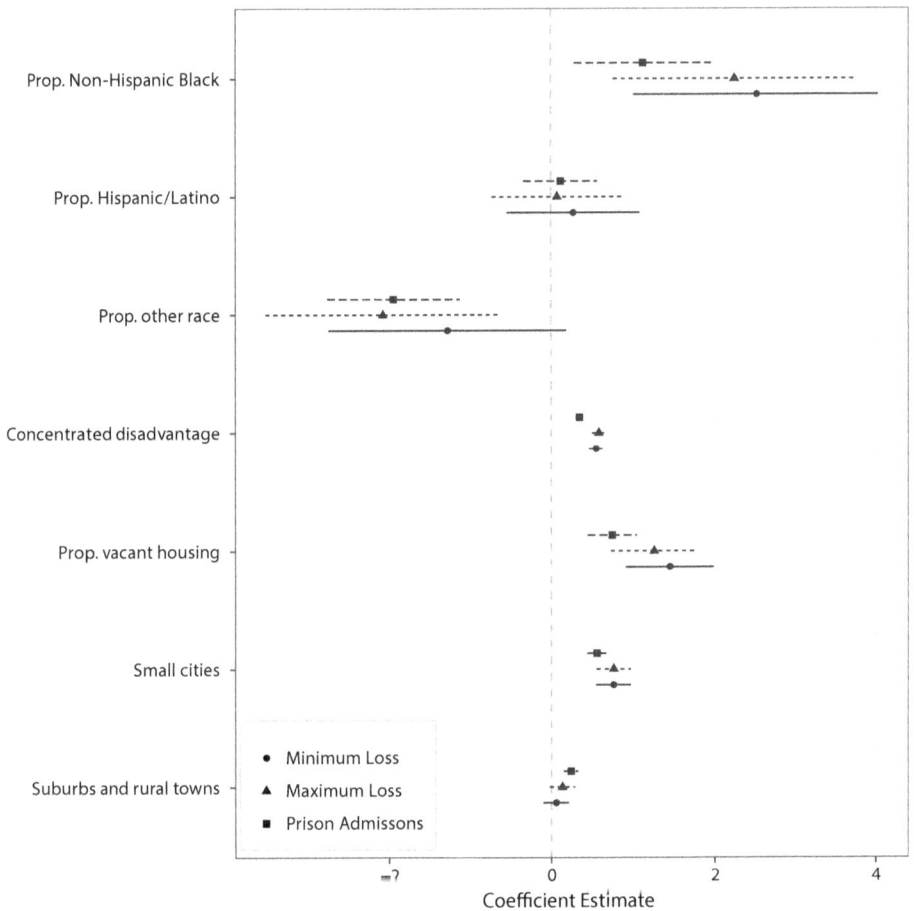

FIGURE 6.1. Estimated associations of community loss and prison admission rates with socioeconomic characteristics of Massachusetts cities and towns, 1997–2009. *Source:* Author's compilation of data from US Census and Massachusetts Department of Correction prison records.

appendix for why neighborhood data on sentencing are not available for years prior to 2009). Figure 6.2 plots a bivariate relationship between the proportion of the census tract population that is Black (top) or Latino (bottom). There is a moderate, positive correlation between the share of the population that is Latino or Black and levels of community loss (.55 and .53 for Latino and Black populations, respectively).

Measuring community loss at the neighborhood level borrows from the work of Eric Cadora and Lauren Kurgan, who produced the Million Dollar

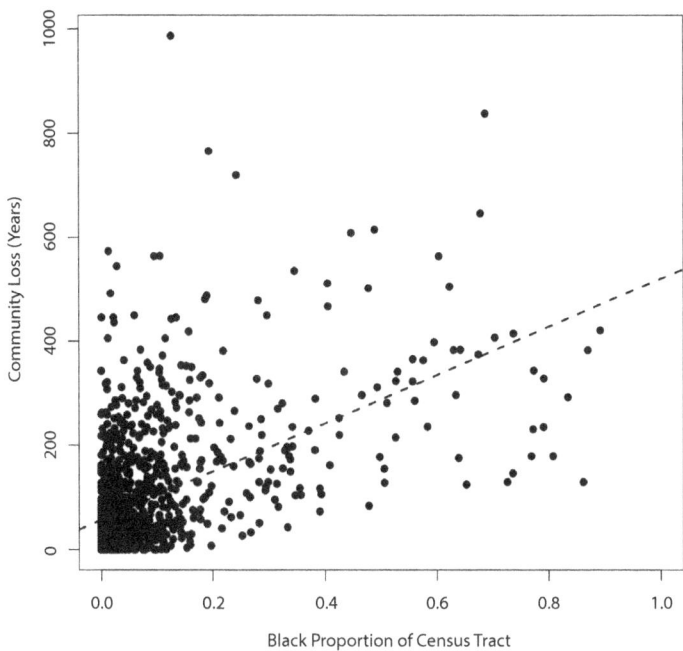

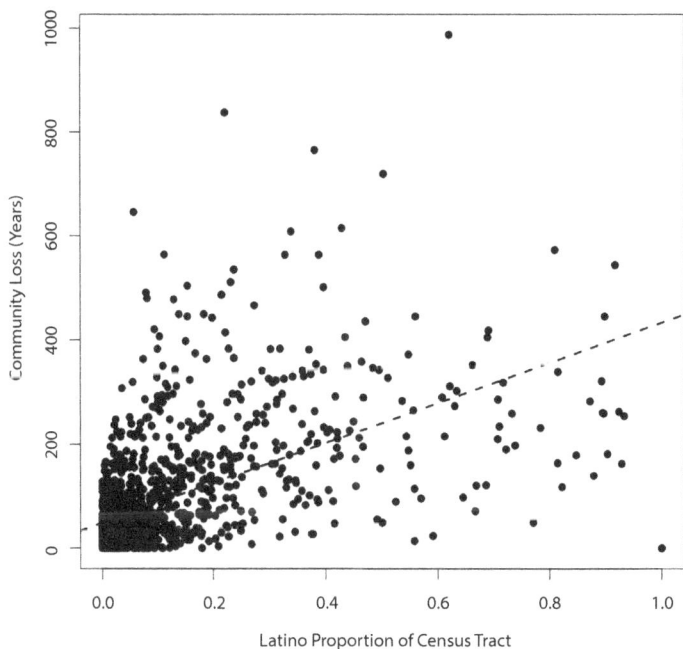

FIGURE 6.2. Community loss in census tracts by the proportion of the tract population that is Black (top) or Latino (bottom), Massachusetts, 2009–2017. *Source:* Author's compilation of data from Massachusetts Department of Correction prison records.

Blocks project and share in the goals of Million Dollar Hoods. Million Dollar Blocks aimed to draw attention to the public expenditures on incarceration at the block level, opening many people's minds to the alarming reality that single neighborhoods were contributing so many people to the prison system that the effort required millions of dollars in state budget expenditures. With this new measure of community loss, I ask for another kind of expansion, one that encourages us to try to fathom the idea that a single neighborhood lost more than 1,000 person-years to incarceration over a period of nine years (2009–2017), when prison admissions had slowed greatly and in the state with the country's lowest imprisonment rate. For many neighborhoods, whole centuries of person-years were lost to imprisonment.

Goffman reflects on the meaning of total institutions (like prisons) in the context of broader society: "Whether a particular total institution acts as a good or bad force in civil society, force it will have, and this will in part depend on the suppression of a whole circle of actual or potential households."[61] Mass incarceration has involved the suppression of whole populations from building families and households, participating in education systems, entering the labor force, and living out their hopes and dreams.

It is not for me to decide if community loss is wholly a net negative for communities, as many of the individuals contributing years to community loss have committed grave acts of harm against their own families, partners, and neighbors.[62] I can only argue that a significant loss of time and population has attended mass incarceration, the direct consequence of deliberate policy actions, and that this loss is felt unevenly through places.

PUNISHMENT VULNERABILITY

In her 2003 presidential address to the Association of American Geographers, Susan Cutter proposed a "science of vulnerability."[63] Building on the multidisciplinary tradition of hazards research, she argues that vulnerability science requires spatial solutions, because "vulnerability manifests itself geographically in the form of hazardous places."[64]

Vulnerability, generally speaking, means the potential or risk for loss. Losses in population vary geographically and over time. *Social vulnerability*, a concept from environmental science, is the degree to which a system, subsystem, or system component is likely to experience harm due to exposure to a hazard, either a perturbation or a stress/stressor. Researchers in environmental science examine how communities are particularly vulnerable (or resilient) to external shocks such as natural disasters, assuming that vulnerability is a social condition and a measure of societal resistance or resilience to hazards.

Typically, though, researchers focus on the vulnerability of individuals or groups rather than the vulnerability of certain places to potential hazards. Thus, in this final discussion I wish to promote a science of *punishment vulnerability*, in which I consider intense formal social control as a hazard akin to industrial waste, toxins, floods, and natural disaster. In other words, I ask what makes people—and the places where they live—vulnerable to violent, harsh, or deadly crime control events, and how could vulnerability and resilience be measured, monitored, and assessed in the field of criminal justice policy?

Owing to the literature on the collateral consequences of mass incarceration, we could consider that mass incarceration is a stressor that reverberates beyond the individual criminals ensnared in the system to mothers, siblings, partners, children, and neighbors.[65] Such a model would direct our attention away from behavioral explanations of rates of punishment and toward understanding the risk of criminal justice contact as the stressor. If we see incarceration as a hazard, we can better see how its own social structure and institutions produce conditions that are unsafe for people.

Viewing punishment as an environmental hazard requires a more articulated discussion of what community harms are associated with imprisonment: the erosion of already-low economic bases, loss of political power, fractured families, and exposure to harsh and violent prison conditions over time (whether as incarcerated people or visitors) are just some of the harms and hazards associated with criminal justice contact for communities. The other side of sensitivity is *resilience*. Just as we should identify communities that are particularly vulnerable to harm, we should identify communities with stories of resistance to this hazard. Their coping strategies could assist in fine-tuning justice responses. Punishment vulnerability fundamentally shifts blame for mass incarceration away from communities and toward a set of structural factors driven by state policies and practices. Such a measure also begins to recognize social needs, including where the provision of economic subsistence has been missing or inadequate. Thus, punishment vulnerability represents a rupture in the value commitment of social welfare in a democratic society.

Susan L. Cutter and colleagues present a social vulnerability indicator with 44 different measures.[66] In table 6.3 I present eighteen concepts that, when

TABLE 6.3 Punishment Vulnerability Concepts and Metrics

Concept	Description	Increases (+) or Decreases (-) Punishment Vulnerability
Poverty	Poverty, and especially deep poverty, limits a community's ability to absorb losses and enhance resilience to punishment (Western 2018; Harris 2016).	Poverty status (+)
Poor health	Poor health, especially mental illness, substance use problems, and chronic pain, may increase exposure to police encounters and the likelihood of incarceration (Teplin 2000; Adams and Ferrandino 2008).	Poor health status (+)
Race/ethnicity	Discrimination, animus, exclusion, threat, and language barriers affect exposure to criminal justice contact and residential location in high-hazard areas (Burch 2014; Goff et al. 2014; Sampson 2012; Pager 2003; Kurwa 2016; Bell 2020).	Non-White (+) Non-Anglo (+)
Employment loss	The loss of employment following punishment exacerbates the number of unemployed workers in a community, contributing to slow recovery in the cycle of incarceration and community return (Western and Sirois 2019; Pettit 2012).	Employment loss (+)
Political power	Voter suppression, removal from participation in elections, and running for office could also greatly affect the ability to enhance resilience to punishment (Manza and Uggen 2006; Behrens, Uggen, and Manza 2003).	Disenfranchisement (+)
Family structure	Families with single-parent households often have limited resources for dependent care and thus may juggle work responsibilities and care for family members who may be exposed to criminal justice contact. It also affects the resilience to and recovery from incarceration (Geller, Garfinkel, and Western 2011; Lee et al. 2015; Wakefield, Lee, and Wildeman 2016).	Single-parent households (+)
Urbanicity	Residents of small/rural areas may be more vulnerable due to persistent poverty and joblessness following deindustrialization, or the conditions of local economy and distance to social infrastructure and health (Simes 2018b; Burton et al. 2013).	Small cities (+) small/midsized counties (+)

TABLE 6.3 *(continued)*

Concept	Description	Increases (+) or Decreases (-) Punishment Vulnerability
Education	Education is linked to socioeconomic status, with higher educational attainment resulting in greater lifetime wealth and earnings, which may insulate communities from incarceration (Pettit and Western 2004).	Little schooling (+)
Job opportunities	Access to job opportunities in a community will enhance community resilience and provide opportunities for financial stability and social integration (Kalleberg 2011; Bartik 2001; Bloome et al. 2007).	Job density (-)
Housing	Access to safe, affordable housing and a stable address create conditions that support community development and reduce residential instability (Sylla et al. 2017; Wood 2014; Geller and Curtis 2011; Roman and Travis 2006).	Affordable housing (-)
Vacancy/ abandonment	Desertification and abandonment leads to community fragmentation and diminished social cohesion, which in turn reduces resilience. High rates of vacancy reduce property values and make neighborhoods vulnerable to quality of life policing (Gomez 2016; Ackerman 1998).	Vacant housing (+) Rapid population loss (+)
Social services	Access to hardship, educational, and employment organizations could intervene in the use of formal social control (Murphy and Wallace 2010; Comfort 2016).	High-density social services (-)
Health care	Access to insurance coverage, emergency and preventative services, screenings, dental visits, mental health counseling and psychiatric care, substance use disorder treatment, and other health-care services can enhance resilience and intervene when punitive institutions may play a role in health-care delivery (Turney 2017b; Wildeman and Wang 2017; Rich et al. 2014).	High-density medical, mental health, and substance use treatment services; insurance coverage (-)
Stigma	Places become stigmatized due to a combination of factors relating to race, poverty, substance use, and concentration effects (Eason 2017; Sampson and Raudenbush 2004).	Stigma (+)

(continued)

TABLE 6.3 *(continued)*

Concept	Description	Increases (+) or Decreases (-) Punishment Vulnerability
Police structure	Overpolicing, hot spots, and militarization of police raise the risk of surveillance and criminalization (Stuart 2016; Alexander 2010; Go 2020).	Greater officers per capita (+)
Court structure	The potential harsh and punitive practices of prosecutors and felony conviction patterns, the over-reliance on misdemeanor legal practices produce harsher punishment outcomes (Kohler- Hausmann 2018; Pfaff 2012).	Harsh or frequent charges and sentencing (+)
Community supervision structure	High rates of community supervision (e.g. parole, probation) increase the level of surveillance and could lead to incarceration for technical violations (Harding, Siegel, and Morenoff 2017; Phelps 2017).	Concentrated or high levels of community supervision (+)
Prison structure	A prison system with greater capacity for incarceration could expose more people to the risk of punishment (Schoenfeld 2018; Eason 2017).	Prison capacity (+) Prison political economy (+)

SOURCE: Adapted from Cutter, Boruff, and Shirley (2003).

examined at the level of counties, cities, or neighborhoods, demonstrate the vulnerability of particular places to punishment.

Using a "hazards of place" model, wherein the hazard is criminalization and punishment, I suggest that *punishment vulnerability* is a multifaceted concept that helps to identify those characteristics and experiences of communities that enable them to respond to and recover from mass incarceration.[67] These correlates have been derived from a broad array of research, including my own, and call for a robust and replicable set of measures that estimate punishment vulnerability in a diverse set of communities. Applying a hazards of place framework takes an important step toward challenging traditional analyses of mass incarceration that too often fall into simplistic discussions of individual blameworthiness, and worse, pathologize people, families, and communities for their misfortune and poor life choices. *Punishment vulnerability* fundamentally recenters the problem of incarceration on the systemic and iterative failures of an array of criminal justice policy

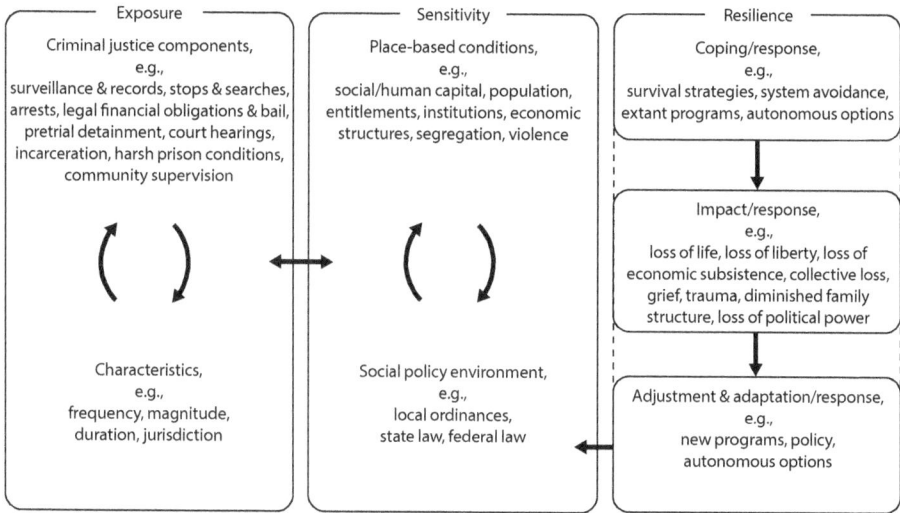

Exposure

Criminal justice components,
e.g.,
surveillance & records, stops & searches,
arrests, legal financial obligations & bail,
pretrial detainment, court hearings,
incarceration, harsh prison conditions,
community supervision

Characteristics,
e.g.,
frequency, magnitude,
duration, jurisdiction

Sensitivity

Place-based conditions,
e.g.,
social/human capital, population,
entitlements, institutions, economic
structures, segregation, violence

Social policy environment,
e.g.,
local ordinances,
state law, federal law

Resilience

Coping/response,
e.g.,
survival strategies, system avoidance,
extant programs, autonomous options

Impact/response,
e.g.,
loss of life, loss of liberty, loss of
economic subsistence, collective loss,
grief, trauma, diminished family
structure, loss of political power

Adjustment & adaptation/response,
e.g.,
new programs, policy,
autonomous options

FIGURE 6.3. Framework for punishment vulnerability. *Source:* Adapted from Turner et al. (2003).

choices that have led to these conditions. It brings direct attention to the complex and interconnected nature of various components of policy and social life that create this vulnerability. It necessitates a direct engagement between quantitative and qualitative scholars and takes seriously the nested scales of both place (neighborhoods, cities, regions) and punishment (police precincts, court districts, prison jurisdictions). Critical to understanding vulnerability is studying the impacts of these hazards; sociology has spent a great deal of time examining these impacts. This kind of research asks: How do people survive in response to state-sponsored suffering, and how might these hazards be mitigated or eliminated?

Figure 6.3 formalizes the punishment vulnerability framework. Exposure is described as a system that begins with labeling and initial contact and can end in the loss of life and liberty. The frequency, duration, magnitude, and jurisdiction all vary and depend on the place. Place-based conditions, described in table 6.3, indicate a multitude of pathways that make some places (and not others) vulnerable to punishment. Communities resist and respond to these conditions with creative adaptations and coping/survival strategies, avoid systems that may contribute to their exposure to the criminal justice system, and engage in programs and autonomous activities aimed at responding to the hazards of criminal justice policy and contact (again, including loss of life, loss of liberty, deepening economic precarity, community grief and trauma, diminished family contact and connection, and the loss of political power). Finally, adjustments and adaptations could yield new policies, reforms, or reimagined justice within communities, which could in turn reduce the vulnerabilities faced by communities.

The goal of this type of analysis is both the empirical study of how *things go together* and a call to action for research and policy.[68] Our disciplines and shared social interest in reducing and perhaps eliminating the penal system as it stands suffer deeply from data silos and data poverty. I do not mean data *on* poverty—but rather, a poverty in our measures, our ability to link data and projects together, and our ability to study incarceration at the community level (largely due to the restrictive data-sharing practices across penal institutions). Few police departments share information disaggregated to spatial markers like the block or longitude/latitude of stops and arrests (though many departments use such data in the practice of predictive policing). Even more challenging, accessing data from any other criminal justice institution (i.e., courts, prisons, jails, probation, parole) is a feat of building and stoking deep relationships and long-standing trust between researchers and institutions. Disciplinary differences have also fractured and siloed research projects, such that sociologists, for instance, are unable to collect the most relevant and up-to-date health data, while their public health colleagues would greatly benefit from the expertise and data of sociologists, geographers, and environmental scientists in their attempts to study community-level phenomena. A science of punishment vulnerability centers the goal on synthesizing research efforts and data collections and sharing strategies for data gathering and dissemination, all while maintaining the highest ethical standards regarding public data sharing.

We can eliminate this stifling data poverty if social scientists work together to ask new and important questions that drill down to the lived experience of suffering and resistance, of deprivation and resilience. We must work together toward crafting a common understanding of the ways that social and economic deprivation produce greater vulnerability and what could and should be done to eliminate suffering.

· · ·

Our social policy levers are too few, our measures and instruments too narrow, and the mindset too individualistic to create the systemic, community-affirming change we need in the American system of punishment and social welfare more broadly. Currently, removal and harsh conditions of confinement are the exclusive tools on offer to communities for transforming safety and justice. However, after decades—and really centuries—of calls for change, the moment is urgent. We must begin to envision and enact a kind of membership in society that does not harm communities, that values liberty and human connection and does not provide safety only to those who can afford to be segregated from violence in communities and immune to the excesses of state violence. Mass incarceration is morally, economically, and politically unsustainable.

In 2020, a pandemic, racial uprising, and looming economic recession led to far louder calls for rethinking policing and punishment and reinvigorating social safety nets. Rather than hot-spot policing, activists and community members wonder whether hot-spot medical care might save lives. As Black Lives Matter protests broke out once again during the 2020 summer and coronavirus pandemic, protestors and activists called for defunding the police and diverting those funds toward, among several other alternatives to police, unarmed mediation and intervention teams who can provide mental health and traffic services and de-escalate community and domestic violence.[69] Therapeutic responses to substance use problems *have* been implemented, suppressing the punitive capacity of the state in order to provide care and reduce the harms of severe and debilitating substance use.[70] And they have been successful. Others imagine housing interventions in which homelessness will not treated as a crime, and transitional housing will be placed in the communities that are home to individuals returning from prison and seeking stable housing. The findings presented in this book are very much along these lines: I ask for a refocusing and reframing of not only the places we study, but the places in which we choose to intervene. We can no longer ignore the clear patterns by which the state interacts with a variety of places and their unique social, political, and economic conditions.

The effectiveness of criminal justice policy has long been measured by lower reported crime rates and incidences of recidivism. Yet this system is remarkably effective at stripping communities of their members and exposing entire places to the specter of punitive responses to social problems. This, too, must be measured.

Reflecting on Monica Bell's impactful essay on safety, justice, and dreams—a quote from which opens this chapter—I wonder how we can ask communities to survive decades of state-sponsored redlining, divestment, restrictive covenants, and state-sanctioned segregation, accompanied and extended by fifty years of mass incarceration, all while being maligned and blamed for their "criminogenic" social conditions, stigmatized by ameliorative policies, and treated as a sociological monolith by the scholars whose findings inform policy. Literally hundreds of thousands of years have been lost to prison life, and this is in Massachusetts—the state with the country's lowest incarceration rate. That is an incomprehensible amount of time in what could be described as the best case scenario for the role of the prison in community life. To the extent that the relationship between state and subject can be described, this is beyond estrangement or neglect. Mass incarceration represents the state's total rejection of whole communities.

Communities have suffered greatly as commentators and scholars continue to conceptualize the effects of mass incarceration as an individual-level vulnerability. The indicators used in my analysis in this chapter begin to describe what a vibrant and healthy community looks like and how incarceration at the scale and concentration found in American neighborhoods harms the health and vibrancy of everyone living in those communities. The dose makes the poison, as they say, and American communities are being poisoned by current conceptions and practices of punishment.

SEVEN

Beyond Punishing Places

A RESEARCH AND REFORM AGENDA

> I urge that we reframe the debate, that we not view it primarily
> in terms of behavior versus structure or the strengths and weak-
> nesses of particular antipoverty measures, but in terms of what
> justice requires and how we, individually and collectively, should
> respond to injustice.
>
> —SHELBY (2016)

SINCE THE 1980S, MASS IMPRISONMENT has transformed the character
of poverty and community life in the United States. In studying the neighborhoods and communities most impacted by crime policy, the scope of mass
incarceration comes into full focus. Whole groups, and thus whole neighborhoods, are bound up in American criminal justice, itself a web of punitive,
criminalizing practices and policies shot through with systemic, historical
racism and inequality. Ultimately, the punitive turn in crime control that
created mass incarceration was *place-based*. The results were far-reaching:
American rural towns, small cities, suburbs, and large metropolises alike, no
matter the cost, organized around a policy agenda that fundamentally seeks
to criminalize and remove people from impoverished and racialized communities. By studying places instead of individuals, by keying in on the *punishing
places*, we can start to envision collective redress and justice for the harms
associated with American incarceration.

Punishment in America has had *collateral consequences*. The concept of
collateral consequences comes from studies of war and describes the unintended destruction of people, property, and places surrounding (but apart
from) those directly involved in combat. The literature on the collateral
consequences of mass incarceration has focused on the effects on the partners and children of criminalized and punished individuals. Few studies
have examined the impacts on neighborhoods and communities.[1] Moreover,
policy *choices* created these conditions, and we have yet to construct effective

social policies in response to the great collective suffering mass incarceration has caused. The data and stories in this book have hinted at the extent and contours of this community suffering, in the hopes that this work compels deep and sustained interest in reforms that could restore justice at the community level, all across the United States.

My main arguments in this book can be summarized fairly tidily. First, the spatial distribution of incarceration in the United States follows the contours of racial segregation, poverty, and rates of criminalized behavior (specifically violence). Second, rather than being limited to urban neighborhoods of major cities, mass incarceration is best understood as a broad mode of governance unevenly applied to communities of all sizes, including rural areas. Third, by reconceptualizing mass incarceration as a broad, place-based policy, we can—and should—estimate and investigate the extensive political, social, and health effects of mass incarceration beyond individual harms.

Chapter 1 describes two sociological research traditions with close empirical connections to the role of justice institutions in poor communities: urban inequality and social control. Because they evolved with little exchange or synthesis, large gaps in the research and theories of punishment emerged. Urban sociologists identified and analyzed the effects of social environments on individual life chances and rates of behavior at the neighborhood level. These urbanists paid insufficient attention to both the dynamic patterns of disadvantage outside of large cities and matters of state power. On the other hand, scholars of social control studied national and state-level demographic trends in punishment and inequality across the United States, but did not fully account for the role of local context in shaping the population dynamics of mass incarceration. Until now, we have had an incomplete picture of how mass incarceration is geographically patterned and how this is important for designing measures for justice in the most punishing places.

Prior research has been designed in ways that reflect built-in assumptions about the "who" and the "where" of criminalized behavior and incarceration (informed, to some degree, by the way punitive crime control strategies were designed to regulate certain people in certain places). Thus, a well-intentioned focus on poor "inner-city" Black neighborhoods, usually in order to draw attention and urgency to racial disparity, can adversely promote a subtle racism in the ideas that these are the *only* places where criminalized behavior exists, that the residents of these places lack political agency or expertise in how to address those conditions, and that reforms can be implemented without questioning the punitive and criminalizing system itself. In *Dark Ghettos: Injustice,*

Dissent, Reform, Tommie Shelby is critical of policy makers who treat the background structure of society as a given and attend only to alleviating the burdens of the disadvantaged. This kind of thinking, Shelby argues, marginalizes the often potent, passionate political agency of those it aims to help.[2] In many ways, this type of analysis avoids taking a stance on the role of the state, denies the differential experiences of state power expressed in neighborhood space, and reinforces a naturalistic notion of neighborhood inequality.

One might come away from reading this book and think that what we need is more research, services, and reforms aimed at the small cities and nonmetropolitan areas described in chapter 3. Generally, I agree. My work aims to bring attention to these forgotten and understudied places in the hope that researchers and policy makers will pay more attention and drive resources and reforms in those places. As the respondents cited in chapter 4 discussed, people coming out of prison who are dealing with poverty and substance use problems need more support and resources, and in some cases, desperately so. But reflecting on the quantitative findings and qualitative accounts presented in these pages, and taking in the implications of the broad scope of mass incarceration, I argue for a more systemic and transformative approach to policy reform. As I asked at the end of chapter 5, what if the state simply punished places *less*, rather than offering supports and resources in response to punishing and criminalizing contexts?

In this way, I seek to inform a research and policy agenda that promotes community-based justice. By the nature of what I called in chapter 6 their *punishment vulnerability*, those who live in the most punishing places have potential, resources, and creative capacities that have been interrupted and undermined by concentrated incarceration—and potential, resources, and creative capabilities that have made them resilient to the state violence under which they live—a resilience painfully and needlessly born out of oppressive state interventions. As Shelby argues, "status quo bias invites us to see dysfunction where perhaps lies resistance to injustice."[3] Such a view of community-based justice understands members of marginalized or disadvantaged communities as people with equal claims and power to implement a just social structure.[4]

BRINGING PLACE INTO MASS INCARCERATION RESEARCH AND REFORM

We organize our lives within places that, in turn, shape our identities, our social groupings, and the trajectories of our economic and social selves. People carry the meaning derived from places—from their communities—for their lifetimes.[5] Our identities respond to city ecology, and our very interactions and modes of living iteratively shape and are shaped by these ecologies. In contexts where social control pervades the community, how have identities and life trajectories been affected? This question has been taken up by very few sociologists, and understanding how concentrated incarceration affects the broader civic and social life within neighborhoods across the rural-urban continuum would be a fruitful and important avenue for future research.[6]

By not studying the relationship between segregation and mass incarceration, scholars have missed how prior social environments provide greater insight into how racial disparities are both cumulative and contextual across the various stages of the criminal justice process. In chapter 5 I argue that racial residential segregation underlies the demographic concentration of punishment, though segregation is rarely theorized or studied as an important driver of racial disparities in incarceration. As Monica Bell argues, policing may indeed reinforce and secure the American system of racial segregation.[7] A racial-spatial divide, coupled with spatially organized criminal justice, means that neighborhoods with distinct ethnoracial compositions are vulnerable to the greatest surveillance and harshest treatment by criminal justice authorities. Racial disparities should be conceptualized as cumulative and contextual over the course of criminal justice contact, beginning with prior neighborhood environments. Looking only at one stage does not fully capture the lived experience of mass criminalization and mass incarceration; it also oversimplifies policy solutions to a focus on biased actors at single stages, such as the police encounter or the sentencing judge. Thus, long-standing debates over the origins of mass criminalization or mass incarceration often analyze race without a cumulative disadvantage perspective, finding in one instance no disparity, but failing to see the profound disparities that lie in the unobserved structure of American communities. This failure of data and analysis leads to incomplete theories, and perhaps most worrisome, to incomplete policy solutions. To do the kind of work that fully captures and seeks to end the realities of systemic racism, innovative methods and data linkages that go beyond single sites and single stages of criminal justice contact will be required.

How does this community-based framing inform a transformative approach to justice and reform? Replicability and scale are the hallmarks of scientifically sound social policy that "works." We ask: *How well does a given policy reform replicate in other settings? Can it scale?* Yet place-based interventions, or those that target specific geographic areas, have come at great cost and with mixed results—struggling to meet either standard.[8] As Laura Tach and Christopher Wimer summarize in their review of policies aiming to transform distressed urban neighborhoods, "Targeted place-based interventions have made incremental change, but few have been transformative."[9] Thus, debates arise over the relative effectiveness of individual and place-based policy reforms. Margery Austin Turner proposes an alternative, "place-conscious approach" to reconcile the individual versus place debate in American public policy.[10] Community boundaries are porous, and people move to seek new opportunities or get pushed out of their neighborhoods for various reasons. As Margery Austin Turner argues, "We must think differently about the boundaries of a community and recognize that linkages between people and services operate between different governmental levels."[11] Further, Turner proposes that place-conscious initiatives could link neighborhood residents to city and regional opportunities, rather than simply focus all resources within a single geographic area such as a single neighborhood. The concept of *place-conscious* (as opposed to *place-based,* which links to a single geographic area) aligns with this book's arguments that criminal justice contact is similarly porous, spilling across neighborhood, city, county, and sometimes state boundaries. Understanding, and intervening in, the lived experience of poverty, criminalization, and punishment necessarily means not simply targeting individuals, or *individual neighborhoods*, but a broader notion of community and place that spans boundaries, activity and work spaces, families, and residential trajectories.[12] With a place-conscious approach, we must prioritize the broad community burdens of frequent and pervasive contact with the criminal justice system. This kind of research and reform practice does not ask how to triage individual encounters with police or prisons, but demands bold and innovative public health and social welfare solutions to the core problem of mass incarceration. It means defining incarceration as a social determinant of health and fully capturing that in community health investments at every level of government. It also means that future policy and practice must affirm the agency of communities to define their own visions of justice.

Designing a singular policy as a panacea for mass incarceration could prove futile. There are a number of possible mechanisms explaining the spatial dimensions of incarceration and imprisonment. Distinctive patterns of punishment vulnerability, unfolding along different timelines and institutional arrangements, created these conditions, challenging the goal of replicability. Moreover, we simply have not done enough to integrate the communities that have been coping with mass incarceration for decades into the research and policy reform conversation. The pressure to find one theory or one policy reform for all places detracts from the more realistic goal of place-conscious reform to a place-based system.

Many will balk at this prescription; as I stated earlier, place-based solutions are costly and have mixed results. But in fact, mass incarceration resulted from a combination of place-based policies that has come at perhaps the greatest costs: human life and liberty and the vitality of communities that remain significantly vulnerable. As chapter 6 demonstrated, hundreds of thousands of person-years that could have been put toward health care and substance treatment or economic and social development have been lost to the carceral system, though no measures of the local, state, and federal expenditures for crime control and punishment include those years in their calculus.[13] In some sense, it's an unimaginable, incalculable cost. With this as our referent, all other large-scale, place-based social interventions begin to seem rather thriftier. We must envision community-based justice reforms that engage the public and democratize our strategies for public safety, that go beyond the well-rehearsed analysis of structural conditions and shift reductive thinking around the origins of harmful behaviors and violence away from individualistic theories and stereotypes.

BRINGING THE STATE AND SMALL CITIES
INTO URBAN INEQUALITY RESEARCH

As an urban sociologist interested in understanding social inequality, I found myself wading into a study of state policy and then into the geography of urban inequality: the places *not* accounted for but undoubtedly contributing to mass incarceration's collateral consequences. Patterns of incarceration, drug arrests, and other forms of state control exist in places far removed from the types of cities my intellectual predecessors had extensively explored. I hope to promote an urban and community sociology that takes seriously the contiguity of place and space, incorporates data and analysis of places where state jurisdictions cross-cut, and examines the totality of social control without arbitrary boundaries. Extreme levels of incarceration and state social control should be considered a form of deprivation in neighborhoods, a measure that would fortify our estimates of durable neighborhood inequality.[14] Pervasive incarceration is not a status quo, "natural" condition of cities, neighborhoods, and towns; it results from policy choices across an array of institutions (police, courts, prisons) and jurisdictions (local, state, federal). An analysis of the conditions and effects of neighborhoods must consider seriously the role of state actions in perpetuating persistent inequality.

Chapter 3 demonstrated that in all regions of the country, suburban, rural, and small to midsized counties outpace incarceration in large urban metro areas. Why have these stories gone untold? There are several possibilities. Research suggests that the demise of local newspapers, media consolidation, and the rise of digital media have stripped many places of journalistic investigations and reporting.[15] Data activists, responding to the inadequacies of traditional data sources, must mine local news to gather and crowdsource reports of police violence; the demise of local news could play a significant role in keeping small cities' social control regimes and practices hidden from view, let alone review.

The historical trajectory of place and punishment may lend important insight into the practice of law enforcement in the United States. The historical data in chapter 3 demonstrated the importance of a broadened approach to the study of neighborhoods, poverty and inequality, and punishment. This has significant implications for social policy. For instance, large cities like Boston have experienced concurrent trends of declining imprisonment and declining levels of reported violence. Future research and policy analysis could aim to explain this coincidence as well as why other urban and suburban areas have not followed suit.

Incarceration, like mortality, is the "deep end" of a complex web of experiences, hazards, and vulnerabilities. There are some events in the life course of the criminal justice process that are particularly instrumental in determining the outcome of incarceration, and these have been tied to the spatial distribution of prison entrances. Some suggest that prosecutors are to blame for the intense rates of felony convictions in some places and not others, some have focused heavily on patterns of policing, and still others point to variation in sentencing guidelines and other legislative efforts to limit the power of judges and other court actors and enhance the punitive conditions of the criminal legal system.

However, the idea that by intervening in one of those steps (the discretionary moments in which a cop decides whom to arrest, a prosecutor determines what charges to seek, or a judge imposes a sentence), we can wholly reform the deep and highly structured relationship between conditions of incarceration and disadvantage in neighborhoods, is both unreasonable and myopic. The main question at the heart of this book is: *Under what conditions do extreme (or even moderate) levels of incarceration* improve *conditions of public safety in neighborhoods?* This means seeking out and researching other possibilities for enhancing safety and redress, ones that do not require the extraction of people from their communities, placement in harsh prison conditions for significant periods of time, or return to punishing places. Rejecting the retributive model, why not change the outcome possibilities to a more expansive, community-enhancing rather than community-fragmenting, response? This would look something like community-based justice, rooted in the idea that promoting social integration and affirming the political agency and humanity of all people and communities may result in what Bruce Western calls for: a "thick" kind of public safety.[16]

COMMUNITY JUSTICE: REPARATIONS, RESTORATIVE JUSTICE, AND ABOLITION

Social movements during 2020 have called for a national dialogue about what America must do to respond to historic injustice and promote an antiracist agenda, pointing to mass incarceration and criminalization as prime examples of the unresolved racism saturating American public policy. In the final passages of his essay on the Black family in the age of mass incarceration, Ta-Nehisi Coates gestures toward reparations as a possible model of response to the historic injustice heaped upon them by the "justice" system.[17] The idea that African Americans have been uniquely harmed by mass incarceration suggests reparative justice as a reasonable and productive response to past harms. How could adopting a community-level focus yield promising avenues for reparative justice?

Incarceration legacies are heritable through the social and spatial conditions of American society.[18] Specific policies, such as the War on Drugs, have led to a "racialized criminalization of people and communities [and] have impacted all Black people in the United States, not just those who can prove their ancestors were slaves."[19] And just as there are strong normative arguments for reparations in the case of the latter, I argue that there are strong normative arguments supporting reparations for the harms of mass incarceration and criminalization enacted upon the former. For example, in the case of police killings, political theorist Jennifer Page writes that reparations are owed when a person who is not otherwise liable to being killed is, in fact, killed by an agent of the state.[20] Unjustifiable shootings are cognizable from a civil law framework, but Page argues that without reparations, police killings will continue to escape accountability or justice. And moreover, in any civil liability settlement, states and police departments require plaintiffs to release the state from any blame—the exact *opposite* of what reparations would do. Specifically, in the context of mass incarceration, Black reparations are owed.[21]

Reparations for mass incarceration can be difficult to imagine from the national vantage point. Slavery, Jim Crow, and apartheid segregation unfolded across vastly different geographic and historical conditions, and both state action *and* neglect—say, for example, in regulating the housing market—have impacted whole groups on the basis of their status as a race for several generations. The uncoordinated—yet similarly spirited—policies surrounding harsh policing, charging, sentencing, and prison confinement all vary and often work independently. It is only when we drill down to the lived experience of individuals and their communities that we can grasp, for example, that in one part of the country reform to fines and fees is crucially important for the community's survival and economic sustainability, while in other parts, the conditions of harsh policing and police violence may be the area in which a community determines it must demand reparations. Often local communities must come to define what is owed and how the state can materially and symbolically repair the harms it has caused.

Reparations enacted at the local level could bolster a national reparations program because local-level resiliencies pinpoint specific community needs and best bolster the case for reparations. A system of reparations must be built on the capacity of communities to express the pain, grief, and suffering that mass incarceration has wrought as well as their visions for a collective future.

Some activists argue otherwise: that a federal or national program is best suited for reparations. One such effort, House Resolution 40, aims to designate a federal committee to study and develop reparations proposals.[22] William Darity Jr. and A. Kirsten Mullen argue that the federal government sponsored segregation and sustained the wealth gap through centuries of federal public policy, and that local initiatives cannot compensate for past harms at that scale. While I fundamentally agree with this perspective, the current political climate features few champions for a federal reparations policy, even on the Left. I think local initiatives could be grouped and later serve as models for effective community support and the development of reparative justice programs, perhaps even at the federal level, but federal reparations are not yet politically viable.

The Movement for Black Lives's "Reparations Now Toolkit" lists the non-negotiable components of reparations:

- *Cessation*: a complete, full, and final end to continuing violations.

- *Guarantee of nonrepetition*: assurance that violations will not be repeated in the future, including reviewing and reforming laws contributing to or allowing violations.

- *Restitution*: restoring the survivor to the original situation before the violations occurred, including, as appropriate: restoration of liberty, enjoyment of human rights, identity, family life, and citizenship, return to one's place of residence, restoration of employment, and return of property.

- *Compensation*: payment appropriate and proportional to the gravity of the violation and circumstances, if damage is not made good through restitution.

- *Satisfaction*: needed in some instances when cessation, restitution, and compensation do not bring full repair. Apology falls under the reparative category of satisfaction. Satisfaction is part of full reparations under international law for moral damage, such as emotional or mental suffering.

- *Rehabilitation*: legal, medical, psychological, and other care and services.[23]

It is abundantly clear that reparations are not solely about financial compensation. Elsewhere in their detailed and deeply researched toolkit, the authors warn, "Reparations cannot be achieved simply through an apology or 'investment in underprivileged communities.'"[24] All these necessary components of reparations are in place to strengthen the likelihood that reparations actually respond to injustice. With the overwhelming knowledge that mass incarceration harms and has harmed millions of lives, regardless of an individual's direct, personal experience of confinement, the components of cessation and nonrepetition imply that *abolition* is a necessary step toward repairing the state-sponsored injustices. The state must, in this model, take an active role in ending the suffering it is causing. Only then can communities address what restitution, satisfaction, and rehabilitation would respond to their specific needs.

The case of drug decriminalization demonstrates the incomplete justice of cessation without reparations. With the widespread decriminalization of cannabis, reparative justice asks not just for the abolition of criminalization, but what must be done to repair past harms to those who were criminalized and incarcerated for now legal acts. One example of community-based reparations suggests the creative ways other places could respond to the reach of mass incarceration. In Evanston, Illinois, the community demanded reparations for the overpolicing of cannabis prior to its legalization in the state, which disproportionately impacted Black residents and placed many young men and women in prison. In addition, Evanston's history is rife with redlining practices, and contemporary economic inequality has displaced working-class Black people from their homes. In June 2019, the Evanston City Council adopted a resolution to establish a committee to assist with the reparations process. In turn, the reparations committee recommended funding housing and economic development initiatives by designating tax revenue collected from the sale of now-legal recreational cannabis.[25]

What does community-based justice reform look like on the ground? One detailed example of how it can work is found in Restorative Justice City, a model developed by the Ella Baker Center for Human Rights in Oakland, California. The RJC is a decentralized infrastructure that embeds restorative practices directly into every neighborhood of a given city.[26] To usher in a new model of "anytime, anywhere" justice, elders become designated arbiters in civil strife and offer interventions, and places for peacebuilding and justice are embedded in schools, community centers, libraries, and homes.[27] The RJC focuses on "collective ownership for change as opposed to traditional revitalization efforts," as Darris Young of the Ella Baker Center puts it.[28] This model, adapted by place and populace, would bring justice out of an individual framework and recast it as an outcome that restores and repairs whole communities.

Both reparations and restorative justice practices require that tangible steps be taken to safeguard against repeating past harms. Applied to an analysis of mass incarceration as a state-sponsored injustice, the principle of nonrepetition implies an end to prior practices: abolition. That is, the abolition of the institution of criminal justice as it stands is a potential way to end the injustice for future generations. Models of justice that affirm communities and their capacity to govern and enact justice—for example, through community-based justice, expanded political power via expanded enfranchisement and voter protection, and full participation in local governance—begin to envision a new kind of justice system that affirms communities rather than punishes and criminalizes them in perpetuity. An abolitionist vision means immediately divesting from the status quo to pursue community-based justice models pointing us toward how we want to live in the future.

. . .

In this book, I have uncovered the spatial dynamics of incarceration, particularly as they relate to patterns of social inequality. This close convergence of social disadvantages lays bare the reality of divergent social worlds, deeply divided experiences of mass incarceration, and the durability of impactful community-level effects stemming from living within our most punishing places. I have shown how the spatial concentration of imprisonment is not restricted to large, metropolitan areas—though it largely has been in the past. Accounting for these spatial dynamics is imperative if we are to capitalize on recent (though spatially limited) patterns of decarceration and a nascent political will to pursue this course. Understanding place and punishment will help reveal the casualties and collateral damage still accruing from a decades-long failure in criminal justice policy: mass incarceration.

The implications of *punishing places* call not just for forward-thinking reform, but also for a deep and significant look back at how flawed crime control efforts have driven the concentration of community grief, loss, hardship, and perpetual, generationally consistent poverty that characterizes the racialized organization of contemporary American society. Even one arrest, conviction, or incarceration can permanently change a person's life for the worse, creating lifelong barriers to employment, schooling, and housing. When this is scaled up to neighborhoods, entire communities suffer. From this morass, what kind of state can we *reimagine*?

Crime is not the result of individual depravity, and social control is not the exclusive province of the criminal. We are talking about social forces, social determinants, social control, and social harm. Now it's time to talk about a radically transformed, community-based notion of justice, building from the collective wisdom accrued in the resistance and resilience of marginalized communities.

Data and Methodology

In this methodological appendix, I provide detailed descriptions of my datasets, discuss ethical considerations inherent in the use of geographic data on prison admissions, and consider the ethical use and dissemination of these data. I close with detailed methodological descriptions for chapters 2, 3, 4, and 6. Detailed results tables, figures, and additional maps are available online at http://punishingplaces.org.

DATA

The book relies on several datasets developed from administrative records, census data, reported crime incidents, and police employee data.

Massachusetts Department of Correction Administrative Records

Throughout the book, I rely on a dataset constructed from Massachusetts prison records. Corrections data provided by the Massachusetts Department of Correction (MADOC) include information about individuals who were sent to prison, key among this being the last known street address for admittees, as provided in their intake processing (alongside their religious affiliation, place of birth, citizenship status, marital status, level of education, and number of children). Some are entering prison directly from jail custody, so the data reflect their community address prior to the intermediate jail stay, and others, of course, enter prison without any prior community address to report. If an individual reported being homeless but named a shelter as their last known address, the shelter's address was used as the last known address. The prison record data required significant data cleaning. Two percent of the admissions address data were erroneous or missing; a portion of these missing or incorrect addresses may be due to admitted persons who were homeless or weakly tied to a single address, while others may result from a refusal to report or data entry error.

Typically, researchers use the county or city of commitment when studying pre-prison community environments. While many individuals are convicted in their county or city of residence, the last known address is a unique feature of the Massachusetts data, and it allowed me the rare opportunity to study where individuals said they were last living before incarceration. In all of my empirical chapters, the data are restricted to those previously living at a Massachusetts address, thus removing the small number of people admitted who reported a last known address in other states.

I have been working with the MADOC since 2011, and these data were provided over the course of several years. The reports were uneven: they covered different time spans and included different variables. Data collection practices and standards have changed greatly across the years. Electronic record keeping in the MADOC became much more standardized in 1997, and in 2009, the collection of address data became standard practice at intake. I constructed datasets from publicly available reports and electronic records from these different time periods in order to study the spatial patterns of incarceration across time and place. I provide detailed descriptions of each of these datasets in this appendix, and table A.1 summarizes the data availability across three time periods of data.

Prison records from 1973 to 1996. Historical data for 1973–1996 come from publicly available reports published on the MADOC website. The first report, from 1973, recorded admissions for nearly every city and town in the Commonwealth. As the years went on, the MADOC reported data on the top ten cities (in terms of prison population size). I extracted these data from pdf reports to conduct time series analyses and study the changing rates and disproportionalities of prison admissions in Massachusetts (chapter 3).

Prison records from 1997 to 2008. The MADOC provided data on commitments to state prison from 1997 to 2008. These records were saved by early computer data systems as dat files, which required me to carefully extract and develop the data into data tables. These tables included several variables that later years' data did not contain, and vice versa. Thus these earlier records included the zip code and cities of prior residences, but very few addresses. Making matters more complicated, the type of data entry used in this period—a drop-down list of zip codes, which led to frequent misselection—for prison intake makes these data unreliable without a manual review. After geocoding addresses, I discovered numerous incorrect zip codes. For example, an address that was associated with the Allston neighborhood of Boston might list, in the data, a zip code associated with downtown. Thus, for analyses using these earlier data (years prior to 2009), I only use geographic information on the city of residence prior to incarceration. These data also included the exact minimum and maximum dates associated with each prison commitment, along with key demographic information such as the committed person's race/ethnicity, sex, and date of birth. Another difficulty with these data is that many

Massachusetts Department of Correction Prison
Record Data Descriptions by Time Period, 1973–2017

	1973–1996	1997–2008	2009–2017
Address-level data			✓
City-level data (all cities)		✓	✓
City-level data (10 largest)	✓	✓	✓
Demographic data (e.g., race, age, sex)		✓	✓
Complete sentencing data (months/years)		✓	
Partial sentencing data (ordinal categories)		✓	✓

women sentenced to a house of correction (jail) were under the jurisdiction of
the MADOC in this period (though not in later years), and so their intakes were
recorded as prison admissions, inflating the number of women sentenced to state
prisons. Because these women were nevertheless incarcerated in a prison and not a
local house of corrections, I choose to report these data as prison admissions despite
differences in sentencing.

Prison records from 2009 to 2017. Data from 2009 offer the most complete and
detailed spatial data associated with Massachusetts prison intake records. Address
data from 2009 onward are particularly reliable (only 2 percent of the data are missing), so any neighborhood-level analyses throughout this book use data from 2009
to 2017 (neighborhoods are operationalized as census tracts). This later period of
data, however, did not include variables recording the exact minimum and maximum sentencing date (as in prior years' data), but as categorical variables (e.g., less
than 3 years, 3–5 years, and so on). This is particularly important for my estimations
of community loss (chapter 6), in which local rates of loss are measured with much
greater bias for these years than the prior years of data (1997–2008), with the exception of 2009. Thus, for the community loss analysis presented in chapter 6, data on
loss are analyzed for cities in 1997–2009, and for neighborhoods in 2009–2017.

On the Validity of Address Data

A central assumption underlying all of the work presented in this book is that the
address information collected during the prison intake process reflects the actual
address of a person prior to incarceration. There are several reasons to be concerned
that this address could be inaccurate. First, this population tends to be highly
disadvantaged, particularly in the area of housing security.[1] Addresses reported
during prison intake could reflect any number of the following: a person's actual
home address; the address of a partner, parent, or other family member; the last
household address; or any number of the institutional, community, and household
arrangements an individual might access (e.g., shelters, rooming houses, friends, on

the street). Because individuals are asked to supply their "last known address," we can be reasonably sure that it was their address at some point, if not immediately proximate to their prison admission. Still, the measurement validity of the address cannot be fully determined. This is the greatest limitation to using administrative records to study neighborhood trajectories. However, studies that use household surveys to study prior neighborhood environments are only observing a subset of the incarcerated sample, excluding individuals in these administrative records who report group housing (e.g., a rooming house, assisted living) or emergency shelter. I instead capture that address and geocode it to its respective census tract and city. Understanding the residential and housing patterns of recently incarcerated people using residential life histories could improve our understanding of the validity of address data collected by prisons and jails.

Prison Admissions

To study rates of imprisonment in places, I use data on prison admissions, rather than total prison populations or other measures. I do not distinguish individuals, who may be admitted to prison repeatedly throughout the course of the data, for several conceptual and methodological reasons. First, I am interested in the process of removal for communities, so I am not focused on estimates of the total numbers of people who go to prison in these time periods, but rather on the repeated removal of people from individual communities. Second, the MADOC data make individual-level analyses (as opposed to prison admissions) difficult; attempts to that end would introduce measurement error into the analysis. Thus, when I report a rate of admission, it is possible that a single individual contributed multiple observations. To reduce bias, I only analyze data on individuals sent to prison for a new criminal violation; this reduces the number of very short stays in the data but nevertheless includes individuals who enter multiple times in the data.

Reported Crime, Arrest, and Police Employee Data

To estimate the relationship between reported violent crime, drug arrest rates, and prison admissions, my analysis uses four sets of data. First, I created a measure of tract-level reported violent crime by merging data from the National Incident-Based Reporting System (NIBRS), provided by the Massachusetts State Crime Reporting Unit, with data from the Boston Police Department (BPD). The NIBRS data include all Part I violent crimes (murder and nonnegligent manslaughter, forcible rape, robbery, and aggravated assault) known to police agencies participating in the NIBRS data program. Because data were provided with longitude/latitude information, they were geocoded to yield tract-level reported crime rates. In order to include Boston in the analysis, additional data mirroring the NIBRS data were gathered from the BPD (Boston does not participate in NIBRS). Second, the Massachusetts Crime Reporting Unit provided a measure of drug arrest data, also at the address level, for the 302 agencies participating in the NIBRS reporting program. The BPD provided data identical to the NIBRS measures. These combined data—reported violent crime and drug arrest rates per 1,000 inhabitants—are observed at the census tract level for 93 percent of census tracts in Massachusetts.

A third set of measures includes agency-level (i.e., cities and towns) violent crime rates (reported complaints of violent crime per 100,000 residents) from the Uniform Crime Reports (UCR). The UCR violent crime rate includes murder and non-negligent manslaughter, forcible rape, robbery, and aggravated assault (limited to Part I crimes to mirror the tract-level crime measure). Data are missing for 192, or 14 percent, of all census tracts, though the UCR data provide coverage of all major municipalities and central cities in Massachusetts.

A final set of data are employee data collected by the FBI. Each year, law enforcement agencies across the United States report to the UCR program the total number of sworn law enforcement officers and civilians in their agencies. These data were calculated at the agency level to estimate the number of sworn officers per capita in cities from 1997 to 2017 (chapter 3).

Incarceration Trends Data

To contextualize the Massachusetts analyses, I use data from the Vera Institute of Justice's Incarceration Trends dataset. This project uses data collected by the US Department of Justice Bureau of Justice Statistics (BJS), supplemented with data from state sources when federal data are not available. From BJS, the data used for this analysis include data from the National Corrections Reporting Program (NCRP), which has collected individual-level data on admissions since 1983; the Annual Survey of Jails; and the Census of Jails. In addition to jail and prison admission data, the dataset includes crime data reported through the UCR and census data on population counts by race and gender in counties. For more information on this publicly available dataset, go to http://trends.vera.org.

US Decennial Census and American Community Survey Data

Data on the social and economic conditions of census tracts, cities, and counties were derived from the US Decennial Census and the American Community Survey (ACS). Total population counts from the census were used to calculate rates of prison admissions for all people, as well as by racial/ethnic subgroup. For chapters that analyzed annual data on prison admissions, I used linear interpolation to construct annual data on cities and census tracts, using data from the Census and ACS.

The table "Descriptive Statistics of Massachusetts Census Tracts" in the online appendix at http://punishingplaces.org reports descriptive statistics of the variables used in my regression analyses of prison admission rates and describes the social and economic characteristics of Massachusetts census tracts. The tract-level reported violent crime rate averages 4.7 per 1,000, and the tract-level drug arrest rate is 3.3 per 1,000 inhabitants. The average reported municipal violent crime rate for each municipality is 585 per 100,000 persons. The non-Hispanic Black population averages 6.4 percent in the sample of census tracts (lower than the national percentage, which is 12.6 percent). Similarly, the average Latino population within census tracts is 9.5 percent, or 6.7 percentage points lower than the national percentage. On average, one-quarter of a tract's population identified as having recently moved into the tract.

To measure concentrated disadvantage for each geographic area, I conducted a principal component analysis of five key measures of concentrated disadvantage in neighborhoods: the proportion of families living in poverty, the proportion of civilians age sixteen and over who are unemployed, the proportion of female-headed family households, the proportion of individuals over the age of twenty-five without a high school degree, and the proportion of households receiving public assistance.[2] Consistent with prior research, these poverty-related conditions are highly correlated and load on the same factor (see the table "Concentrated Disadvantage Measures" in the online appendix at http://punishingplaces.org for the factor pattern from the ACS 2005–2009 data). With an eigenvalue greater than 3, the first factor is dominated by high loadings (>0.75) for family poverty, female-headed households, low educational attainment, and public assistance receipt. I calculated a factor regression score that weighted each variable by its factor loading and joined this measure to the associated census tract or city.

Spatial Data Analysis, Geocoding, and Mapping

Analyses presented in the empirical chapters (chapters 2-6) were conducted using R and Stata. Spatial lag modeling, in which the average admission rate of surrounding neighborhoods was used as a predictor of a neighborhood's own admission rate, was conducted using a combination of R and GeoDa software, the latter producing a spatial weights matrix that allowed me to identify contiguous tracts. All address data were geocoded using ArcGIS and spatially joined to census tracts, cities and towns, and counties, which were then associated with census and reported crime data. Maps were generated in both ArcMap and R.

The table "Distribution of Spatial Indicators in Massachusetts" in the online appendix at http://punishingplaces.org describes the key spatial indicators for various types of localities in the state of Massachusetts. Regional indicators are used to contextualize tract- and city-level prison admission rates in regression analyses.

Tracts are indicated as residing in the following regions: (1) Boston (11.5 percent of tracts), (2) Greater Boston suburbs and towns (17.3 percent of tracts), (3) small cities outside Greater Boston (20.8 percent of tracts), and (4) suburban and rural towns outside Greater Boston (50.4 percent of tracts). For tract-level analyses, Boston serves as the reference category. For city-level analyses, Greater Boston (Boston and its surrounding suburbs) is used as a reference category.

STUDYING PUNISHING PLACES: ETHICAL CONSIDERATIONS

Analyzing data on race, place, and incarceration—even in the aggregate—requires the utmost care in the social sciences. Incarceration is a highly stigmatizing event, and it compounds and reinforces racialized stereotypes about places already facing stigma associated with racial segregation, poverty, and violence.[3] Throughout the book, I have declined to name specific census tracts and am restricted from ever revealing information about individuals. Online maps I have constructed use a technique called geo-masking, so that data are randomly displaced by several miles to mask the actual location of prior neighborhood environments.

When a person enters prison, they supply information that is pertinent to the institution. Presumably, they are not told that eventually their information may be used by researchers. Their lack of informed consent is an ethical consideration, as is the question of whether the personhood of incarcerated people is affirmed when their data can be shared by these nonvoluntary institutions with researchers. The public availability of criminal records negatively impacts the lives of formerly incarcerated, convicted, or even just arrested people.[4] I have to weigh this ethical consideration against another: the ethical costs of locking this information into silos, where the public, policy makers, and scholars are unable to see the spatial dependence of incarceration rates. This lack of information and data has allowed those who support punitive policies to lean on, for example, Massachusetts's low overall rate of incarceration. Leaving these data unexplored masks the degree of inequality found in the most vulnerable places.

Throughout this book, I have included careful protections to ensure that individual prison records are not exposed outside of the research environment. Address data, once aggregated, are stored on nonnetworked hard drives inside a locked drawer in a locked office. To protect the identities of all people who enter prison in the write-up, data are aggregated to census tracts at the lowest level of spatial aggregation. These data are stored and analyzed under special agreement with the MADOC and the Criminal Offender Record Information (CORI) office, and my data practices are regularly monitored by Boston University's Institutional Review Board.

To test hypotheses outlined in the social control and urban inequality literature, the analysis in chapter 2 writes census tract-level prison admission rates as a function of local rates of criminalized violence, drug arrest rates, spatial dependence in prison admissions, and other social and economic predictors. For census tract i, I fit the following regression to the count of prison admissions, Y_i,

$$\log \widehat{Y_i} = \log P_i + \beta_0 + \beta_1 \log \bar{y}_i + \beta_2 \log C_i + \beta_3 \log A_i + \beta_4 N_i + r_i' \beta_5 + s_i' \beta_6,$$

where the regression contains an offset term for the tract total population, P, and thus the coefficients can be interpreted as the association of the predictors with the log admission rate.[5] Predictors include a spatial lag, $\bar{y}$, a measure of reported crime, C, a measure of arrests, A, a concentrated disadvantage factor regression score, N, a vector of racial and ethnic characteristics, r, and a vector of spatial characteristics, s. Because prison admissions represent counts of individuals incarcerated in a given tract and are distributed with substantial overdispersion, prison admissions were fit with negative binomial regressions.[6] This overdispersed model tends to increase standard errors as compared to the Poisson regression.[7]

The spatial lag, $\bar{y}$, records the average log admission rate in contiguous census tracts. A Moran's I score of 0.63 (p<.001) for tract-level prison admissions indicates significant spatial autocorrelation. I hypothesized that the spatial organization of formal social control would induce a correlation among contiguous tracts net of other predictors. Similar to lagged dependent variables in time series analysis, the spatial lag coefficient indicates the correlation of neighboring prison admissions net of other predictors in the model, supporting my hypothesis.

In the urban inequality perspective, prison admissions are clustered in areas of high rates of criminalized behavior and violence. The analysis estimates the effects of reported crime, C, with two measures of violence. Detailed in the following, reported violent crime measures include data from the NIBRS and the BPD.

In the social control perspective, prison admissions are strongly related to a pattern of policing, beyond patterns of criminalized behavior. This analysis estimates the effects of drug arrests, A, on rates of prison admissions, using data derived from the NIBRS and BPD arrest records.

The predictors measuring concentrated disadvantage, N, and racial minority concentration, r, are motivated by prior research from both the urban inequality and social control perspectives, and test for the presence of punishment beyond that attributable to reported crime within a given neighborhood context. Measures of racial, ethnic, and immigrant composition include the proportion of Black, Latino, and other race residents, as well as the proportion of foreign-born residents per tract.

Finally, a vector of spatial characteristics of tracts, *s*, records two separate measures relating to urbanicity and residential instability. Residential instability is measured as the proportion of new residents in the tract.[8]

As derived from the theoretical discussion, the prison should draw overwhelmingly from Boston tracts. The analysis includes indicators of a tract location in particular community areas to address this hypothesis, identifying whether or not a tract falls within the boundaries of Boston, Greater Boston suburbs and cities, small cities outside of Greater Boston (e.g., Springfield, Worcester, Fall River), and other suburbs and rural towns beyond the Greater Boston area.

The regressions should be interpreted as describing the spatial structure of prison admission and its relationship to reported crime and socioeconomic disadvantage. The table "The Urban Model: Regression Analysis" in the online appendix at http://punishingplaces.org shows the results of negative binomial regression models of statewide prison admissions on measures of socioeconomic disadvantage, racial segregation, arrests, and reported crime. A first model analyzes prison admissions without the spatial fixed effects, while Model 2 (results used to produce figure 2.2) introduces the spatial context fixed effects. The results of each of the models show that concentrated neighborhood disadvantage (measured by poverty, unemployment, and low schooling among adults) and high proportions of non-Hispanic Black residents in the population are associated with higher rates of prison admissions at the tract level, net of arrest rates and multiple measures of criminalized violence. These results offer support for hypotheses linking formal social control efforts to the spatial concentration of social and economic disadvantage, net of the local conditions of criminalized violence and arrest. But these models do not account for all of the difference in prison admissions; unmeasured differences in the types of cities and regional inequalities (as show in the size and direction of the spatial indicators) suggest that, even after accounting for the contiguity of prison admissions and conditions within neighborhoods, significant regional differences remain.

Model 2 (the full model results presented in figure 2.2) indicates the close association between prison admissions, reported crime, race, and poverty. The crime coefficient indicates that a 1 percent change in the log violent crime rate is associated with over a quarter of a percentage point (.26) increase in the expected admission rate, showing that tracts with high reported crime have significantly higher rates of prison admission. A 1 percent change in the log drug arrest rate in tracts is associated with a .03 percent increase in the tract's expected admission rate, and this relationship is not significant after taking into account other factors.

Concentrated neighborhood disadvantage is strongly associated with prison admissions. In Model 2, net of reported violent crime, arrest, and prison admission spatial autocorrelation, a 1 point increase in the neighborhood disadvantage score is associated with a 54 percent increase in the admission rate ($\exp[.44] = 1.55$).

Residential instability, or the proportion of the tract's population who are new residents, is significantly related to higher prison admissions.

These models also indicate the positive association between prison admissions and the non-Hispanic Black population of tracts, net of other controls. In Model 2, two hypothetical census tracts that differ by 20 percentage points in the share of the Black population would differ, on average, by 17 percent in prison admissions (exp[.2*0.76] = 1.17). The positive association between these racial characteristics of neighborhoods and imprisonment supports the social control hypothesis (that the presence of racial minorities is associated with greater prison admissions, controlling for multiple measures of reported violent crime, concentrated disadvantage, and spatial autocorrelation in prison admissions). The proportion of Latino and foreign-born populations in a tract is not associated with prison admissions, but prison admissions are significantly lower as the proportion of a given tract's non-Hispanic other-race population increases.

Beyond the patterns of reported crime and socioeconomic disadvantage, the results also show that imprisonment is spatially clustered. The spatial autocorrelation for Model 1 indicates that a 1 percent increase in the log average prison admission rate of contiguous tracts is associated with a .25 percent increase in a given tract's expected admission rate. In this statewide analysis, all three models indicate significant spatial autocorrelation net of tracts' reported violent crime, socioeconomic, and racial characteristics. These results offer evidence for the diffusion of punishment, suggested by the urban inequality perspective—an ecological condition of social control that cannot be fully explained by the internal characteristics of a neighborhood.

A set of regional spatial dummies in Model 2 indicates whether a tract resides in one of four key areas: Boston (omitted as reference category), Greater Boston suburbs, small cities of Massachusetts, and suburbs and rural towns. Model 2 indicates that tracts in both Greater Boston and other suburbs and towns have significantly lower rates of prison admissions than those found in Boston. Small cities, however, have significantly *higher* prison admissions. A census tract in a small city outside Greater Boston has an estimated 22 percent higher prison admission rate than Boston tracts, even after taking into account the neighborhood ecology of disadvantage, racial segregation, violent crime, and surrounding neighborhood incarceration rates.

My results demonstrate a strong empirical association between prison admissions and neighborhood disadvantage, though future research could usefully address measurement limitations. Researchers could study intermediate stages of criminal processing, such as filings, arraignments, and sentencing, which are more causally proximate to criminalized behavior. The urban focus of previous research has been driven, in large part, by a dearth of geographically granular and available prison or reported crime data (disaggregated to zip codes, tracts, or neighborhoods for all jurisdictions). Making data of this sort available to researchers could greatly expand the scope of analysis in studies of place and punishment.

CHAPTER 3—SMALL CITIES AND MASS INCARCERATION

To understand the differences in prison admission rates for a spatially diverse sample of cities, I model the rate of prison admissions in cities, with a linear regression written as follows:

$$\log \hat{Y}_{it} = \beta_0 + u'_i\beta_1 + \beta_2 C_{it} + \beta_3 S_i + \tau_t,$$

where τ_t are fixed effects for each year. The urban inequality conditions are represented as a vector, u, which considers several measures. First, racial and ethnic composition are measured as the proportion of the city that is non-Hispanic Black and Latino.[9] A set of measures indicates conditions in cities related to disadvantage, including an index of correlated adversity and rates of vacancy in the city's housing stock.[10] Criminalized violence is measured as the annual rate of reported violent crime in the city according to the Uniform Crime Reports.[11] Next, C introduces a measure of the social control environment—the number of uniformed officers per 10,000 inhabitants—time-varying in these models.[12] A final measure, S, indicates whether the city is one of Massachusetts's small cities outside Greater Boston or a suburb or rural town outside Greater Boston. In the models reported later in this appendix, Greater Boston is the reference category for these regional controls.

The table "Small Cities and Mass Incarceration: Regression Analysis" in the online appendix at http://punishingplaces.org displays the results of linear regression analyses of the log prison admission rate in years 1997–2006 and 2008–2017. The cities in the models are restricted to those for which there are complete crime and criminal justice data for the 20 years of data (102 total cities).

I plotted the main model for two time periods: 1997–2006 and 2007–2017. These results are plotted in figure 3.5. With the exception of vacant housing rates, the proportion of the city that is Latino, and the reported violent crime rate, results are comparable for the two time periods.

CHAPTER 4—SOCIAL SERVICES BEYOND THE CITY: ISOLATION AND REGIONAL INEQUITY

Chapter 4 presents an analysis of interview data collected during the summer of 2019. With Erin Tichenor, an undergraduate research assistant, I reached out to 365 organizations located throughout Massachusetts, with a particular focus on small cities with very high incarceration rates according to my analysis of Massachusetts prison admissions data. We received a high response rate, and we completed interviews with 64 people associated with 47 different organizations representing rural, suburban, and small cities across the state. Five interviews were conducted with Boston-based organizations to provide comparison to small cities. We spoke to individuals from Andover, Brockton, Chelsea, Chicopee, Framingham, Gardner, Greenfield, Holyoke, Hyannis, Lawrence, Lowell, Lynn, New Bedford, Northampton, Pittsfield, Springfield, Sudbury, and Worcester. To supplement our interviews, we conducted fieldwork and attended site visits with several organizations in all key regions of the state.

The organizations were diverse in terms of size, services offered, faith-based orientation, and whether or not they explicitly worked with people leaving prison or jail. The vast majority of the 64 respondents were presidents or directors of their programs or organizations, while some were case managers, coaches, and direct service providers. We conducted interviews with sheriffs and reentry program officers working in corrections. Thirteen of the organizations we engaged with were explicitly providing reentry services, and eleven provided substance use recovery services to low-income community members. The remainder were housing, mental health, job-training, anti-poverty, justice, and community-development organizations.

Interviews were conducted in person either at Boston University, at the organization's office or site, or over the phone. The following is the interview protocol for all interviews:

1. How long have you worked in your current role at your current agency?
   Probes: Have you worked in other industries?

2. In your current job, approximately how many people have you worked with who are returning from prison?

3. Could you describe your role and the types of services you provide?
   Probes: Could you walk me through a typical day at work?

4. Could you describe barriers you see formerly incarcerated people facing when they come home from prison?
   Probes: Has this varied across different cities you've worked in? What are the main challenges to accessing housing?

5. What are some of the main barriers you face in providing these services?

6. How would you describe the availability of reentry services generally for people returning from prison in your city?
   Probes: How does this compare to Boston?

7. How would you describe the availability of funding for services like yours across the state?
   Probes: In what cities are resources for housing/recovery/reentry concentrated? Where do you receive funding from? Has funding from private and

public sponsors changed in the last decade? How does this affect your work? What do you do to cope with your funding situation?

8. What would you consider to be the top cause for return to custody in your region?

9. What are some of the most pressing issues facing the residents of your community? (drug addiction, overdose, crime, violence, poverty, incarceration, homelessness)

10. What neighborhoods are dealing with the most social problems in your city?

11. Are there areas where there have been significant improvements or particular attention paid to provide resources and services? Which neighborhoods?

12. How do your clients describe their neighborhood and community?
Probes: Do they talk about certain challenges or positives? How do they describe their relationship to home?

13. What are the relationships like between police, parole/probation, corrections, courts, and residents? How closely do you work with police/DOC to maintain safety, provide services, refer people?
Probes: How do you perceive relationships between police and communities in small cities? In your experience, does this differ in Boston?

14. How would you describe the racial, ethnic, and nationality makeup of your city? Has this changed?
Probes: Do you think this affects relationships with police? Availability of services? Relationships with service providers?

15. What are the main public services available in your city (public/affordable housing, transportation, libraries, public hospitals/emergency services)?

16. Is there anything else about the resources in cities and for programs that you would like to share with me?

17. Is there anything that I should be asking that I haven't asked about?

18. Could you provide three contacts through your organization or at others you work closely with who might be interested in participating in this study?

19. Why did you choose to participate in the study?

CHAPTER 6—PUNISHING PLACES

Community Loss

The table "Community Loss: Regression Analysis" (in the online appendix at http:// punishingplaces.org) displays the results from a linear regression analysis that regressed the log community loss (years sentenced to state prison) between 1997 and 2009. In this analysis, the greatest community loss was experienced where the share of the Black population was greater, where the city had high levels of concentrated disadvantage, and in cities outside of the Greater Boston area. Specifically, two hypothetical cities that differ by 20 percent in the share of the non-Hispanic Black population would differ on average by 66 percent in the years of community loss (exp[.2*2.524] = 1.66).

The results indicate that, at least for years 1997–2009 in Massachusetts, race is a strong predictor of community loss. Vacancy is also strongly associated with community loss, a measure of community abandonment. On average, small cities experience twice the rate of community loss as cities comprising Greater Boston (exp[.762] = 2.14). Note that all of these estimates use the minimum years sentenced (community loss) in a given city (Model 1).

NOTES

PREFACE

1. Travis, Western, and Redburn (2014, 355).
2. Travis, Western, and Redburn (2014, 356).
3. For a review, see Morenoff and Harding (2014).
4. Spatial Information Design Lab (2007).
5. Cadora, Swartz, and Gordon (2003).
6. Clear (2007, 68); Sampson and Loeffler (2010).

INTRODUCTION

1. Bureau of Justice Statistics (2020).
2. Shannon et al. (2017).
3. Shannon et al. (2017).
4. Western (2006).
5. Bonzcar (2003); Shannon et al. (2017).
6. Garland (2001a).
7. Travis, Western, and Redburn (2014, 355).
8. McGraw (2019).
9. NBC Chicago (2020).
10. Clines (1992).
11. Fagan, West, and Holland (2003, 1568n87).
12. These selections demonstrate the scholarly (and legislative) tendency to promote a view of mass incarceration as primarily unfolding within urban neighborhoods. Loïc Wacquant's historical account (2001, 97) of the emergence of hyperincarceration draws a clear link between urban places and incarceration: "sweeping economic and political forces have reshaped *the structure and function of the urban 'Black Belt' of mid-century* to make the ghetto more like a prison, while the racial inequities of postwar 'inmate society' makes the prison more

like a ghetto." Michelle Alexander (2010, 77) states: "Drug arrests skyrocketed, as *SWAT teams swept through urban housing projects*, highway patrol agencies organized drug interdiction units on the freeways, and stop-and-frisk programs were set loose on the streets." Alice Goffman (2014, 195) argues: "The United States embarked on a new and highly punitive era in regard to poor communities of color—signifying a profound change in *how American society governs segregated urban areas* and those living within them." Historian Elizabeth Hinton (2016, 25) draws a link between anti-poverty initiatives and the choice to police and punish urban neighborhoods: "Ultimately, *policymakers were determined to police urban space* and eventually to remove an entire generation of young men of color from their communities."

13. Sampson (2012).
14. Manduca and Sampson (2019).
15. Frase (2009).
16. Subramanian, Henrichson, and Kang-Brown (2015).
17. Rotman (1998, 160).
18. Bureau of Justice Statistics (2020).
19. See Muller (2012), Jacobs (1977), and Rothman (2002).
20. Abel (2017).
21. Phelps (2013, 2017).
22. Schoenfeld (2018).
23. Formisano (1991).
24. Bacon and Chen (2013).
25. Wong (2016).
26. Frase (2009).
27. Lerman and Weaver (2014a).
28. Nellis (2016).
29. Bridges and Crutchfield (1988).
30. Prison Policy Initiative (2014).
31. Massachusetts District Attorneys Association to State Senator William S. Brownsberger, October 23, 2017, www.wbur.org/radioboston/2017/10/24/da-letter -justice.
32. Mass Inc. (2015). When multiple convictions result from the same case, a "governing offense" is the most serious offense according to the severity of crimes in a jurisdiction.
33. NAACP Legal Defense Fund (2018).
34. Travis, Western, and Redburn (2014); Beckett and Western (2001).
35. Turner (2015).

CHAPTER 1. A SPATIAL VIEW OF PUNISHMENT

1. Fyfe (1991).
2. Johnson (2006).

3. See, for example, Papachristos and Bastomski (2018). Among scholars who have begun to look beyond bounded neighborhoods and specific zip codes, Papachristos and Bastomski find that spatial analysis helps reveal co-offending networks that durably span neighborhoods within the same city—in their study of Chicago.

4. Harcourt (2001, 18).

5. Cohen and Felson (1979); Tonry (1995).

6. Beckett and Herbert (2010).

7. Dubber (2001, 865).

8. Beckett and Western (2001).

9. Porter and Clemons (2013); Greene, Pranis, and Zeidenberg (2006).

10. Commonwealth of Massachusetts General Laws, Part 1, Title XV, Chapter 94C, Section 32J: Controlled substances violations in, on, or near school property or public parks or playgrounds.

11. Beckett and Herbert (2010, 49).

12. Beckett and Herbert (2010, 49).

13. Blakely and Snyder (1998).

14. Sanchez, Lang, and Dhavale (2005).

15. Sanchez, Lang, and Dhavale (2005, 283).

16. Youngerman (2012).

17. Beck (2020).

18. See Wooldredge (2007, 2012); Wooldredge and Thistlethwaite (2004).

19. Omori (2017).

20. Wacquant (2001, 384).

21. Wacquant (2001, 384).

22. Gilmore (2007, 17).

23. Gilmore (2007, 17.

24. Gilmore (2007, 126).

25. Cohen (1985, 206).

26. See also Irwin (1985).

27. Cohen (1985, 212).

28. Cohen (1985, 211).

29. Hinton (2016, 2).

30. President's Commission on Law Enforcement and Administration of Justice (1967, 5).

31. Muhammad (2011).

32. Hinton (2016); Flamm (2005); Weaver (2007).

33. Flamm (2005, 141).

34. Stuart (2016).

35. Politico (2016).

36. Politico (2016).

37. Politico (2016).

38. Buchanan, Bui, and Patel (2020).

39. Baker, Kanno-Youngs, and Davey (2020).

40. Levinson, Wilson, and Haas (2020).

41. Wacquant (2001, 2007, 2009); Alexander (2010). See also Forman (2012).

42. Garland (2001b); Feeley and Simon (1992).

43. Beckett and Western (2001).

44. Uggen and Manza (2002); Behrens, Uggen, and Manza (2003); Weaver (2007).

45. See Muhammad (2011), Alexander (2010), and Hinton (2016).

46. See, for example, Jacobs and Helms (1996), Sutton (2000), and Western (2006).

47. Clinard (1944); Steffensmeier and Jordan (1978); Truman and Planty (2012); Morgan and Truman (2020).

48. Travis, Western, and Redburn (2014, ch. 10).

49. In particular, the work of Traci Burch, Eric Cadora, Todd Clear, Jeffrey Fagan, and Sampson and colleagues has focused on these correlations among local conditions of segregation and disadvantage as they relate to imprisonment.

50. See Sampson (2012) and Sampson and Loeffler (2010).

51. Omi and Winant ([1986] 2015, 66); Bonilla-Silva (1997); Massey and Denton (1997).

52. Peterson and Krivo (2010).

53. Sampson and Wilson (1995); Sampson (2012).

54. Massey and Denton (1997).

55. Chetty and Hendren (2018); Sharkey (2013); Western (2018); Manduca and Sampson (2019).

56. Peterson and Krivo (2010).

57. Sampson (2012).

58. Wilson (1985).

59. *Terry v. Ohio* (1968); *Floyd v. the City of New York* (2013).

60. For an in-depth discussion of contemporary debates over policing practices, see Weisburd and Braga (2019).

61. Cohen (1999); Sampson (2012).

62. For a review, see Braga, Papachristos, and Hureau (2012) and Walker and Katz (2012).

63. See arguments made by Korver-Glenn, Dantzler, and Howell (2021).

64. Especially the work of Sampson (2012).

65. Velez, Krivo, and Peterson (2003); Peterson and Krivo (2010); Sharkey (2010); Sharkey et al. (2012).

66. Forman (2012); Gottschalk (2015, 169).

67. Sharkey (2013); Western (2015, 2018).

68. Clear (2007); Clear et al. (2003).

69. See Eason (2012, 2017) and Weidner and Frase (2003).

70. Simes (2020).

71. Sinyangwe (2020); Rios (2020); Boyles (2015, 2019).

72. Eason (2010, 2012, 2017).

73. Subramanian, Henrichson, and Kang-Brown (2015).

74. Keller and Pearce (2016).

75. Murphy and Wallace (2010); Burton et al. (2013).

76. Dobkin and Nicosia (2009); Gruenwald et al. (2010); Garriott (2011); Mauer (2013); Reding (2010).

77. See Frederick and Mooney (2018).

78. Planas (2016).

79. See Blumstein (2006).

80. See Morgan and Truman (2020).

81. See Kneebone and Berube (2013) and Murphy (2007).

82. Jargowsky (2013).

83. Caldwell et al. (2016).

84. See Pfaff (2012); Subramanian, Henrichson, and Kang-Brown (2015).

85. Park and Burgess (1925, 190).

86. Park and Burgess (1925, 7).

87. Hunter (1974, 113).

88. Cromartie and Buchholtz (2008). See also McIntyre, Knowles-Yánez, and Hope (2000).

89. Hall, Kaufman, and Ricketts (2006).

90. Cromartie and Bucholtz (2008).

91. Baldassare (1992).

92. Hall and Lee (2010); Orfield and Luce (2013).

93. Terbeck (2020).

94. See, for example, Kneebone and Berube (2013).

95. Terbeck (2020, 594).

96. Clark et al. (2009, 179).

97. Eason (2017, 62).

98. De Marco and De Marco (2010, 107).

99. Eason (2017). While urban jails are common, rural jails are also proliferating. See, for example, Vera (2017).

100. Mitchelson (2012); Spatial Information Design Lab (2007).

101. Campbell and Schoenfeld (2013).

102. Schoenfeld (2018).

103. Small (2014).

104. A nonexhaustive list of recent works in the area of criminalization, criminal justice, race, and Chicago includes Stuart (2020); Sampson (2012); Shedd (2015); Vargas (2016); Gonzalez Van Cleve (2016); Venkatesh (2000); Papachristos, Hureau, and Braga (2013); and Papachristos (2009).

105. See, for example, Trancik (1986) and Ford (2001).

106. Gilmore (2008, 55).

107. Gilmore (2008, 32).

108. Bacon and Chen (2013).

109. Parkes, Burnley, and Walker (1985).

110. Weisheit, Falcone, and Wells (2005).

111. Garland (1991, 134).

CHAPTER 2. THE URBAN MODEL

1. Ellis (1998).
2. Ellis (1998).
3. Spatial Information Design Lab (2007); Cooper and Lugalia-Hollon (n.d.); Lytle Hernandez and Dupuy (n.d.).
4. US Bureau of the Census (2010).
5. Foreman et al. (2007).
6. Bacon and Chen (2013); Foreman et al. (2007).
7. For examples of analyses that incorporate new forms of geographic variation, see Eason (2017), Marrow (2011), Murphy (2007), Murphy and Wallace (2010), Lichter et al. (2007), Sharkey (2014), Brown-Saracino (2018), and Beckett and Beach (2021).
8. Ellis (1998).
9. Simes (2016).
10. Lytle Hernandez and Dupuy (2020).

CHAPTER 3. SMALL CITIES AND MASS INCARCERATION

1. Boyles (2015, 2019); Lung-Amam and Schafran (2019); Rios (2020).
2. US Department of Justice, Civil Rights Division (2015).
3. Keller and Pearce (2016).
4. Sampson and Loeffler (2010); Sampson (2012); Spatial Information Design Lab (2007); Cadora, Swartz, and Gordon (2003); Clear (2007); Goffman (2014); Rios (2011); Wacquant (2000, 2001).
5. Feeley and Simon (1992, 450).
6. Brayne (2020).
7. Irwin (1985).
8. Boyles (2015); Lung-Amam and Schafran (2019); Sherman (2018).
9. Paternoster et al., (2004, 33).
10. See, for example, Weidner and Frase (2003); Subramanian, Henrichson, and Kang-Brown (2015); and Keller and Pearce (2016).
11. Eason (2017).
12. In a recent article, Beckett and Beach (2020) make a similar argument studying patterns of decarceration in comparative case studies of prison admissions.
13. The bulk of these cities were part of the first wave of industry in the United States; therefore they are geographically concentrated in the Northeast (Connecticut, Maine, Massachusetts, New Hampshire, Rhode Island, and Vermont), mid-Atlantic (New Jersey, New York, and Pennsylvania), and Midwest (Illinois, Indiana, Michigan, Ohio, and Wisconsin).
14. Hoyt and Leroux (2007).
15. Davis (2016); see also Davis (2021).
16. Welburn and Seamster (2016); Davis (2021).

17. Davis (2021).
18. Booker (2021).
19. Trounstine (2016).
20. Murphy and Wallace (2010).
21. Harris (2016).
22. See Mauer (2013) and Subramanian, Riley, and Mai (2018).
23. Pfaff (2012).
24. Rota (2015).
25. Rosenberg (2017).
26. Rosenberg (2017).
27. MacQuarrie (2016).
28. Southcoast Urban Indicators Project (n.d.).
29. Torname (2011).
30. Atkinson (2012); Bidgood (2012).
31. Rivera (2019).
32. Beck (2020).
33. Iluminacion Lawrence (n.d.; emphasis added).
34. Black (2009, 33–34).
35. Borges-Mendez (1994).
36. Borges-Mendez (1994).
37. Christensen (2019).
38. Kaufman (2017).
39. Sawyer and Wagner (2020).
40. Mitchelson (2012).
41. Subramanian, Henrichson, and Kang-Brown (2015).
42. Beckett and Beach (2021).
43. Toukabri and Medina (2020).
44. Eason (2017); Lichter et al. (2007); Brennan, Hackler, and Hoene (2005); Kneebone and Berube (2013); Murphy and Wallace (2010).
45. Evidence about the harshness of nonmetropolitan sentencing practices is mixed. A literature finds that harsher sentencing, and in particular the death penalty, is most commonly sought in rural and suburban counties, in comparison to their metropolitan counterparts. See, for example, Ulmer (1997); Songer and Unah (2006); Paternoster and Brame (2008); Barnes, Sloss, and Thaman (2009); Ulmer, Zajac, and Kramer (2020). Indeed, Barnes, Sloss, and Thaman (2009) find that geography is a stronger predictor of seeking the death penalty than race. In capital cases, which are extremely rare but often high profile, conservative political strongholds in rural counties may influence democratically elected prosecutors to push for harsher sentencing (Ulmer 1997; Weidner and Frase 2003). However, Barry C. Feld (1991) finds in the case of juvenile justice that urban counties, which have more formalized and bureaucratized due process, produced *greater* severity in pretrial detention and sentencing than in rural counties. Yunmei Lu (2018) finds in a study of Pennsylvania localities that women experience greater leniency in sentence length in the smallest and most rural localities.

46. See, for example, Murakawa (2014); Gottschalk (2015); Pfaff (2017); Schoenfeld (2018).

CHAPTER 4. ISOLATION AND REGIONAL INEQUITY

1. Bureau of Justice Statistics (2020).
2. Harris (2016).
3. Pager (2003); Western and Sirois (2019).
4. Herbert, Morenoff, and Harding (2015); Sirois (2019).
5. Western and Simes (2019).
6. Durose, Cooper, and Snyder (2014).
7. Comfort (2016).
8. Western (2018); Comfort (2016).
9. Ehrenhalt (2012); Hyra (2015); Walker (2017); Blumenberg et al. (2019).
10. The rate of opioid-related deaths has increased twenty-twofold in the United States since 1979 (Alexander, Kiang, and Barbieri 2018). While the opioid epidemic has been stereotyped as typically befalling rural, low-income communities, opioid mortality is particularly pronounced in the northeastern cities (Kiang et al. 2019).
11. Vance and Schuster (2018).
12. Vance and Schuster (2018).
13. Western and Sirois (2019).
14. See for example, Vargas (2019), who demonstrates in Chicago how nonprofits vie for power through competition over limited funding resources.
15. Wu (2019).
16. Chapple (2017); Hyra (2015).
17. Dobkin and Nicosia (2009); Gruenewald et al. (2010); Garriott (2011).

CHAPTER 5. COMMUNITIES OF PERVASIVE INCARCERATION

1. Muhammad (2011).
2. Gibson and Jung (2005).
3. Muhammad (2011).
4. Muhammad (2011).
5. Muhammad (2011, 5; emphasis added).
6. Pager (2003); Eberhardt et al. (2004); Goff et al. (2014); Del Toro et al. (2019).
7. Manduca and Sampson (2019).
8. Traci Burch (2014) has provided one of the most comprehensive studies to date on the relationship between racial segregation and incarceration rates, studying patterns of prison admissions in a sample of neighborhoods in North Carolina. Meares (1997) and recent work by Bell (2020) and Johnson et al. (2019) also point toward the relationship between segregation and the carceral system.

9. Alexander (2010); Burch (2014, 244).

10. See also Bell (2020) and Kurwa (2016).

11. Bonilla-Silva (1997); Massey and Denton (1997); Omi and Winant ([1986] 2015).

12. Garland (2001a).

13. Alexander (2010).

14. See Gottschalk (2015) and Forman (2012).

15. Mauer (2006, 2013).

16. Gottschalk (2015, 4).

17. Clegg and Usmani (2019).

18. Clegg and Usmani (2019).

19. Clegg and Usmani (2019).

20. Muller (2012).

21. Beckett and Western (1999); Garland (2001b); Flamm (2005); Hinton (2016).

22. Travis, Western, and Redburn (2014).

23. Wacquant (2009); Alexander (2010); Wacquant (2000).

24. Bell (2017); Wacquant (2009).

25. Edwards, Esposito, and Lee (2018); Jacobs and O'Brien (1998); Kirk (2008); Legewie (2016).

26. Steffensmeier and Demuth (2000); Spohn and Holleran (2000); Tonry and Melewski (2008).

27. Pager (2003).

28. Spencer, Charbonneau, and Glaser (2016); James (2017). See the work of the National Initiative for Building Community Trust & Justice (https://trustandjustice .org/) and the Center for Policing Equity (https://policingequity.org/).

29. See the work of Meares (1997), Burch (2014), Johnson et al. (2019), and Bell (2020).

30. Sampson (2012); Sharkey (2013).

31. Gonzalez Van Cleve and Mayes (2015). See also, for example, Fryer (2019).

32. Ludwig et al. (2013); Kirk (2015).

33. Clear (2007).

34. Turner (2015).

35. Sampson and Wilson (1995); see also Peterson and Krivo (2010).

36. Peterson and Krivo (2010).

37. Wilson (1987, citing a personal communication with Mark Testa).

38. Sampson (2012).

39. Wilson (1987, 59).

40. For this analysis I use child poverty as a measure of the level of poverty in a community.

41. Beckett and Western (2001).

42. Killewald and Bryan (2016); Oliver and Shapiro (2006).

43. Chetty and Hendren (2018).

44. Mun͂oz et al. (2015, 2).

45. Burch (2014).

46. Logan (2012).

47. Anselin (1995).

48. Bacon and Chen (2013).

49. Roediger (1999); Omi and Winant ([1986] 2015); Bonilla-Silva (1997); Oliver and Shapiro (2006).

50. See, for example, the work of Junia Howell (2019), who finds that contextual and structural effects of White advantage have greater explanatory power than the concentration of disadvantage in understanding the effects of neighborhood conditions on educational attainment.

CHAPTER 6. PUNISHING PLACES

1. Visher (2007, 97).

2. Visher (2007, 97).

3. Travis, Western, and Redburn (2014, 341).

4. Schwartz et al. (2016).

5. Schwartz et al. (2016, 256).

6. Douglas (2009).

7. Personal communication from Dr. Betty A. J. Adams, March 31, 2020.

8. Personal communication from Adams.

9. Watkins (1993).

10. For a nonexhaustive set of reviews, see Lichter (1997), Charles (2003), Pager and Shepard (2008), Elo (2009), Wakefield and Uggen (2010), Western et al. (2012), and Desmond and Western (2018).

11. Uggen and Manza (2002); Lerman and Weaver (2014b).

12. Pettit and Western (2004).

13. Travis, Western, and Redburn (2014).

14. Bureau of Justice Statistics (2015); Travis, Western, and Redburn (2014).

15. Travis, Western, and Redburn (2014).

16. An explosion of excess mortality research examines mortality estimates due to the COVID-19 pandemic. See, for example, Wrigley-Field (2020) and Rivera, Rosenbaum, and Quispe (2020).

17. Note that these are two highly simplified ideal types, and many scholars and policy makers fit in both perspectives. For example, reformers who advocate for abolition and the improved conditions of prisons simultaneously, or police abolition but reforms around police practices, may find themselves in either camp. I use these two ideal types as a purposeful oversimplification as I explore models of each, though I do not place any particular scholar or advocate in either camp.

18. As a clear example of the centering of abolition among scholarly work, Haymarket Books initiated a new Abolitionist Papers book series, edited by Naomi Murakawa. In 2021 the series published Ruth Wilson Gilmore's newest book, *Change Everything: Racial Capitalism and the Case for Abolition*.

19. For example, a Gallup poll in summer 2020 found that while most Americans say policing needs "major changes," fewer were in support of defunding the police (47%), and even fewer supported abolishing the police (15%) (Crabtree 2020). A Reuters poll in June 2020 found only one in five respondents agreed the United States should use "taxpayer money to pay damages to descendants of enslaved people in the United States" (Johnson 2020).

20. McLeod (2015, 1161).

21. Davis (2003, 21).

22. Davis (2003); Gready and Robins (2014); Kim (2018); Brown (2019).

23. Travis, Western, and Redburn (2014, 323). See also Morris (1974).

24. Travis, Western, and Redburn (2014).

25. Beckett and Western (2001).

26. Holzer (2020).

27. Garland (2005).

28. Erez and Ibarra (2014); Jones (2014).

29. Klockars (1996).

30. Klockars (1996).

31. Klockars (1996).

32. Skolnick and Fyfe (1994).

33. Sawyer and Wagner (2020).

34. See, for example, Skolnick and Fyfe (1994). Advocates propose alternatives to excessive policing in communities, such as professional training, the use of reasonable restraint, and the abolition of policing in its current form.

35. Lenner (1990).

36. McCord and Freeman (1990).

37. Pridemore (2014); Patterson (2010).

38. Following Vogel and Porter (2016), who find in their study of US incarceration rates that age structure accounts for 20 percent of the Latino-White disparity and 8 percent of the Black-White disparity in incarceration.

39. Note that this analysis does not construct mortality rates by geographic area, though there is significant geographic variation in mortality (and incarceration); for simplicity, these are calculated using the overall rates for men and women in the entire state.

40. Comfort (2008).

41. Sykes (2007, 65).

42. Goffman (1961, 30).

43. Travis, Western, and Redburn (2014, ch. 13).

44. Pettit (2012); Western (2006).

45. Lytle Hernandez and Dupuy (2020).

46. Pettit (2012); Western (2006).

47. Abramovitz and Albrecht (2013).

48. Abramovitz and Albrecht (2013).

49. Abramovitz and Albrecht (2013).

50. Boss (1999).

51. Eddy and Reid (2003). See also Turney (2017a).

52. See, for example, Gjelsvik et al. (2014).

53. Arditti (2012, 2003, 128).

54. Doka (1989); Arditti (2012).

55. Abramovitz and Albrecht (2013).

56. Manduca and Sampson (2019).

57. Jahn et al. (2020).

58. Wakefield and Wildeman (2013a); Comfort (2008); Wildeman, Schnittker, and Turney (2012).

59. Abramovitz and Albrecht (2013); Bell (2016).

60. For an empirical study of the effects of prison gerrymandering on political efficacy, see Remster and Kramer (2018).

61. Goffman (1961, 30).

62. Sampson (2011).

63. Cutter (2003).

64. Cutter (2003, 6).

65. Travis, Western, and Redburn (2014, chs. 9–11).

66. Cutter, Boruff, and Shirley (2003).

67. Cutter, Boruff, and Shirley (2003).

68. Sampson (2012).

69. See defundthepolice.org for examples of alternatives to policing.

70. For example, concepts such as "harm reduction" and "housing first" are innovations that remove punitive aspects of prior public health and social work frameworks in the areas of substance use and housing, respectively.

CHAPTER 7. A RESEARCH AND REFORM AGENDA

1. Travis, Western, and Redburn (2014, ch. 13).

2. Shelby (2016, 2).

3. Shelby (2016, 2).

4. Shelby (2016, 2).

5. Brown-Saracino (2018); Sampson (2012).

6. Rios (2011); Stuart (2016).

7. Bell (2020).

8. See, for example, discussions by Sampson (2008) and Greene (2008).

9. Tach and Wimer (2017).

10. Tach and Wimer (2017). See also Turner (2015).

11. Turner (2015, n.p.).

12. See also recent work by Rachel Ellis (2021), which argues that prisons have too often been characterized as total institutions, and that prison gates open daily and operate in the overlapping contexts of surveillance and control typically studied only in community settings.

13. See also Lytle Hernandez and Dupuy (2020).

14. Similarly to Manduca and Sampson (2019).
15. Nielson (2015).
16. Western (2018, 182).
17. Coates (2015).
18. Wakefield and Wildeman (2013).
19. Movement for Black Lives (2019).
20. Page (2019).
21. Page (2019). See also King and Page (2018).
22. Darity and Mullen (2020).
23. Movement for Black Lives (2019, 26).
24. Movement for Black Lives (2019, 27).
25. Note that cannabis remains a Schedule I controlled substance at the federal level, demonstrating the patchwork of policy and jurisdiction that governs places.
26. Institute for the Future (2014).
27. Institute for the Future (2014).
28. Institute for the Future (2014).

APPENDIX

1. Herbert, Morenoff, and Harding (2015); Sirois (2019); Simes (2018a).
2. See Sampson, Raudenbush, and Earls (1997) and Wodke, Harding, and Elwert (2011).
3. Quillian and Pager (2001); Mobasseri (2019).
4. Lageson (2020).
5. For example, McCullagh and Nelder (1989, 199).
6. Long (1997).
7. See Berk and MacDonald (2008).
8. See Hipp and Adam (2012).
9. Data based on the the 2006–2010 American Community Survey five-year estimates.
10. 2006–2010 American Community Survey.
11. Data from the Uniform Crime Reports (2009–2014).
12. Uniform Crime Reports (2009–2014).

REFERENCES

Abel, David. 2017. "Water at State's Largest Prison Raises Concerns." *Boston Globe*, June 17. www3.bostonglobe.com/metro/2017/06/17/water-state-largest-prison -raises-concerns/xDEkyL3GFwsqag7qvywl3K/story.html?arc404=true.

Abramovitz, Mimi, and Jochen Albrecht. 2013. "The Community Loss Index: A New Social Indicator." *Social Service Review* 87:677–724.

Ackerman, William V. 1998. "Socioeconomic Correlates of Increasing Crime Rates in Smaller Communities." *Professional Geographer* 50:372–87.

Adams, Kenneth and Joseph Ferrandino. 2008. "Managing Mentally Inmates in Prisons." *Criminal Justice and Behavior* 35:913–27.

Alexander, Michelle. 2010. *The New Jim Crow: Mass Incarceration in the Age of Colorblindness*. New York: New Press.

Alexander, Monica J., Mathew V. Kiang, and Magali Barbieri. 2018. "Trends in Black and White Opioid Mortality in the United States, 1979–2015." *Epidemiology* 29:707–15.

American Community Survey. n.d. www.census.gov/programs-surveys/acs (data from several years used in figures).

Anselin, Luc. 1995. "Local Indicators of Spatial Association—LISA." *Geographical Analysts* 27:93–115.

Arditti, Joyce. 2003. "Locked Doors and Glass Walls: Family Visiting at a Local Jail." *Journal of Loss & Trauma* 8:115–38.

———. 2012. *Parental Incarceration and the Family: Psychological and Social Effects of Imprisonment on Children, Parents, and Caregivers*. New York: New York University Press.

Atkinson, Jay. 2012. "Lawrence, MA: City of the Damned." *Boston Magazine*, February 28. www.bostonmagazine.com/news/2012/02/28/city-of-the-damned -lawrence-massachusetts/.

Bacon, Nick, and Xiangming Chen. 2013. "Introduction: Once Prosperous and Now Challenged." In *Confronting Urban Legacy: Rediscovering Hartford and New England's Forgotten Cities*, edited by Xiangming Chen and Nick Bacon, 1–18. Lanham, MD: Lexington Books.

Baker, Peter, Zolan Kanno-Youngs, and Monica Davey. 2020. "Trump Threatens to Send Federal Law Enforcement Forces to More Cities." *New York Times*, July 24. www.nytimes.com/2020/07/20/us/politics/trump-chicago-portland-federal-agents.html.

Baldassare, Mark. 1992. "Suburban Communities." *Annual Review of Sociology* 18:475–94.

Barnes, Katherine, David Sloss, and Stephen Thaman. 2009. "Place Matters (Most): An Empirical Study of Prosecutorial Decision-Making in Death Eligible Cases." *Arizona Law Review* 51:305–79.

Bartik, Timothy J. 2001. *Jobs for the Poor: Can Labor Demand Policies Help?* New York: Russell Sage Foundation.

Beck, Brenden. 2020. "Policing Gentrification: Stops and Low-Level Arrests during Demographic Change and Real Estate Reinvestment." *City & Community* 19:245–72.

Beckett, Katherine, and Lindsey Beach. 2021. "The Place of Punishment in Twenty-First-Century America: Understanding the Persistence of Mass Incarceration." *Law & Policy* 46:1–31.

Beckett, Katherine, and Steven Herbert. 2010. *Banished: The New Social Control in Urban America*. Oxford: Oxford University Press.

Beckett, Katherine, and Bruce Western. 1999. "Governing Social Marginality: Welfare, Incarceration, and the Transformation of State Policy." *Punishment & Society* 3:43–59.

———. 2001. "Governing Social Marginality: Welfare, Incarceration, and the Transformation of State Policy." In *Mass Imprisonment*, edited by David Garland, 35–50. London: Sage Publications.

Behrens, Angela, Chris Uggen, and Jeff Manza. 2003. "Ballot Manipulation and the 'Menace of Negro Domination': Racial Threat and Felon Disenfranchisement in the United States, 1850–2002." *American Journal of Sociology* 109:559–605.

Bell, Monica C. 2016. "Essays on Police Relations in the Context of Inequality." PhD thesis, Harvard University.

———. 2017. "Police Reform and the Dismantling of Legal Estrangement." *Yale Law Journal* 126:2054–2150.

———. 2019. "Safety, Friendship, and Dreams." *Harvard Civil Rights-Civil Liberties Law Review* 54:703–39.

———. 2020. "Anti-Segregation Policing." *New York University Law Review* 95:650–765.

Berk, Richard A., and John M. MacDonald. 2008. "Overdispersion and Poisson Regression." *Journal of Quantitative Criminology* 24:269–84.

Bidgood, Jess. 2012. "After Seeing a Dismal Reflection of Itself, a City Moves to Change." *New York Times*, May 29. www.nytimes.com/2012/05/30/us/a-massachusetts-city-tries-to-change-its-image.html.

Black, Tim. 2009. *When a Heart Turns Rock Solid: The Lives of Three Puerto Rican Brothers on and off the Streets*. New York: Vintage Books.

Blakely, Edward J., and Gail Snyder. 1998. "Separate Places: Crime and Security in Gated Communities." In *Reducing Crime through Real Estate Development and Management*, 53–70. Washington, DC: Urban Land Institute.

Bloom, Dan, Cindy Redcross, Janine Zweig, and Gilda Azurdia. 2007. "Transitional Jobs for Ex-Prisoners: Early Impact from a Random Assignment Evaluation of the Center for Employment Opportunities (CEO) Prisoner Reentry Program." Technical report, MDRC, Washington, DC.

Blumenberg, Evelyn, Anne Brown, Kelcie Ralph, Brian D. Taylor, and Carole Turley Voulgaris. 2019. "A Resurgence in Urban Living? Trends in Residential Location Patterns of Young and Older Adults since 2000." *Urban Geography* 40:1375–97.

Blumstein, Alfred. 2006. "Disaggregating the Violence Trends." In *The Crime Drop in America*, rev. ed., edited by Alfred Blumstein and Joel Wallman, 13–44. New York: Cambridge University Press.

Bonilla-Silva, Eduardo. 1997. "Rethinking Racism: Toward a Structural Interpretation." *American Sociological Review* 62:465–80.

Bonczar, Thomas P. 2003. "Prevalence of Imprisonment in U.S. Population, 1974–2001." Washington, DC: US Department of Justice. NCJ 197976.

Booker, Brakkton. 2021. "Ex-Michigan Gov. Rick Snyder and 8 Others Criminally Charged in Flint Water Crisis." *National Public Radio*, January 14. www.npr.org /2021/01/14/956924155/ex-michigan-gov-rick-snyder-and-8-others-criminally -charged-in-flint-water-crisi.

Borges-Mendez, Ramon. 1994. "Urban and Regional Restructuring and Barrio Formation in Massachusetts: The Cases of Lowell, Lawrence and Holyoke." PhD thesis, Massachusetts Institute of Technology.

Boss, Pauline. 1999. *Ambiguous Loss: Learning to Live with Unresolved Grief*. Cambridge, MA: Harvard University Press.

Boyles, Andrea S. 2015. *Race, Place, and Suburban Policing: Too Close for Comfort*. Berkeley: University of California Press.

———. 2019. *You Can't Stop the Revolution: Community Disorder and Social Ties in Post-Ferguson America*. Berkeley: University of California Press.

Braga, Anthony A., Andrew V. Papachristos, and David M. Hureau. 2012. "The Effects of Hot Spots Policing on Crime: An Updated Systematic Review and Meta-Analysis." *Justice Quarterly* 31:633–63.

Brayne, Sarah. 2020. *Predict and Surveil: Data, Discretion, and the Future of Policing*. New York: Oxford University Press.

Brennan, Christiana, Darrene Hackler, and Christopher Hoene. 2005. "Demographic Change in Small Cities, 1990 to 2000." *Urban Affairs Review* 40:342–61.

Bridges, George S., and Robert D. Crutchfield. 1988. "Law, Social Standing and Racial Disparities in Imprisonment." *Social Forces* 66:699–724.

Brown, Michelle. 2019. "Transformative Justice and New Abolition in the United States." In *Justice Alternatives*, edited by Pat Carlen and Leandro Ayres França, 73–87. New York: Routledge.

Brownsberger, Will. 2015. "The Massachusetts Legislature Regularly Enacts Criminal Penalty Increases." July 10. https://willbrownsberger.com/the-massachusetts -legislature-has-regularly-enacted-criminal-penalty-increases-for-decades/.

Brown-Saracino, Japonica. 2018. *How Places Make Us: Novel LBQ Identities in Four Small Cities*. Chicago: University of Chicago Press.

Buchanan, Larry, Qyoctrung Bui, and Jugal K. Patel. 2020. "Black Lives Matter May Be the Largest Movement in U.S. History." *New York Times*, July 30. www.nytimes .com/interactive/2020/07/03/us/george-floyd-protests-crowd-size.html.

Burch, Traci. 2014. "The Old Jim Crow: Racial Residential Segregation and Neighborhood Imprisonment." *Law & Policy* 36:223–55.

Bureau of Justice Statistics. 2015. "Use of Restrictive Housing in U.S. Prisons and Jails, 2011–12." Washington, DC: US Department of Justice. NCJ 249209.

———. 2018. "Survey of State Criminal History Information Systems, 2016." Washington, DC: US Department of Justice.

———. 2020. "Prisoners in 2019." Washington, DC: US Department of Justice. NCJ 255115.

Burton, Linda M., Daniel T. Lichter, Regina M. Baker, and John M. Eason. 2013. "Inequality, Family Processes, and Health in the 'New' Rural America." *American Behavioral Scientist* 57:1128–51.

Cadora, Eric, Charles Swartz, and Mannix Gordon. 2003. "Criminal Justice and Health and Human Services: An Exploration of Overlapping Needs, Resources, and Interests in Brooklyn Neighborhoods." In *Prisoners Once Removed: The Impact of Incarceration and Reentry on Children, Families, and Communities*, edited by Jeremy Travis and Michelle Waul, 285–312. Washington, DC: Urban Institute Press.

Caldwell, Julia T., Chandra L. Ford, Steven P. Wallace, May C. Wang, and Lois M. Takahashi. 2016. "Intersection of Living in a Rural versus Urban Area and Race/ Ethnicity in Explaining Access to Health Care in the United States." *American Journal of Public Health* 106:1463–69.

Campbell, Michael C., and Heather Schoenfeld. 2013. "The Transformation of America's Penal Order: A Historicized Political Sociology of Punishment." *American Journal of Sociology* 118:1375–1423.

Carson, E. Ann. 2020. "Prisoners in 2018." Washington, DC: US Department of Justice. NCJ 253516.

Chapple, Karen. 2017. "Income Inequality and Urban Displacement: The New Gentrification." *New Labor Forum* 26:84–93.

Charles, Camile Zubrinsky. 2003. "The Dynamics of Racial Residential Segregation." *Annual Review of Sociology* 29:167–207.

Chetty, Raj, and Nathaniel Hendren. 2018. "The Impacts of Neighborhoods on Intergenerational Mobility II: County-Level Estimates." *Quarterly Journal of Economics* 133:1163–1228.

Christensen, Dusty. 2019. "San Juan Mayor Hails Holyoke as Haven for Hurricane Maria Refugees." *Daily Hampshire Gazette*, November 7. www.gazettenet

.com/Carmen-Yulin-Cruz-speaks-to-the-Gazette-at-Mount-Holyoke-College
-30110795.

Clark, Jill K., Ronald McChesney, Darla K. Munroe, and Elena G. Irwin. 2009. "Spatial Characteristics of Exurban Settlement Pattern in the United States." *Landscape and Urban Planning* 90:178–88.

Clear, Todd R. 2007. *Imprisoning Communities: How Mass Incarceration Makes Disadvantaged Neighborhoods Worse*. New York: Oxford University Press.

Clear, Todd R., Dina R. Rose, Elin Waring, and Kristen Scully. 2003. "Coercive Mobility and Crime: A Preliminary Examination of Concentrated Incarceration and Social Disorganization." *Justice Quarterly* 20: 33–64.

Clegg, John, and Adaner Usmani. 2019. "The Economic Origins of Mass Incarceration." *Catalyst* 3:9–53.

Clinard, Marshall. 1944. "Rural Criminal Offenders." *American Journal of Sociology* 48:202–13.

Clines, Francis X. 1992. "Ex-Inmates Urge Return to Areas of Crime to Help." *New York Times*, December 23, A1.

Coates, Ta-Nehisi. 2015. "The Black Family in the Age of Mass Incarceration." *Atlantic Monthly*, October. www.theatlantic.com/magazine/archive/2015/10/the-black-family-in-the-age-of-mass-incarceration/403246/.

Cohen, Bernard. 1999. "Police Enforcement of Quality-of-Life Offending: A Critique." In *The Criminology of Criminal Law*, edited by William S. Laufer and Freda Adler, 107–34. New Brunswick, NJ: Transaction.

Cohen, Lawrence E., and Marcus Felson. 1979. "Social Change and Crime Rate Trends: A Routine Activities Approach." *American Sociological Review* 44:588–608.

Cohen, Stanley. 1985. *Visions of Social Control: Crime, Punishment and Classification*. Cambridge, UK: Polity Press.

Comfort, Megan. 2008. *Doing Time Together: Love and Family in the Shadow of the Prison*. Chicago: University of Chicago Press.

———. 2016. "'A Twenty-Hour-a-Day Job': The Impact of Frequent Low-Level Criminal Justice Involvement on Family Life." *ANNALS of the American Academy of Political and Social Science* 665:63–79.

Cooper, Daniel, and Ryan Lugalia-Hollon. n.d. "Chicago's Million Dollar Blocks." Accessed February 1, 2020. https://chicagosmilliondollarblocks.com/.

Crabtree, Steve. 2020. "Most Americans Say Policing Needs 'Major Changes.'" *Gallup News*, July 22. https://news.gallup.com/poll/315962/americans-say-policing-needs-major-changes.aspx.

Cromartie, John and Shawn Bucholtz. 2008. "Defining the 'Rural' in Rural America." *Amber Waves* 6:29–34.

Cutter, Susan L. 2003. "Presidential Address: The Vulnerability of Science and the Science of Vulnerability." *Annals of the Association of American Geographers* 93:1–12.

Cutter, Susan L., Bryan J. Boruff, and W. Lynn Shirley. 2003. "Social Vulnerability to Environmental Hazards." *Social Science Quarterly* 84:242–61.

Darity, William A., Jr., and A. Kirsten Mullen. 2020. *From Here to Equality: Reparations for Black Americans in the Twenty-First Century*. Chapel Hill: University of North Carolina Press.

Davis, Angela Y. 2003. *Are Prisons Obsolete?* New York: Seven Stories Press.

Davis, Katrinell M. 2016. "False Assurances: The Effects of Corrosive Drinking Water and Noncompliance with Lead Control Policies in Flint, Michigan." *Environmental Justice* 9:103–8.

———. 2021. *Tainted Tap: Flint's Journey from Crisis to Recovery*. Chapel Hill: University of North Carolina Press.

De Marco, Allison, and Molly De Marco. 2010. "Conceptualization and Measurement of the Neighborhood in Rural Settings: A Systematic Review of the Literature." *Journal of Community Psychology* 38:99–114.

Del Toro, Juan, Tracey Lloyd, Kim S. Buchanan, Summer Joi Robins, Lucy Zhang Bencharit, Meredith Gamson Smiedt, Kavita S. Reddy, Enrique Rodriguez Pouget, Erin M. Kerrison, and Phillip Atiba Goff. 2019. "The Criminogenic and Psychological Effects of Police Stops on Adolescent Black and Latino Boys." *Proceedings of the National Academy of Sciences* 116:8261–68.

Desmond, Matthew, and Bruce Western. 2018. "Poverty in America: New Directions and Debates." *Annual Review of Sociology* 44:305–18.

Dobkin, Carlos, and Nancy Nicosia. 2009. "The War on Drugs: Methamphetamine, Public Health, and Crime." *American Economic Review* 99:324–49.

Doka, Kenneth J. 1989. *Disenfranchised Grief: Recognizing Hidden Sorrow*. Lexington, MA: Lexington Books.

Douglas, Heather E. 2009. *Science, Policy, and the Value-Free Ideal*. Pittsburgh: University of Pittsburgh Press.

Du Bois, W. E. B. 1899. *The Philadelphia Negro: A Social Study*. Philadelphia: University of Pennsylvania Press.

Dubber, Markus Dirk. 2001. "Policing Possession: The War on Crime and the End of Criminal Law." *Journal of Criminal Law and Criminology* 91:829–996.

Durose, Matthew R., Alexia D. Cooper, and Howard N. Snyder. 2014. "Recidivism of Prisoners Released in 30 States in 2005: Patterns from 2005 to 2010." Washington, DC: US Bureau of Justice Statistics. NCJ 244205.

Eason, John. 2010. "Mapping Prison Proliferation: Region, Rurality, Race and Disadvantage in Prison Placement." *Social Science Research* 39:1015–28.

———. 2012. "Extending the Hyperghetto: Toward a Theory of Punishment, Race, and Rural Disadvantage." *Journal of Poverty* 16:274–95.

———. 2017. *Big House on the Prairie: Rise of the Rural Ghetto and Prison Proliferation*. Chicago: University of Chicago Press.

Eberhardt, Jennifer L., Phillip Atiba Goff, Valerie J. Purdie, and Paul G. Davies. 2004. "Seeing Black: Race, Crime, and Visual Processing." *Journal of Personality and Social Psychology* 87:876–93.

Eddy, J. Mark, and John B. Reid. 2003. "The Adolescent Children of Incarcerated Parents: A Developmental Perspective." In *Prisoners Once Removed: The Impact of Incarceration and Reentry on Children, Families, and Communities*, edited by

Jeremy Travis and Michelle Waul, 233–58. Washington, DC: Urban Institute Press.

Edwards, Frank, Michael H. Esposito, and Hedwig Lee. 2018. "Risk of Police-Involved Death by Race/Ethnicity and Place, United States, 2012–2018." *American Journal of Public Health* 108:1241–48.

Ehrenhalt, Alan. 2012. *The Great Inversion and the Future of the American City*. New York: Vintage Books.

Ellis, Edwin. 1998. "An Interview with Eddie Ellis." *Humanity & Society* 22:98–111.

Ellis, Rachel. 2021. "Prisons as Porous Institutions." *Theory and Society* 50:175–99.

Elo, Irma T. 2009. "Social Class Differentials in Health and Mortality: Patterns and Explanations in Comparative Perspective." *Annual Review of Sociology* 35:533–72.

Erez, Edna, and Peter R. Ibarra. 2014. "Electronic Monitoring: International and Comparative Perspectives." *Crime, Law, and Social Change* 62:385–87.

Fagan, Jeffrey, Valerie West, and Jan Holland. 2003. "Reciprocal Effects of Crime and Incarceration in New York City Neighborhoods." *Fordham Urban Law Journal* 30:1551–1602.

Feeley, Malcolm M., and Jonathan Simon. 1992. "The New Penology: Notes on the Emerging Strategy of Corrections and Its Implications." *Criminology* 30:449–74.

Feld, Barry C. 1991. "Justice by Geography: Urban, Suburban, and Rural Variations in Juvenile Justice Administration." *Journal of Criminal Law and Criminology* 82:156–210.

Flamm, Michael. 2005. *Law and Order: Street Crime, Civil Unrest, and the Crisis of Liberalism in the 1960s*. New York: Columbia University Press.

Ford, Larry R. 2001. "Alleys and Urban Form: Testing the Tenets of New Urbanism." *Urban Geography* 22:268–86.

Foreman, Benjamin, Ed Lambert, John Schneider, Dana Ansel Leiserson, Eric McLean Shinaman, David Warren, Mark Muro, and Rebecca Sohmer. 2007. "Reconnecting Massachusetts Gateway Cities: Lessons Learned and an Agenda for Renewal." Mass Inc.

Forman, James. 2012. "Racial Critiques of Mass Incarceration: Beyond the New Jim Crow." *New York University Law Review* 87:101–46.

Formisano, Ronald P. 1991. *Boston against Busing: Race, Class, and Ethnicity in the 1960s and 1970s*. Chapel Hill: University of North Carolina Press.

Frase, Richard S. 2009. "What Explains Persistent Racial Disproportionality in Minnesota's Prison and Jail Populations?" *Crime and Justice* 38:201–80.

Frederick, Brittany, and Heather Mooney. 2018. "16 Miles: Opioids and the Construction of White Users and Racialized Sellers in Small Cities." Paper presented at the American Sociological Association Meetings, Philadelphia.

Fryer, Roland G. 2019. "An Empirical Analysis of Racial Differences in Police Use of Force." *Journal of Political Economy* 127:1210–61.

Fyfe, Nicholas R. 1991. "The Police, Space, and Society: The Geography of Policing." *Progress in Human Geography* 15:249–67.

Garland, David. 1991. "Sociological Perspectives on Punishment." *Crime and Justice* 14:115–65.

———. 2001a. *Mass Imprisonment: Social Causes and Consequences*. Thousand Oaks, CA: Sage Publications.

———. 2001b. *The Culture of Control: Crime and Social Order in Contemporary Society*. Chicago: University of Chicago Press.

———. 2005. "Penal Excess and Surplus Meaning: Public Torture Lynchings in Twentieth-Century America." *Law & Society Review* 39:793–833.

Garriott, William Campbell. 2011. *Policing Methamphetamine: Narcopolitics in Rural America*. New York: New York University Press.

Geller, Amanda, and Mariah A. Curtis. 2011. "A Sort of Homecoming: Incarceration and the Housing Security of Urban Men." *Social Science Research* 40:1196–1213.

Geller, Amanda, Irwin Garfinkel, and Bruce Western. 2011. "Paternal Incarceration and Support for Children in Fragile Families." *Demography* 48:25–47.

Gibson, Campbell, and Kay Jung. 2005. "Historical Census Statistics on Population Totals by Race, 1790 to 1990, and by Hispanic Origin, 1970 to 1990, for Large Cities and Other Urban Places in the United States." US Census Bureau Working Paper no. 76.

Gilmore, Ruth Wilson. 2007. *Golden Gulag: Prisons, Surplus, Crisis, and Opposition in Globalizing California*. Berkeley: University of California Press.

Gilmore, Ruth Wilson. 2008. "Forgotten Places and the Seeds of Grassroots Planning." In *Engaging Contradictions: Theory, Politics, and Methods of Activist Scholarship*, 31–61. Berkeley: University of California Press.

Gjelsvik, Annie, Dora M. Dumont, Amy Nunn, and David L. Rosen. "Adverse Childhood Events: Incarceration of Household Members and Health-Related Quality of Life in Adulthood." *Journal of Health Care for the Poor and Underserved* 25:1169–82. www.ncbi.nlm.nih.gov/pmc/articles/PMC4897769/.

Go, Julian. 2020. "The Imperial Origins of American Policing: Militarization and Imperial Feedback in the Early 20th Century." *American Journal of Sociology* 125:1–62.

Goff, Phillip Atiba, Matthew Christian Jackson, Brooke Allison Lewis DiLeone, Carmen Marie Culotta, and Natalie Ann DiTomaso. 2014. "The Essence of Innocence: Consequences of Dehumanizing Black Children." *Journal of Personality and Social Psychology* 106:526–45.

Goffman, Alice. 2014. *On the Run: Fugitive Life in an American City*. Chicago: University of Chicago Press.

Goffman, Erving. 1961. *Asylums: Essays on the Social Situation of Mental Patients and Other Inmates*. Garden City, NY: Anchor Books.

Gomez, Marisela B. 2016. "Policing, Community Fragmentation, and Public Health: Observations from Baltimore." *Journal of Urban Health* 93:154–67.

Gonzalez Van Cleve, Nicole. 2016. *Crook County: Racism and Injustice in America's Largest Criminal Court*. Stanford, CA: Stanford University Press.

Gonzalez Van Cleve, Nicole, and Lauren Mayes. 2015. "Criminal Justice through 'Colorblind' Lenses: A Call to Examine the Mutual Constitution of Race and Criminal Justice." *Law & Social Inquiry: Journal of the American Bar Foundation* 40:406–32.

Gottschalk, Marie. 2015. *Caught: The Prison State and the Lockdown of American Politics*. Princeton, NJ: Princeton University Press.

Gready, Paul, and Simon Robins. 2014. "From Transitional to Transformative Justice: A New Agenda for Practice." *International Journal of Transitional Justice* 8:339–61.

Greene, Judith, Kevin Pranis, and Jason Zeidenberg. 2006. "Disparity by Design: How Drug-Free Zone Laws Impact Racial Disparity—and Fail to Protect Youth." Washington, DC: Justice Policy Institute.

Greene, Matthew H. 2008. "The Hope VI Paradox: Why Do HUD's Most Successful Housing Developments Fail to Benefit the Poorest of the Poor?" *Journal of Law and Policy* 17:191–229.

Gruenewald, Paul J., Fred W. Johnson, William R. Ponicki, Lillian G. Remer, and Elizabeth A. LaScala. 2010. "Assessing Correlates of the Growth and Extent of Methamphetamine Abuse and Dependence in California." *Substance Use and Misuse* 45:1948–70.

Hall, Matthew, and Barrett Lee. 2010. "How Diverse Are US Suburbs?" *Urban Studies* 47:3–28.

Hall, Susan A., Jay S. Kaufman, and Thomas C. Ricketts. 2006. "Defining Urban and Rural Areas in U.S. Epidemiologic Studies." *Journal of Urban Health* 83:162–75.

Harcourt, Bernard E. 2001. *Illusion of Order: The False Promise of Broken Windows Policing*. Cambridge, MA: Harvard University Press.

Harding, David J., Jonah A. Siegel, and Jeffrey D. Morenoff. 2017. "Custodial Parole Sanctions and Earnings after Release from Prison." *Social Forces* 96:909–34.

Harris, Alexes. 2016. *A Pound of Flesh: Monetary Sanctions as Punishment for the Poor*. New York: Russell Sage Foundation.

Herbert, Claire W., Jeffrey D. Morenoff, and David J. Harding. 2015. "Homelessness and Housing Instability among Former Prisoners." *Russell Sage Foundation Journal* 1:45–79.

Hinton, Elizabeth. 2016. *From the War on Poverty to the War on Crime: The Making of Mass Incarceration in America*. Cambridge, MA: Harvard University Press.

Hipp, John R., and Boessen Adam. 2012. "Immigrants and Social Distance: Examining the Social Consequences of Immigration for Southern California Neighbors over Fifty Years." *ANNALS of the American Academy of Political and Social Science* 641:192–219.

Holzer, Jenny. 2020. "Unnecessary Death Can't Be Policy." Electronic sign, Washington, DC. https://spruethmagers.com/exhibitions/jenny-holzer-trucks-and-truisms-online/.

Howell, Junia. 2019. "The Truly Advantaged: Examining the Effects of Privileged Places on Educational Attainment." *Sociological Quarterly* 60:420–38.

Hoyt, Lorlene and Andre Leroux. 2007. "Voices from Forgotten Cities: Innovative Revitalization Coalitions in America's Older Small Cities." New York: PolicyLink.

Hunter, Albert. 1974. *Symbolic Communities: The Persistence and Change of Chicago's Local Communities*. Chicago: University of Chicago Press.

Hyra, Derek. 2015. "The Back-to-the-City Movement: Neighborhood Redevelopment and Processes of Political and Cultural Displacement." *Urban Studies* 52:1753–73.

Iluminacion Lawrence. n.d. "Mission." We Are Lawrence. Accessed January 1, 2020. www.wearelawrence.org/iluminacion.

Institute for the Future. 2014. "The Restorative Justice City: From Punitive to Restorative Justice." Oakland, CA.

Irwin, John. 1985. *The Jail: Managing the Underclass in American Society*. Berkeley: University of California Press.

Jacobs, David, and Ronald E. Helms. 1996. "Toward a Political Model of Incarceration: A Time-Series Examination of Multiple Explanations for Prison Admission Rates." *American Journal of Sociology* 102:323–57.

Jacobs, David, and Robert M. O'Brien. 1998. "The Determinants of Deadly Force: A Structural Analysis of Police Violence." *American Journal of Sociology* 103:837–62.

Jacobs, James B. 1977. *Statesville: The Penitentiary in Mass Society*. Chicago: University of Chicago Press.

Jahn, Jaquelyn L., Jarvis T. Chen, Madina Agénor, and Nancy Krieger. 2020. "County-Level Jail Incarceration and Pre-term Birth among Non-Hispanic Black and White U.S. Women, 1999–2015." *Social Science & Medicine* 250:1–8.

James, Tom. 2017. "Can Cops Unlearn Their Unconscious Biases?" *Atlantic Monthly*, December 23. www.theatlantic.com/politics/archive/2017/12/implicit-bias -training-salt-lake/548996/.

Jargowsky, Paul. 2013. "Concentration of Poverty in the New Millennium: Changes in the Prevalence, Composition, and Location of High-Poverty Neighborhoods." The Century Foundation.

Johnson, Katanga. 2020. "U.S. Public More Aware of Racial Inequality But Still Rejects Reparations: Reuters/Ipsos Polling." *Reuters*, June 25. www.reuters.com/article/us -usa-economy-reparations-poll/u-s-public-more-aware-of-racial-inequality-but -still-rejects-reparations-reuters-ipsos-polling-idUSKBN23W1NG.

Johnson, Michael P. 2006. "Decision Models for the Location of Community Corrections Centers." *Environment and Planning B: Planning and Design* 33:393–412.

Johnson, Odis, Christopher St. Vil, Keon L. Gilbert, and Melody Goodman. 2019. "How Neighborhoods Matter in Fatal Interactions Between Police and Men of Color." *Social Science & Medicine* 220:226–35.

Jones, Richard. 2014. "The Electronic Monitoring of Offenders: Penal Moderation or Penal Excess?" *Crime, Law, and Social Change* 62:475–88.

Kalleberg, Arne. 2011. *Good Jobs, Bad Jobs: The Rise of Polarized and Precarious Employment Systems in the United States, 1970s to 2000s*. New York: Russell Sage Foundation.

Kang-Brown, Jacob, and Ram Subramanian. 2017. "Out of Sight: The Growth of Jails in Rural America." Vera Institute of Justice.

Kaufman, Jill. 2017. "Holyoke Schools Prepare for Influx of Puerto Rican Families after Hurricane Maria." *WBUR*, September 27. www.wbur.org/edify/2017/09/27 /holyoke-schools-maria.

Keller, Josh, and Adam Pearce. 2016. "A Small Indiana County Sends More People to Prison Than San Francisco and Durham, N.C., Combined: Why?" *New York Times*, September 2. www.nytimes.com/2016/09/02/upshot/new-geography-of -prisons.html.

Kiang, Mathew V., Sanjay Basu, Jarvis Chen, and Monica J. Alexander. 2019. "Assessment of Changes in the Geographical Distribution of Opioid-Related Mortality across the United States by Opioid Type, 1999–2016." *JAMA Network Open* 2:e190040.

Killewald, Alexandra, and Brielle Bryan. 2016. "Does Your Home Make You Wealthy?" *RSF: The Russell Sage Foundation Journal of the Social Sciences* 2:110–28.

Kim, Mimi E. 2018. "From Carceral Feminism to Transformative Justice: Women-of-Color Feminism and Alternatives to Incarceration." *Journal of Ethnic & Cultural Diversity in Social Work* 27:219–33.

King, Desmond S., and Jennifer M. Page. 2018. "Towards Transitional Justice? Black Reparations and the End of Mass Incarceration." *Ethnic and Racial Studies* 41:739–58.

Kirk, David. 2008. "The Neighborhood Context of Racial and Ethnic Disparities in Arrest." *Demography* 45:55–77.

———. 2015. "A Natural Experiment of the Consequences of Concentrating Former Prisoners in the Same Neighborhoods." *Proceedings of the National Academy of Sciences* 112:6943–48.

Klockars, Carl B. 1996. "A Theory of Excessive Force and Its Controls." In *Police Violence: Understanding and Controlling Police Abuse of Force*, edited by William A. Geller and Hans Toch, 1–22. New Haven, CT: Yale University Press.

Korver-Glenn, Elizabeth, Prentiss Dantzler, and Junia Howell. 2021. "A Critical Intervention for Urban Sociology." SocArXiv. January 12. doi: 10.31235/osf.io /zrj7s.

Kneebone, Elizabeth, and Alan Berube. 2013. *Confronting Suburban Poverty in America*. Washington, DC: The Brookings Institution.

Kohler-Hausmann, Issa. 2018. *Misdemeanorland: Criminal Courts and Social Control in an Age of Broken Windows Policing*. Princeton, NJ: Princeton University Press.

Kurwa, Rahim. 2016. "Segregatory Consequences of the Carceral State." In *Housing Justice in Unequal Cities*, edited by Ananya Roy and Hilary Malson, 127–34. Los Angeles: Institute on Inequality and Democracy.

Lageson, Sarah. 2020. *Digital Punishment: Privacy, Stigma, and the Harms of Data-Driven Criminal Justice*. Oxford: Oxford University Press.

Lee, Hedwig, Tyler McCormick, Margaret T. Hicken, and Christopher Wildeman. 2015. "Racial Inequalities in Connectedness to Imprisoned Individuals in the United States." *Du Bois Review: Social Science Research on Race* 12:269–82.

Legewie, Joscha. 2016. "Racial Profiling and Use of Force in Police Stops: How Local Events Trigger Periods of Increased Discrimination." *American Journal of Sociology* 122:379–424.

Lenner, Per. 1990. "The Excess Mortality Rate: A Useful Concept in Cancer Epidemiology." *Acta Oncologica* 29:573–76.

Lerman, Amy E., and Vesla Weaver. 2014a. "Race and Crime in American Politics: From Law and Order to Willie Horton and Beyond." In *The Oxford Handbook of Ethnicity, Crime, and Immigration*, edited by Sandra M. Bucerius and Michael Tonry, 41–69. New York: Oxford University Press.

———. 2014b. "Staying Out of Sight? Concentrated Policing and Local Political Action." *ANNALS of the American Academy of Political and Social Science* 651:202–19.

Levinson, Jonathan, Conrad Wilson, and Ryan Haas. 2020. "50 Days of Protest in Portland: A Violent Police Response; This Is How We Got Here." *Oregon Public Broadcasting*, July 19. www.opb.org/news/article/police-violence-portland -protest-federal-officers/.

Lichter, Daniel T. 1997. "Poverty and Inequality among Children." *Annual Review of Sociology* 23:121–45.

Lichter, Daniel T., Domenico Parisi, Steven Michael Grice, and Michael C. Taquino. 2007. "National Estimates of Racial Segregation in Rural and Small-Town America." *Demography* 44:563–81.

Logan, John R. 2012. "Making a Place for Space: Spatial Thinking in Social Science." *Annual Review of Sociology* 38:507–24.

Long, J. Scott. 1997. *Regression Models for Categorical and Limited Dependent Variables*. Thousand Oaks, CA: Sage Publications.

Lu, Yunmei. 2018. "Rural and Urban Differences in Gender-Sentencing Patterns of Pennsylvania." *Rural Sociology* 83:402–30.

Ludwig, Jens, Greg J. Duncan, Lisa A. Gennetian, Lawrence F. Katz, Ronald C. Kessler, Jeffrey R. Kling, and Lisa Sanbonmatsu. 2013. "Long-Term Neighborhood Effects on Low-Income Families: Evidence from Moving to Opportunity." *American Economic Review* 103:226–31.

Lung-Amam, Willow, and Alex Schafran. 2019. "From Sanford to Ferguson: Race, Protect, and Democracy in the American Suburbs." In *The Routledge Companion to the Suburbs*, edited by Bernadette Hanlon and Thomas J. Vicino, 220–29. New York: Routledge.

Lytle Hernandez, Kelly, and Danielle Dupuy. n.d. "Million Dollar Hoods." Accessed August 1, 2020. https://milliondollarhoods.pre.ss.ucla.edu/.

MacQuarrie, Brian. 2016. "Fall River Gets Assistance to Confront and Old Foe: Heroin." *Boston Globe*, February 21. www.bostonglobe.com/metro/2016/02/21 /fall-river-confronts-old-foe-heroin/ZthYcAb8kWAL5EJtLNeypO/story.html.

Manduca, Robert, and Robert J. Sampson. 2019. "Punishing and Toxic Neighborhood Environments Independently Predict the Intergenerational Social Mobility of Black and White Children." *Proceedings of the National Academy of Sciences* 115:7772–77.

Manza, Jeff, and Christopher Uggen. 2006. *Locked Out: Felon Disenfranchisement and American Democracy*. New York: Oxford University Press.

Marrow, Helen. 2011. *New Destination Dreaming: Immigration, Race, and Legal Status in the Rural American South*. Stanford, CA: Stanford University Press.

Mass Inc. 2015. "Crime, Cost & Consequences: A Two Year Progress Report."

Massey, Douglas S., and Nancy A. Denton. 1997. *American Apartheid: Segregation and the Making of the Underclass*. Cambridge, MA: Harvard University Press.

Mauer, Marc. 2006. *Race to Incarcerate*. New York: New Press.

———. 2013. *The Changing Racial Dynamics of Women's Incarceration*. The Sentencing Project.

McCord, Colin, and Harold P. Freeman. 1990. "Excess Mortality in Harlem." *New England Journal of Medicine* 322:173–77.

McCullagh, Peter, and John A. Nelder. 1989. *Generalized Linear Models*. 2nd ed. Boca Raton, FL: CRC Press.

McGraw, Meridith. 2019. "President Trump Defends His Attacks against Cummings, Sharpton, and Baltimore; Claims He's the 'Least Racist' Person." *ABC News*, July 30. https://abcnews.go.com/Politics/president-trump-defends-attacks-cummings-sharpton-baltimore-claims/story?id=64654878.

McIntyre, Nancy E., Kimberly Knowles-Yánez, and Diane Hope. 2000. "Urban Ecology as an Interdisciplinary Field: Differences in the use of 'Urban' between the Social and Natural Sciences." *Urban Ecosystems* 4:5–24.

McLeod, Allegra M. 2015. "Prison Abolition and Grounded Justice." *UCLA Law Review* 62:1156–1239.

Meares, Tracey L. 1997. "Place and Crime." *Chicago-Kent Law Review* 73:669–705.

Mitchelson, Matthew L. 2012. "Research Note—The Urban Geographer of Prisons: Mapping the City's 'Other' Gated Community." *Urban Geography* 33:147–57.

Mobasseri, Sanaz. 2019. "Race, Place, and Crime: How Violent Crime Events Affect Employment Discrimination." *American Journal of Sociology* 125:63–104.

Morenoff, Jeffrey D., and David J. Harding. 2014. "Incarceration, Prisoner Reentry, and Communities." *Annual Review of Sociology* 40:1–20.

Morgan, Rachel E., and Jennifer L. Truman. 2020. "Criminal Victimization, 2019." Washington, DC: US Department of Justice. NCJ 255113.

Morris, Norval. 1974. *The Future of Imprisonment*. Chicago: University of Chicago Press.

Movement for Black Lives. 2019. "Movement for Black Lives Reparations Now Toolkit." https://m4bl.org/wp-content/uploads/2020/05/Reparations-Now-Toolkit-FINAL.pdf.

Muhammad, Khalil Gibran. 2011. *The Condemnation of Blackness: Race, Crime, and the Making of Modern Urban America*. Cambridge, MA: Harvard University Press.

Muller, Christopher. 2012. "Northward Migration and the Rise of Racial Disparity in American Incarceration, 1880–1950." *American Journal of Sociology* 118:281–326.

Muñoz, Ana Patricia, Marlene Kim, Mariko Chang, Regine O. Jackson, Darrick Hamilton, and William A. Darity Jr. 2015. "The Color of Wealth in Boston." Federal Reserve Bank of Boston.

Murakawa, Naomi. 2014. *The First Civil Right: How Liberals Built Prison America*. New York: Oxford University Press.

Murphy, Alexandra K. 2007. "The Suburban Ghetto: The Legacy of Herbert Gans in Understanding the Experience of Poverty in Recently Impoverished American Suburbs." *City & Community* 6:21–37.

Murphy, Alexandra K., and Danielle Wallace. 2010. "Opportunities for Making Ends Meet and Upward Mobility: Differences in Organizational Deprivation across Urban and Suburban Poor Neighborhoods." *Social Science Quarterly* 91:1164–86.

NAACP Legal Defense Fund. 2018. *Case: Prison-Based Gerrymandering Reform.*

NBC Chicago. 2020. "President Trump Says Chicago Violence Worse Than Afghanistan." July 13. www.nbcchicago.com/news/local/president-trump-says-chicago-violence-worse-than-afghanistan/2304459/.

Nellis, Ashley. 2016. "The Color of Justice: Racial and Ethnic Disparity in State Prisons." The Sentencing Project.

Nielson, Rasmus Kleis, ed. 2015. *Local Journalism: The Decline of Newspapers and the Rise of Digital Media.* London: I. B. Tauris.

Oliver, Melvin, and Thomas Shapiro. 2006. *Black Wealth/White Wealth: A New Perspective on Racial Inequality.* 2nd ed. New York: Routledge.

Omi, Michael, and Howard Winant. (1986) 2015. *Racial Formation in the United States.* 3rd ed. New York: Routledge.

Omori, Marisa. 2017. "Spatial Dimensions of Racial Inequality: Neighborhood Racial Characteristics and Drug Sentencing." *Race and Justice* 7:35–58.

Orfield, Myron, and Thomas F. Luce. 2013. "America's Racially Diverse Suburbs: Opportunities and Challenges." *Housing Policy Debate* 23:395–430.

Page, Jennifer M. 2019. "Reparations for Police Killings." *Perspectives on Politics* 17:958–72.

Pager, Devah. 2003. "The Mark of a Criminal Record." *American Journal of Sociology* 108:937–75.

Pager, Devah, and Hana Shepard. 2008. "The Sociology of Discrimination: Racial Discrimination in Employment, Housing, Credit, and Consumer Markets." *Annual Review of Sociology* 34:181–209.

Papachristos, Andrew V. 2009. "Murder by Structure: Dominance Relations and the Social Structure of Gang Homicide." *American Journal of Sociology* 115:74–128.

Papachristos, Andrew V., and Sara Bastomski. 2018. "Connected in Crime: The Enduring Effect of Neighborhood Networks on the Spatial Patterning of Violence." *American Journal of Sociology* 124:517–68.

Papachristos, Andrew V., David M. Hureau, and Anthony A. Braga. 2013. "The Corner and the Crew: The Influence of Geography and Social Networks on Gang Violence." *American Sociological Review* 78:1–31.

Park, Robert E. and Ernest W. Burgess. 1925. *The City.* Chicago: University of Chicago Press.

Parkes, D. N., I. H. Burnley, and S. R. Walker. 1985. *Arid Zone Settlement in Australia: A Focus on Alice Springs.* Tokyo: United Nations University Press.

Paternoster, Raymond, and Robert Brame. 2008. "Reassessing Race Disparities in Maryland Capital Cases." *Criminology* 46:971–1008.

Paternoster, Raymond, Robert Brame, Sarah Bacon, and Andrew Ditchfield. 2004. "Justice by Geography and Race: The Administration of the Death Penalty in Maryland, 1978–1999." *University of Maryland Law Journal of Race, Religion, Gender, and Class* 4:1–98.

Patterson, Evelyn. 2010. "Incarcerating Death: An Analysis of Mortality in United States' State Correctional Facilities, 1985–1998." *Demography* 47:587–607.

Peterson, Ruth D., and Lauren J. Krivo. 2010. *Divergent Social Worlds Neighborhood Crime and the Racial-Spatial Divide*. New York: Russell Sage Foundation.

Pettit, Becky. 2012. *Invisible Men: Mass Incarceration and the Myth of Black Progress*. New York: Russell Sage Foundation.

Pettit, Becky, and Bruce Western. 2004. "Mass Imprisonment and the Life Course: Race and Class Inequality in US Incarceration." *American Sociological Review* 69:151–69.

Pfaff, John. 2012. "The Causes of Growth in Prison Admissions and Populations." Working paper. SSRN: 1990508.

———. 2017. *Locked In: The True Causes of Mass Incarceration and How to Achieve Real Reform*. New York: Basic Books.

Phelps, Michelle S. 2013. "The Paradox of Probation: Community Supervision in the Age of Mass Incarceration." *Law and Policy* 35:51–80.

———. 2017. "Mass Probation: Toward a More Robust Theory of State Variation in Punishment." *Punishment & Society* 19:53–73.

Planas, Antonio. 2016. "Suspect: 2,000 bags of Heroin Help Pay Bills." *Boston Herald*, October 28. www.bostonherald.com/2016/10/28/suspect-2000-bags-of-heroin-help-pay-bills/.

Politico. 2016. "Full text: Donald Trump 2016 RNC Draft Speech Transcript."

Porter, Nicole D., and Tyler Clemons. 2013. "Drug Free Zone Laws: An Overview of State Policies." Washington, DC: The Sentencing Project.

President's Commission on Law Enforcement and Administration of Justice. 1967. *The Challenge of Crime in a Free Society: A Report by the President's Commission on Law Enforcement and Administration of Justice*. Washington, DC: US Government Printing Office.

Pridemore, William Alex. 2014. "The Mortality Penalty of Incarceration: Evidence from a Population-Based Case-Control Study of Working-Age Males." *Journal of Health and Social Behavior* 55:215–33.

Prison Policy Initiative. 2014. "Tracking State Prison Growth in 50 States."

Quillian, Lincoln, and Devah Pager. 2001. "Black Neighbors, Higher Crime? The Role of Racial Stereotypes in Evaluations of Neighborhood Crime." *American Journal of Sociology* 107:717–67.

Reding, Nick. 2010. *Methland: The Death and Life of an American Small Town*. New York: Bloomsbury USA.

Remster, Brianna, and Rory Kramer. 2018. "Shifting Power: The Impact of Incarceration on Political Representation." *Du Bois Review* 15:417–39.

Rich, Josiah D., Redonna Chandler, Brie A. Williams, Dora Dumont, Emily A. Wang, Faye S Taxman, Scott A. Allen, Jennifer G. Clarke, Robert B. Greifinger, Christopher Wildeman, Fred C. Osher, Steven Rosenberg, Craig Haney, Marc Mauer, and Bruce Western. 2014. "How Health Care Reform Can Transform the Health of Criminal Justice-Involved Individuals." *Health Affairs* 33:462–67.

Rios, Jodi. 2020. *Black Lives and Spatial Matters: Policing Blackness and Practicing Freedom in Suburban St. Louis*. Ithaca, NY: Cornell University Press.

Rios, Victor. 2011. *Punished: Policing the Lives of Black and Latino Boys*. New York: New York University Press.

Rivera, Dan. 2019. Interview on Gateways podcast, September 10.

Rivera, Roberto, J. E. Rosenbaum, and Walter Quispe. 2020. "Excess Mortality in the United States During the First Three Months of the COVID-19 Pandemic." *Epidemiology & Infection* 148:1–9.

Robinson, Zandria F. 2014. *This Ain't Chicago: Race, Class, and Regional Identity*. Chapel Hill: University of North Carolina Press.

Roediger, David R. 1999. *The Wages of Whiteness: Race and the Making of the American Working Class*. London: Verso.

Roman, Caterina Gouvis, and Jeremy Travis. 2006. "Where Will I Sleep Tomorrow: Housing, Homelessness, and the Returning Prisoner." *Housing Policy Debate* 17:389–417.

Rosenberg, Eli. 2017. "Brockton Police to Get Aid from Massachusetts State Police in Battle Against Violence." New England News Channel, July 12. www.nbcboston.com/news/local/brockton-police-to-get-aid-from-massachusetts-state-police-in-battle-against-violence/23393/.

Rota, Katelyn. 2015. "The Brockton Shoe Industry." *Brockton's Great Migration* (blog). http://brocktonsgreatmigration.blogspot.com/p/historical-10.html.

Rothman, David J. 2002. *Conscience and Convenience: The Asylum and Its Alternatives in Progressive America*. Rev. ed. New York: Aldine de Gruyter.

Rotman, Edgardo. 1998. "The Failure of Reform: United States, 1865–1965." In *The Oxford History of the Prison*, edited by Norval Morris and David J. Rothman, 151–77. New York: Oxford University Press.

Sampson, Robert J. 2008. "Moving to Inequality: Neighborhood Effects and Experiments Meet Social Structure." *American Journal of Sociology* 114:189–231.

———. 2011. "The Incarceration Ledger: Toward a New Era in Assessing Societal Consequences. *Criminology & Public Policy* 10:819–28.

———. 2012. *Great American City: Chicago and the Enduring Neighborhood Effect*. Chicago: University of Chicago Press.

Sampson, Robert J., and Charles Loeffler. 2010. "Punishment's Place: The Local Concentration of Mass Incarceration." *Daedalus* 139: 20–31.

Sampson, Robert J., and Stephen W. Raudenbush. 2004. "Seeing Disorder: Neighborhood Stigma and the Social Construction of 'Broken Windows.'" *Social Psychological Quarterly* 67:319–42.

Sampson, Robert J., Stephen W. Raudenbush, and Felton Earls. 1997. "Neighborhoods and Violent Crime: A Multilevel Study of Collective Efficacy." *Science* 277:918–24.

Sampson, Robert J., and William Julius Wilson. 1995. "Toward a Theory of Race, Crime, and Urban Inequality." In *Crime and Inequality*, edited by John Hagan and Ruth D. Peterson, 37–56. Stanford, CA: Stanford University Press.

Sanchez, Thomas W., Robert E. Lang, and Dawn M. Dhavale. 2005. "Security versus Status? A First Look at the Census's Gated Community Data." *Journal of Planning Education and Research* 24:281–91.

Sawyer, Wendy, and Peter Wagner. 2020. "Mass Incarceration: The Whole Pie 2020." Prison Policy Initiative.

Schoenfeld, Heather. 2018. *Building the Prison State: Race and the Politics of Mass Incarceration*. Chicago: University of Chicago Press.

Schwartz, Sharon, Seth J. Prins, Ulka B. Campbell, and Nicolle M. Gatto. 2016. "Is the 'Well-Defined Intervention Assumption' Politically Conservative?" *Social Science & Medicine* 166:254–57.

Shannon, Sarah K. S., Christopher Uggen, Jason Schnittker, Melissa Thompson, Sara Wakefield, and Michael Massoglia. 2017. "The Growth, Scope, and Spatial Distribution of People with Felony Records in the United States, 1948–2010." *Demography* 54:1795–1818.

Sharkey, Patrick. 2010. "The Acute Effect of Local Homicides on Children's Cognitive Performance." *Proceedings of the National Academy of Sciences* 107: 11733–38.

———. 2013. *Stuck in Place: Urban Neighborhoods and the End of Progress Toward Racial Equality*. Chicago: University of Chicago Press.

———. 2014. "Spatial Segmentation and the Black Middle Class." *American Journal of Sociology* 119:903–54.

Sharkey, Patrick, Nicole Tirado-Strayer, Andrew V. Papachristos, and C. Cybele Raver. 2012. "The Effect of Local Violence on Children's Attention and Impulse Control." *American Journal of Public Health* 102:2287–93.

Shedd, Carla. 2015. *Unequal City: Race, Schools, and Perceptions of Injustice*. New York: Russell Sage Foundation.

Shelby, Tommie. 2016. *Dark Ghettos: Injustice Dissent, and Reform*. Cambridge, MA: Harvard University Press.

Sherman, Lawrence W. 2018. "Reducing Fatal Police Shootings as System Crashes: Research, Theory, and Practice." *Annual Review of Criminology* 1:421–49.

Simes, Jessica T. 2016. *Essays on Place and Punishment in America*. PhD thesis, Harvard University.

———. 2018a. "Place after Prison: Neighborhood Attainment and Attachment During Reentry." *Journal of Urban Affairs* 41:443–63.

———. 2018b. "Place and Punishment: The Spatial Context of Mass Incarceration." *Journal of Quantitative Criminology* 34:515–33.

———. 2020. "The Ecology of Race and Punishment Across Cities." *City & Community* 19:169–90.

Sinyangwe, Samuel. 2020. "Police Are Killing Fewer People in Big Cities, But More in Suburban and Rural America." FiveThirtyEight, June 1. https://fivethirtyeight.com/features/police-are-killing-fewer-people-in-big-cities-but-more-in-suburban-and-rural-america/.

Sirois, Catherine. 2019. "Household Support and Social Integration in the Year after Prison." *Sociological Forum* 34:838–60.

Skolnick, Jerome H., and James J. Fyfe. 1994. *Above the Law: Police and the Excessive Use of Force*. New York: Free Press.

Small, Mario Luis. 2014. "No Two Ghettos Are Alike." *Chronicle Review*, March 17. www.chronicle.com/article/no-two-ghettos-are-alike/.

Songer, Michael J., and Isaac Unah. 2006. "The Effect of Race, Gender, and Location on Prosecutorial Decisions to Seek the Death Penalty in South Carolina." *South Carolina Law Review* 58:161–210.

Southcoast Urban Indicators Project. n.d. "Substance Abuse." Accessed February 1, 2020. http://southcoastindicators.org/health/substance-abuse/.

Spatial Information Design Lab. 2007. "The Pattern." Justice Mapping Center, Columbia University.

Spencer, Katherine B., Amanda K. Charbonneau, and Jack Glaser. 2016. "Implicit Bias and Policing." *Social & Personality Psychology Compass* 10:50–63.

Spohn, Cassia, and David Holleran. 2000. "The Imprisonment Penalty Paid by Young, Unemployed Black and Hispanic Male Offenders." *Criminology* 38:281–306.

Steffensmeier, Darrell, and Stephen Demuth. 2000. "Ethnicity and Sentencing Outcomes in U.S. Federal Courts: Who Is Punished More Harshly?" *American Sociological Review* 65:705–29.

Steffensmeier, Darrell J., and Charlene Jordan. 1978. "Changing Patterns of Female Crime in Rural America." *Rural Sociology* 43:87–102.

Stuart, Forrest. 2016. *Down, Out, and Under Arrest: Policing and Everyday Life in Skid Row*. Chicago: University of Chicago Press.

———. 2020. *Ballad of the Bullet: Gangs, Drill Music, and the Power of Online Infamy*. Princeton, NJ: Princeton University Press.

Subramanian, Ram, Christian Henrichson, and Jacob Kang-Brown. 2015. "In Our Own Backyard: Confronting Growth and Disparities in American Jails." Vera Institute of Justice.

Subramanian, Ram, Kristine Riley, and Chris Mai. 2018. "Divided Justice: Trends in Black and White Jail Incarceration, 1990–2013." Vera Institute of Justice.

Sutton, John. 2000. "Imprisonment and Social Classification in Five Common Law Democracies, 1955–1985." *American Journal of Sociology* 106:350–86.

Sykes, Gresham M. 2007. *The Society of Captives: A Study of a Maximum Security Prison*., Princeton Classic ed. Princeton, NJ: Princeton University Press.

Sylla, Laurie, René Franzen, Debra Srebnik, Marla Hoffman, and Amnon Shoenfeld. 2017. "Creating a Regional Model to Coordinate and Prioritize Access to Permanent Supportive Housing." *Journal of Behavioral Health Services & Research* 44:564–73.

Tach, Laura, and Christopher Wimer. 2017. "Evaluating Policies to Transform Distressed Urban Neighborhoods." US Partnership on Mobility from Poverty.

Teplin, Linda A. 2000. "Keeping the Peace: Police Discretion and Mentally Ill Persons." *National Institute of Justice Journal* 244:8–15.

Terbeck, Fabian J. 2020. "Defining Suburbs: An Evaluation and Comparison of Four Methods." *Professional Geographer* 72:586–97.

Tonry, Michael. 1995. *Malign Neglect: Race, Crime, and Punishment in America.* New York: Oxford University Press.

Tonry, Michael, and Matthew Melewski. 2008. "The Malign Effects of Drug and Crime Control Policies on Black Americans." *Crime and Justice* 37:1–44.

Torname, Joe. 2011. "A Little City with Big Potential: A Publication of the New Lynn Coalition." New Lynn Coalition.

Toukabri, Amel, and Lauren Medina. 2020. "America: A Nation of Small Towns." US Census Bureau.

Trancik, Roger. 1986. *Finding Lost Space: Theories of Urban Design.* New York: Van Nostrand Reinhold.

Travis, Jeremy, Bruce Western, and Steve Redburn, eds. 2014. *The Growth of Incarceration in the United States: Exploring Causes and Consequences.* Washington, DC: National Academies Press.

Trounstine, Jessica. 2016. "How Racial Segregation and Political Mismanagement Led to Flint's Shocking Water Crisis." *Monkey Cage* (blog), *The Washington Post*, February 8. www.washingtonpost.com/news/monkey-cage/wp/2016/02/08/heres-the-political-history-that-led-to-flints-shocking-water-crisis/.

Truman, Jennifer L., and Michael Planty. 2012. "Criminal Victimization, 2011." Washington, DC: US Department of Justice. NCJ 239437.

Turner, Margery Austin. 2015. "A Place-Conscious Approach Can Strengthen Integrated Strategies in Poor Neighborhoods." Economic Studies at Brookings.

Turner, B. L., II, Roger E. Kasperson, Pamela A. Matson, James J. McCarthy, Robert W. Corell, Lindsey Christensen, Noelle Eckley, Jeanne X. Kasperson, Amy Luers, Marybeth L. Martello, Colin Polsky, Alexander Pulsipher, and Andrew Schiller. 2003. "A Framework for Vulnerability Analysis in Sustainability Science." *Proceedings of the National Academy of Sciences* 100:8074–79.

Turney, Kristin. 2017a. "The Unequal Consequences of Mass Incarceration for Children." *Demography* 54:361–89.

———. 2017b. "Unmet Health Care Needs among Children Exposed to Parental Incarceration." *Maternal and Child Health Journal* 21:1194–1202.

Uggen, Christopher, and Jeff Manza. 2002. "Democratic Contraction? Political Consequences of Felon Disenfranchisement in the United States." *American Sociological Review* 67:777–803.

Ulmer, Jeffery T. 1997. *Social Worlds of Sentencing: Court Communities under Sentencing Guidelines.* Albany: State University of New York Press.

Ulmer, Jeffery T., Gary Zajac, and John H. Kramer. 2020. "Geographic Arbitrariness? County Court Variation in Capital Prosecution and Sentencing in Pennsylvania." *Criminology & Public Policy* 19:1073–112.

Uniform Crime Reports. n.d. www.fbi.gov/services/cjis/ucr (data from various years used in tables).

US Bureau of the Census. 2010. "Census 2010: Summary File 1."

———. n.d. www.census.gov (data from several years used in figures).

US Department of Justice, Civil Rights Division. 2015. *Investigation of the Ferguson Police Department.* Washington, DC: US Department of Justice.

Vance, Anise, and Luc Schuster. 2018. "Opioid Addiction Is a National Crisis: And It's Twice as Bad in Massachusetts." Boston Indicators. www.bostonindicators.org /-/media/indicators/boston-indicators-reports/report-files/opioids-2018.pdf?la =en&hash=82606AB8DC4B6AC57B5E462A43E008B63EDBF903.

Vargas, Robert. 2016. *Wounded City: Violent Turf Wars in a Chicago Barrio*. New York: Oxford University Press.

———. 2019. "Gangstering Grants: Bringing Power to Collective Efficacy Theory." *City & Community* 18: 369–91.

Velez, Maria B., Lauren J. Krivo, and Ruth D. Peterson. 2003. "Structural Inequality and Homicide: An Assessment of the Black-White Gap in Killings." *Criminology* 41:645–72.

Venkatesh, Sudhir Alladi. 2000. *American Project: The Rise and Fall of a Modern Ghetto*. Cambridge, MA: Harvard University Press.

Vera Institute of Justice. n.d. Incarceration Trends Dataset: County- and Jurisdiction-Level Jail Data (1970–2018) and Prison Data (1983–2016). https://github.com /vera-institute/incarceration-trends.

Visher, Christy A. 2007. "Returning Home: Emerging Findings and Policy Lessons about Prisoner Reentry." *Federal Sentencing Reporter* 20:93–102.

Vogel, Matt, and Lauren C. Porter. 2016. "Toward a Demographic Understanding of Incarceration Disparities: Race, Ethnicity, and Age Structure." *Journal of Quantitative Criminology* 32:515–30.

Wacquant, Loïc. 2000. "The New 'Peculiar Institution': On the Prison as Surrogate Ghetto." *Theoretical Criminology* 4:377–89.

———. 2001. "Deadly Symbiosis: When Ghetto and Prison Meet and Mesh." *Punishment and Society* 3:95–133.

———. 2007. *Urban Outcasts: A Comparative Sociology of Advanced Marginality*. London: Polity.

———. 2009. *Punishing the Poor: The Neoliberal Government of Social Insecurity*. Durham, NC: Duke University Press.

Wagner, Peter, and Wendy Sawyer. 2018. "States of Incarceration: The Global Context 2018." June. Prison Policy Initiative. www.prisonpolicy.org/global/2018.html ?gclid=CjwKCAjw47eFBhA9EiwAy8kzNMNFB2EgA1YwAVqSUsX86H8a00q KZpUjIVBlDAqnjEFBmPNOCSiNlxoCYxUQAvD_BwE.

Wakefield, Sara, Hedwig Lee, and Christopher Wildeman. 2016. "Tough on Crime, Tough on Families? Criminal Justice and Family Life in America." *Annals of the American Academy of Political and Social Science* 665:8–21.

Wakefield, Sara, and Christopher Uggen. 2010. "Incarceration and Stratification." *Annual Review of Sociology* 36:387–406.

Wakefield, Sara, and Christopher Wildeman. 2013. *Children of the Prison Boom: Mass Incarceration and the Future of American Inequality*. New York: Oxford University Press.

Walker, Kyle E. 2017. "The Shifting Destinations of Metropolitan Migrants in the U.S., 2005–2011." *Growth and Change* 48:532–51.

Walker, Samuel, and Charles Katz. 2012. *The Police in America: An Introduction.* 8th ed. New York: McGraw-Hill Higher Education.

Watkins, Susan Cotts. 1993. "If All We Knew about Women Was What We Read in Demography, What Would We Know?" *Demography* 30:551–77.

Weaver, Vesla. 2007. "Frontlash: Race and the Development of Punitive Crime Policy." *Studies in American Political Development* 21:230–65.

Weidner, Robert R., and Richard S. Frase. 2003. "Legal and Extralegal Determinants of Intercountry Differences in Prison Use." *Criminal Justice Policy Review* 14:377–400.

Weisburd, David, and Anthony Braga, eds. 2019. *Police Innovation: Contrasting Perspectives.* 2nd ed. Cambridge, UK: Cambridge University Press.

Weisheit, Ralph A., David N. Falcone, and L. Edward Wells. 2005. *Crime and Policing in Rural and Small-Town America.* 3rd ed. Long Grove, IL: Waveland Press.

Welburn, Jessica, and Louise Seamster. 2016. "How a Racist System Has Poisoned the Water in Flint, Mich." *The Root,* January 9. www.theroot.com/how-a-racist-system -has-poisoned-the-water-in-flint-mi-1790853824.

Western, Bruce. 2006. *Punishment and Inequality in America.* New York: Russell Sage Foundation.

———. 2015. "Lifetimes of Violence in a Sample of Released Prisoners." *RSF: The Russell Sage Foundation Journal of the Social Sciences* 1:14–30.

———. 2018. *Homeward: Life in the Year after Prison.* New York: Russell Sage Foundation.

Western, Bruce, Deirdre Bloome, Ben Sosnaud, and Laura Tach. 2012. "Economic Insecurity and Social Stratification." *Annual Review of Sociology* 38: 341–59.

Western, Bruce, and Jessica T. Simes. 2019. "Drug Use in the Year After Prison." *Social Science & Medicine* 235:112357.

Western, Bruce, and Catherine Sirois. 2019. "Racialized Reentry: Labor Market Inequality after Incarceration." *Social Forces* 94:1517–42.

Wildeman, Christopher, Jason Schnittker, and Kristin Turney. 2012. "Despair by Association? The Mental Health of Mothers with Children by Recently Incarcerated Fathers." *American Sociological Review* 77:216–43.

Wildeman, Christopher, and Emily A. Wang. 2017. "Mass Incarceration, Public Health, and Widening Inequality in the USA." *Lancet* 389:1464–74.

Wilson, James Q. 1985. *Thinking about Crime.* Rev. ed. New York: Vintage Books.

Wilson, William Julius. 1987. *The Truly Disadvantaged: The Inner City, the Underclass, and Public Policy.* Chicago: University of Chicago Press.

Wodke, Geoffrey T., David J. Harding, and Felix Elwert. 2011. "Neighborhood Effects in Temporal Perspective: The Impact of Long-Term Exposure to Concentrated Disadvantage on High School Graduation." *American Sociological Review* 76:713–36.

Wong, Alia. 2016. "What Are Massachusetts Public Schools Doing Right?" *Atlantic Monthly.* May 23, www.theatlantic.com/education/archive/2016/05/what-are -massachusetts-public-schools-doing-right/483935/.

Wood, Holly. 2014. "When Only a House Makes a Home: How Home Selection Matters in the Residential Mobility Decisions of Lower-Income, Inner-City African American Families." *Social Service Review* 88:264–94.

Wooldredge, John. 2007. "Neighborhood Effects on Felony Sentencing." *Journal of Research in Crime and Delinquency* 44:238–63.

———. 2012. "Distinguishing Race Effects on Pre-trial Release and Sentencing Decisions." *Justice Quarterly* 29:41–75.

Wooldredge, John, and Amy Thistlethwaite. 2004. "Bilevel Disparities in Court Dispositions for Intimate Assault." *Criminology* 42:417–56.

Wrigley-Field, Elizabeth. 2020. "US Racial Inequality May Be as Deadly as COVID-19." *Proceedings of the National Academy of Sciences* 117:21854–56.

Wu, Viviana Chiu-Sik. 2019. "The Geography and Disparities of Community Philanthropy: A Community Assessment Model of Needs, Resources, and Ecological Environment." *VOLUNTAS: International Journal of Voluntary and Nonprofit Organizations* 32: 351–71.

Youngerman, Zach. 2012. "Did Bad Neighborhood Design Doom Trayvon Martin?" *Boston Globe*, April 7. www.bostonglobe.com/opinion/editorials/2012/04/06/did-bad-neighborhood-design-doom-trayvon-martin/8TSIJBEdBla6NBb1z1VH0O/story.html.

INDEX

NOTE: Figures, tables and maps are denoted in italics: *fig, tab* and *map*.

reparative justice, 166–68

Republican National Convention 2016, 25

research approaches: community-level, 5–9, 15–17; glossary of terms, 36–42; guided by urban inequality and social control theories, 45–46, 133; maps, 118; methods, 50–51, 83–84, 110; place comparisons, 33; semistructured interviews, 16, 82, 83–89, 95–96; theory development, 30–35

research focus on large cities, 2–4, 6, 30–31, 33, 39–40, 58, 79–80

research questions: about conditions of small cities, 58, 108–9; about generalizability, 74; about high incarceration rates in small cities, 83; about punishment as hazard, 132; about racial disparities in incarceration, 126–27; about reentry services, 84; about social control, 19, 162, 165–66; about spatial patterns, 96, 106

residual analysis, 51

resilience, 151, 152*fig*, 155*fig*

restitution, 168. *See also* reparations

Restorative Justice City, 168

Retreat, The at Twin Lakes, 21

Revere, Massachusetts, 41

Rivera, Dan, 67

Robinson, Zandria F., 40

Romney, Mitt, 15

Roxbury, Massachusetts, 12

rural areas, 31, 34, 37–38, 46, 60

Safer Cities Initiative, 25

safe streets acts, 24–25

Salem, Massachusetts, 41

Sampson, Robert J., 27, 105, 143

Sanford, Florida, 21

Scandinavia, 136

schools, 12, 20, 28, 54, 153*fig*

Schwartz, Sharon, 129

science, role of, 129–30

science of vulnerability, 150

Second Chance Act, 90–91

semistructured interviews, 16, 82, 83–89, 95–96

sentencing practices, 26, 39, 154*tab*, 165

sentencing rates, 22

services, access to, 28, 85–91, 137, 153*tab*

Seven Neighborhoods Study, 43, 54

sex offenders, 94

Sharkey, Patrick, 105

Shelby, Tommie, 159, 160–61

shelters, funding for, 90. *See also* housing; services, access to

Silicon Valley, 87

silos, research and data, 156. *See also* data

Simon, Jonathan, 59

Sirois, Catherine, 88

Skid Row, 25

slavery, 167

Small, Mario Luis, 40

small cities. *See under* cities

Snyder, Rick, 61

social contracts, 135

social control: in Black neighborhoods, 103–5, 108; definition, 4; deviance and, 32; evidence of, 119; as managing urban underclass, 42; measured by number of police officers, 72; metrics of, 52*fig*, 132; perspectives on place and punishment, 19–27; prison admissions rates and, 73*fig*, 74; racial aspects of, 81; in small cities, 58–59, 62*tab*, 72, 80; spatial nature of, 5, 17, 125; spatial variation in, 54; theory, 45, 46, 160; *vs.* urban inequality theory, 30

social environments, 102, 105–10

social exclusion. *See* exclusion in small cities

social hazards, 132

social inequality, 12, 35, 102. *See also* inequality, neighborhood; racial disparities in health and living conditions; urban inequality

social institutions, 137, 141

social marginality. *See* marginalization in small cities

social policy investments, 101

social service providers, 83–84, 95

social vulnerability, 150–51

socioeconomic deprivation. *See* poverty

sociology of punishment, 6, 17, 39–40, 60, 129–30, 136

South Africa, 14*fig*

South Boston, Massachusetts, 12

South Bronx, New York, 3, 44

South Jamaica, New York, 3, 44

US Department of Justice, 25
Usmani, Adaner, 100–101

vacant housing, 148*fig*, 153*tab*. *See also* housing
values, driving research, 130–31
Vera Institute of Justice, 34, 74, 80
Vermont, 88, 89
violence: in Brockton, Massachusetts, 66; criminalized, 32, 33, 34, 53, 64; declines in Boston in, 79; de-escalation of, 157; differences between White and Black neighborhoods, 105, 109–10; gun and gang, 25; impacts of in isolated places, 42; intergenerational, 32; lead exposure and, 143; as marker of social disadvantage, 2–3, 23; as predictor of incarceration rates, 28; as preventable, 134; role in punishing places theory, 31–32; in small cities, 80; state use of, 26, 30, 56; urban/inner city, 9
violent crime rates, 14, 27, 33, 34–35, 66–67, 72, 108*fig*
Visher, Christy, 128
Visions of Social Control (Cohen), 23
vulnerability science, 150

Wacquant, Loïc, 22
Walsh, Martin J., 91
War on Drugs, 99, 100, 166
water supply, 61

wealth disparities, 28, 101, 109–10
well-being of communities, 5, 98
Western, Bruce, 88, 166
Westfield, Massachusetts, 41
Westmoreland County, Pennsylvania, 116
"wet housing," 93. *See also* housing
When a Heart Turns Rock Solid (Black), 68
White disproportionality, 114*fig*, 115*fig*, 121*map*
White flight, 28
White incarceration rates, Massachusetts, 1, 13
White neighborhoods, 117–18, 117*fig*, 119, 119*tab*, 125–26
Wilson, Darren, 56
Wilson, James Q., 28–29
Wilson, William Julius, 27, 87, 105, 106
Wimer, Christopher, 163
Worcester, Massachusetts: community loss of, 145*tab*; disproportionality in prison admissions, 112*tab*; as "forgotten city," 41; funding for social services in, 90–91; Latino neighborhoods of, 117; prison admissions rates, 47, 49*tab*
working-class Americans, 100–101
Wu, Viviana Chui-Sik, 90
Wyden, Ron, 26

Young, Darris, 169
Youngerman, Zach, 21
young men and boys. *See* men

Founded in 1893,
UNIVERSITY OF CALIFORNIA PRESS
publishes bold, progressive books and journals
on topics in the arts, humanities, social sciences,
and natural sciences—with a focus on social
justice issues—that inspire thought and action
among readers worldwide.

The UC PRESS FOUNDATION
raises funds to uphold the press's vital role
as an independent, nonprofit publisher, and
receives philanthropic support from a wide
range of individuals and institutions—and from
committed readers like you. To learn more, visit
ucpress.edu/supportus.

www.ingramcontent.com/pod-product-compliance
Lightning Source LLC
Chambersburg PA
CBHW020855270326
41928CB00006B/717